Preparing Instructional Text

Preparing Instructional Text

Document Design Using Desktop Publishing

Earl R. Misanchuk
University of Saskatchewan

Educational Technology Publications
Englewood Cliffs, New Jersey 07632

Library of Congress Cataloging-in-Publication Data

Misanchuk, Earl R.
    Preparing instructional text : document design using desktop
publishing / Earl R. Misanchuk.
        p.   cm.
    Includes bibliographical references and indexes.
    ISBN 0-87778-241-5 : $32.95
    1. Desktop publishing. 2. Instructional systems--Design--Data
processing. 3. Printing, Practical--Layout--Data processing.
I. Title
Z286.D47M59 1992
686.2'2544--dc20   91-32872
                                                              CIP

Printed in the United States of America.

Library of Congress Catalog Card Number:
91-32872.

International Standard Book Number:
0-87778-241-5.

First Printing: January 1992.

This book is dedicated to my mother
and the memory of my father.

Preface

This book had its origin in an attempt to develop guidelines for instructional developers creating text-based instruction on desktop computers. Trying to achieve some degree of uniformity of appearance and functionality among documents produced by a small, often part-time, work group triggered the project. In reviewing the writing of desktop publishing experts, I sometimes found advice that made intuitive sense for certain kinds of publications, but no sense for instructional materials. Yet only rarely did the writers stipulate what kinds of materials they were referring to, and almost never was the material instructional. To confirm my intuitions about good and bad practices for text-based instruction, I undertook a review of the research literature on text used for instruction. Along with that came the realization that we, in our work group, were probably not the only ones who didn't really know how to make the best use of the desktop publishing tools we now had available to us, and the book took on a life of its own.

As powerful desktop computers empower educators to produce documents that rival those that are professionally designed and typeset, they also raise the potential for misuse of that power, either intentionally or unintentionally. Educators using desktop publishing systems to prepare instructional materials now have many more choices available for how their documents will look than they did in the day of the typewriter. Sometimes those choices are made wisely; other times they are not. Sometimes choices are not made at all, and software defaults prevail. The results vary from excellent to terrible. This book has as its goal to maximize the number of the former and minimize the number of the latter.

Although, strictly speaking, this book itself is not the kind of document that I am writing about—it is more of a professional library/reference work than instructional material per se—I have tried to incorporate into the design and layout of the book most of the principles about

which I write. This book may therefore look different than most you've
read. I hope you will analyze the effectiveness with which it communicates, in terms of the design principles applied. While you're at it, try
not to let convention interfere with your judgment. For example, some
pages will appear to have large amounts of blank space, for reasons that
will become apparent as you read the book. As you look at these, ask
yourself: Do I approve or disapprove of these differences? Are they
logical and functional? Above all, do they make sense in terms of
instruction?

A number of commercial hardware and software products are
mentioned in this book by name. Attaching the customary trademark
(™ or ®) symbols to them each time they were used seemed to make for
tedious reading. I therefore appended the appropriate symbol the first
time I used a name, and omitted it thereafter. Mention of a particular
product in this book does not constitute an endorsement of it, nor does
failure to mention a product imply the contrary.

A number of people contributed to the existence of this book. As is the
case for many writers, my immediate family was affected most, and I
want to thank Linda, Melanie, and Michael for their support and understanding of why the realization of promises was sometimes deferred.

I want to acknowledge the support and assistance of the Extension
Division, University of Saskatchewan, and the Audio-Visual Center,
Indiana University, during my sabbatical leave from the former
organization. In particular, the cooperation of the directors of the two
units, Bob Brack and Tom Schwen, respectively, facilitated the
preparation of this book considerably.

Grateful thanks are also extended to Richard Schwier, Ruth Epstein,
and Margareth Peterson for their critical reviews of a draft of the
manuscript, and to Melanie Misanchuk, who served ably as occasional
research assistant and general factotum.

ERM
Saskatoon, Saskatchewan
and Bloomington, Indiana

Contents

3. Using the Computer Wisely   33

4. Initial Design Considerations   69

5. Access Structure and Orienting Devices   97

6. Fonts and Type   125

7. Leading and Kerning   155

8. Principles of Page Layout   167

11. Illustrations and Other Graphics   237

Figures and Tables

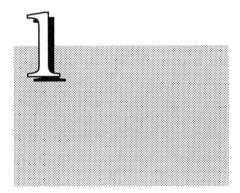

Teachers and Typographers, Professors and Printers

What do grade-school teachers have in common with graphic designers? Educators with editors? Instructors with compositors, trainers with proofreaders, teachers with typographers, and professors with printers? At first blush, perhaps not very much. Yet, on reflection, we see that one group is concerned with the "consumption" of the product of the other group. Despite that relationship, the two groups operate in completely different worlds, with different perspectives, concerns, and terminology.

Despite educators' traditional reliance on the printed word, most of us have been content to accept what publishers provide us. While we may occasionally quibble with the content of published material, we usually accept its format as a given.

We are largely ignorant of what goes into designing, laying out, and printing a page of text. That is not necessarily a bad thing; educators have not in the past been expected to have technical expertise in such matters—and rightly so. Today, with the advent of microcomputers and desktop publishing (DTP), things are changing. It is not so much that educators are expected to produce professional-looking text materials, as it is that educators want to capitalize on the opportunity to do so. Now that DTP is accessible to educators, it behooves us to learn enough about it to be able to prepare good-looking instructional materials, or at least to avoid preparing ugly ones—or worse, instructionally counter-productive ones!

A number of very powerful word processing and desktop publishing programs for microcomputers are now affordable to educators and their institutions. Laser printers exist that are capable of reproducing very high-quality images. There are many recent books available on design, on desktop publishing in general, and on desktop publishing with particular software and hardware, to help us learn how to use these tools (e.g., Bove and Rhodes, 1989; Collier and Cotton, 1989; Cowart and Cummings, 1989; Davies, 1989; Davis, Barry, and Wiesenberg, 1986; Felici and Nace, 1987; Hewson, 1988; Kleper, 1987; Lang, 1987; Latif-Pembry, 1989; Sans, 1988; Shushan and Wright, 1989; Swann, 1987; Zimmerman, 1989). Much of the advice in some of those books is good—Lichty (1989) and Miles (1987) provide an especially high proportion of good advice—and educators can and should follow it.

At the same time, a central thesis of this book is that desktop publishing (DTP) as practiced by publishers of newsletters, magazines, newspapers, brochures, pamphlets, and even some books, is fundamentally different from desktop publishing for instruction (DTPI). Some of the rules of thumb and generalizations that are held sacred in the publishing industry, and hence in DTP, are either ill-founded from a pedagogical point of view, or have been shown through research to be counter-productive in an instructional situation.

Where, then, can an educator turn to learn the difference between the good advice and the bad? The answer, I hope, is this book.

Is This Book for You?

Page 3 is as good a place as any to find out whether you want to invest any time in reading this book or not. I will describe the type of person for whom it is written; you can decide how well that description applies to you.

First and foremost, you are an educator. Whether you are a kindergarten teacher or a university professor, whether you teach diploma courses in a technical college or conduct workshops with adults for the YWCA, whether you are a trainer in industry or government or an instructional developer who designs tutorial guides for computer software, whether your instruction is formal or informal, for children or for adults: Your primary purpose in our context is to produce good text materials for instruction, be they class handouts, laboratory manuals, individualized instruction packages, or even textbooks.

Second, you are primarily responsible for the preparation of the instructional materials, using desktop publishing (DTP) techniques. You probably operate within a typical school, college, or other institutional environment, and don't have access to either elaborate printing facilities or highly-trained specialists in typography, graphic design, or printing. You do, however, have access to a DTP system, which may be as simple as an Apple® Macintosh® and a LaserWriter® printer with appropriate software. Since one of the by-products of DTP is to set people free of dependence on highly qualified—but scarce or expensive—individuals, you are willing to invest a modest amount of time learning how to design and lay out better instructional materials.

Third, your aspirations are to produce effective instructional materials, but not necessarily to win awards for outstanding graphic design of your publications. In other words, you want to produce good instructional materials as part of your role as an educator, but you are not particularly interested in becoming a graphic designer. This is not to say you are willing to produce ugly publications. Rather, your first priority is instructional effectiveness. Attractive, attention-getting design, while still important, is a secondary concern.

Finally, I have made a number of assumptions about you and your environment that influence what is and isn't in this book:

- Your instructional materials will probably be used again—next month, next semester, or next year—but are subject to change before they are re-printed. In education, instructional materials are constantly undergoing formative evaluation and revision as they are used. What you publish this time is likely not cast in stone, and may have to be revised before the next publication, which may be next week or next year. Hence your layout cannot be complex or labor-intensive, or easily disrupted by such changes.

- Your print run is limited (i.e., the instructional materials you produce will be used with relatively small audiences). You are not planning to print thousands of copies and distribute them widely, as a publisher might. Hence your binding is simple and inexpensive: loose-leaf ring binder, tubular or comb binding (e.g., Cerlox®), slide-on plastic spines, saddle-stitching (magazine-style), or perhaps merely a single staple in the upper-left corner. (This assumption is not terribly restrictive. It can be violated with relative impunity—see the next point.)

- You are limited to simple printing processes, like xerography (or perhaps offset press), and to commonplace paper sizes, like letter-size (8 $1/2$" × 11"), legal (8 $1/2$" × 14"), or A4 International. (Like the last assumption, this one is not very restrictive. If you are printing thousands of copies, you might need to use a higher-definition printer than the LaserWriter. You may also employ more elaborate reproduction and binding processes. If so, consult printing professionals for help.)

- You are not contemplating using color, or if you are, you are planning to use a single color as a highlight only. The design of multi-color printed materials is beyond the scope of this book.

- You are comfortable with and experienced at the basic operation of your DTP system, including word processing and perhaps page-layout software. This book will not teach you how to use the DTP system, merely how to optimize its use for instructional materials. This book was produced on a Macintosh/LaserWriter system, using Microsoft® Word 4.0 (MS Word) as both the word processing and page layout software, and frequently examples and tips will pertain to that combination. Occasional reference will be made to PageMaker® 4.0, a more specialized and powerful page-layout package. However, most of the principles and practices described in this book are easily generalizable to other DTP systems.

- You are uncertain about your skills in design and page layout and want to learn more about what you should and should not do to produce instructional materials that are both effective and attractive.

Why Was This Book Necessary?

Two main considerations prompted this book. The first is that much of the advice given in other DTP books seemed to me to be arbitrary, and based on gut instinct. Rules and guidelines existed without explanation, or when explanations were given, they were couched in terms that might be used by an art critic, without any supporting evidence. A good sense of design, being something that few were born with and even fewer could acquire (so the attitude went), was necessarily handed down through rules and guidelines from those who had it to those of us who didn't. Other rules and guidelines apparently existed only because "that's the way it has always been done" in the publishing industry. It seemed to me more reasonable that rules developed from research results should prevail over arbitrary rules.

The second consideration is that there is a good deal of conflicting advice being given in the DTP literature. One writer gives a rule, and another one contradicts it, or states it sufficiently differently to be confusing to the aspiring designer. Which rule is right? Again, research may give an answer.

Research vs. "Trusting Your Tummy"

Lichty's (1989) descriptions of the Bookman font (typeface) is an excellent example of value-laden statements with no explanation or justification. In an otherwise excellent, even-handed, and helpful book, he characterizes Bookman thus:

> See Dick present his dissertation on thermonuclear devices
> using Bookman. No one is reading it. Even Jane fails to take it
> seriously. See Jane throw the thermonuclear device for her dog
> Spot. Fetch, Spot, fetch! Boom! Dick should have used a
> typeface with more authority. (p. 33)

> Use Bookman to complement any text where a warm, comfort-
> ing, solid character without pretense is appropriate. Bookman
> has a Mom-and-apple-pie/Dick-and-Jane personality. (p. 34)

Puzzled and somewhat disturbed that statements of such obvious
opinion were being presented as fact, I looked for either empirical
evidence or reasoned arguments in support of them, but found none. My
typical response to assessing the value of one person's opinion is to
gather similar data from a number of people. Since you are a consumer
of sorts, reading this, let me ask you: Does it bother you that the text you
are reading is set in Bookman? Do you get a Dick-and-Jane feeling
(whatever that is) from reading it? Or Mom-and-apple-pie? If I could
hear your answer, I would have another person's opinion. If I could do
that with many people, I could find out what the "average" opinion
was—that's empirical research—and use that knowledge to guide my
actions. (And there has been some research done on this topic; it will be
examined later.)

There are a number of practices in the publishing industry that are
simply traditions. For example, according to Kleper (1987), the
tradition of having text right-justified (i.e., text forming a straight edge
down the page at the right margin) originated with the scribes who
copied text by hand before the invention of movable type. Because paper
was expensive at that time, the scribes attempted to put as much as
possible onto a page, filling each line completely, and giving rise to
what amounted to a right-justified margin. Since that time, anything
else has been regarded as "unprofessional." Later on, the use of metal
type required that the right edges of type align in the page form so that
the type could be locked into place (Burns, Venit, and Hansen, 1988).
Recently, computers have made right-justification quite easy to do,
giving everyone the ability to look "professional." Following that
tradition, most DTP books wax enthusiastic about right justification,
and spend a number of pages discussing it and its consequences, and
illustrating how those consequences should be dealt with.

Yet there is reason to believe that perhaps that "professional" look may
be counter-productive, at least for instructional materials. Hartley

(1978; Hartley and Burnhill, 1977a) argues that right-justified text is not a good idea for instructional materials, for two reasons:

- The variable inter-word spacing that is inevitable with right-justified margins impedes smooth reading progress, since the eye has to continually adjust to the different spacing.

- The use of hyphenation—another inevitability of right-justified margins—makes reading more difficult, since often upon encountering the first part of a hyphenated word, readers make incorrect assumptions about the remainder of the word and have to make subsequent mental corrections.

This is a topic that has been researched, and the results are somewhat mixed. However, at least some research studies have shown that right justification does interfere with reading speed and/or comprehension, at least for some kinds of readers (Gregory and Poulton, 1970; Muncer, Gorman, Gorman, and Bibel, 1986; Trollip and Sales, 1986).

Discrepancies in Advice

Even a superficial review of the plentiful literature available on DTP will show that while rules of thumb abound, they are not always consistent across advisors. Consider, for example, the advice on how wide a column of text should be.

Some authors state that a column of text should be 35–40 characters long (West, 1987). Others suggest that it should not be more than about one and one-half lower-case alphabets long (i.e., the space occupied by typing the lower-case characters *a* through *z* followed by *a* through *m*)—about 40 characters (*Printing layout and design*, 1968; Walker, 1990); others say 50 (Parker, 1988); still others say up to 60 characters (Burns, Venit, and Hansen, 1988). One advisor says that 60–65 characters is the most comfortable line length for reading (Miles, 1987), while another source will permit as many as 75 characters in a line (*Publish!*, 1989b).

The range of recommendations represents a difference of 114%. Which one is right?

Tinker (1963, 1965), whose recommendations are based on the results of empirical research, suggests that there is a whole range of answers to the question, depending on the size of the font and the vertical spacing of the line. We will examine Tinker's recommendations in detail later.

Sometimes advice given by one DTP expert is contradicted by another. For example, Davis, Barry, and Wiesenberg (1986, p. 50) suggest that as few fonts as possible be used in a single document, but that three or four fonts per publication are not excessive; Burns, Venit, and Hansen (1988) flatly state that more than two should not be used (p. 92). One writer suggests that the Bookman font should be "...principally reserved for headlines and display boxes of text" (Hewson, 1988, p. 81), but another suggests it can be used successfully for all kinds of jobs (*Printing layout and design*, 1968, p. 135). Burns, Venit, and Hansen concur with the latter point of view, calling Bookman "sturdy" and "readable." However, Lichty suggests Bookman is "...almost too easy to read," and (as already noted) says it has a "Dick and Jane" personality (Lichty, 1989, p. 33) and should not be used for any work that is to be taken seriously.

As we will see later, similar contradictions exist on the advice regarding margin size.

Unspecified "Evidence"

Sometimes the statements made in other DTP guides are suspiciously glib. In a discussion about whether the right margin of a column of text should be justified or ragged, Burns, Venit, and Hansen (1988) say "Legibility studies have found that there is no noticeable difference in legibility (reading speed and comprehension) between justified and ragged-right text, and the average reader does not even notice whether text is justified or not" (p. 107), but they give no indication as to how or where they obtained that generalization. Miles (1987) says "there is no evidence to suggest that unjustified (flush left) setting is any more or less readable than justified..." (p. 27). As already noted above, there is at least some research evidence that some readers are negatively affected by right justification.

Questionable Advice (...at Least from an Educator's Point of View)

Occasionally advice offered by DTP experts is, from an educator's point of view, of dubious merit. This is not to say that the expert proffering the advice is necessarily unknowledgeable or deliberately misleading. Sometimes, a suggestion is offered that may be effective in a certain kind of publication (e.g., an advertisement) merely as an idea stimulator; if it were applied to instructional materials, the outcome would likely be somewhere between ludicrous and disastrous. For example, Collier and Cotton (1989) say:

> The first paragraph doesn't necessarily have to be at the top of the page. As long as it is set different from the body text, the viewer will know that this is the introductory paragraph and go to it first. Using conventions like a larger point size of bold type will help signpost the way. (p. 39)

The statement is accompanied by a thumbnail sketch similar to Figure 1–1, in which the darker gray bands are to be interpreted as the first paragraph of the contents of the page.

Figure 1–1. First paragraph of an article centered on the page, in the manner recommended by Collier and Cotton (1989).

Any educator who unthinkingly follows the advice (because it was given by DTP experts) will probably have some very confused students! On the other hand, to apply such a design to a magazine article may have less serious consequences.

Collier and Cotton provide another example of questionable layout advice (for educators, at least) by example. In their book, virtually every two-page spread within a section (or chapter) has exactly the same format: the spread consists of a column containing a checklist (ostensibly identifying the key points made), a full column of text, and a half-page containing three graphic displays, on the left-hand page, and six similar displays on the right-hand page. The layout sounds complicated, and it is. But the important point is not how complicated the layout is; rather, the point is how invariant the layout is, regardless of the subject-matter being treated. Each spread is devoted to a separate topic, except in a few circumstances where a topic has to be distributed across several two-page spreads. The net effect of this unvarying format is that the content is either condensed or expanded to fit the space available, often to the detriment of effective communication. As an intellectual design exercise leading to a conversation-provoking coffee-table book, such an effort might be effective; as a model for how instructional materials might be laid out, it is counter-productive. To be fair, Collier and Cotton do not claim to be illustrating how instructional materials should be laid out, and likely would be quick to deny the effectiveness of their layout for such a purpose. Still, uncritical mimicking of these experts' layout by an educator could happen.

Backgrounds and Perspectives

The contents of any book are a reflection of the background of its author. Anyone who sets out to communicate brings to bear his or her unique perspective; I believe that your understanding of my comments in this book will be enhanced by your knowing a little about my background and my beliefs.

Most of the other DTP books on the market are written by graphic designers or by writers intimately familiar with the publishing industry and its practices. I'm an educator, not a graphic designer; my background is in instructional design and educational technology.

I have for a number of years applied desktop publishing concepts and practices to the preparation of printed distance education materials, and through that experience developed an appreciation that desktop publishing for instruction is a very special sub-category of desktop publishing, one that has its own rules and guidelines.

I have taught high school courses, university courses in instructional technology and instructional design, and adult education courses on various related topics. I've also examined the literature for advice on how text and layout affect the teaching process. I value research, and believe it should be used more often to guide educators' actions, rather than relying on "what your tummy tells you." At the same time, I recognize that research may not have all the answers, and that sometimes research findings are colored by the way the research was conducted. I have tried to take these factors into account in presenting the advice in this book.

I also believe that an educator doesn't need to know how things were done in the printing industry before DTP, or even necessarily how they are done today with DTP, in order to make effective use of DTP. In this book, I may well use terminology that would make graphic designers cringe, but hopefully will be completely understandable to educators, and I will gloss over points that typographers might consider fundamental, but will not make a big difference to the lives of teachers. After all, what does it matter that I will encourage you to measure pages in inches or centimeters, when the publishing industry uses picas, points, and ciceros? How would your job of preparing effective instructional materials be facilitated by knowing that page numbers are called folios, and that recto and verso are the names given in the publishing industry to the left-hand and right-hand pages of a spread? Unless you are a fan of the game Trivial Pursuit, I don't think it does matter, and that attitude carries over into the terminology I've chosen to use in this book.

As I hinted on the first page of this book, some of the common practices of the publishing industry have actually been shown through research to be bad ideas vis-à-vis instruction. Since I value design decisions based on the findings of research, this book is necessarily somewhat more academic in appearance and tone than the typical DTP book. Educators who wish to delve further into the research that produced a generalization need the typically academic references provided.

However, I have tried to make this book more readable than the typical textbook or research summary. Feel free to gloss right over the references if that is your preference.

Sources of Information

I have used three general categories of sources:

- educational and psychological research;

- publishing industry practice, rules of thumb, and opinions, as published in numerous books on DTP; and

- my own opinions, which are founded on experience in teaching, designing printed instructional materials, and common sense applied to the teaching environment.

It is my intent to make plain throughout this book what category I am drawing from when offering advice in the form of rules or guidelines. When the evidence is from research, the wording should make that clear, and references will typically be given. When I am passing on publishing industry guidelines or rules, or describing widespread practice, I will typically say so. I will give references when the opinions seem to be minority opinions, but will generally not do so when the opinions are widely held. Finally, when the advice is of my own making, I will preface it with such statements as "I believe...", "in my opinion...", or "I think...." Usually, when my personal conclusions run counter to industry practice or advice, I will present an argument for my position, and let you be the final arbiter. In general, however, my belief is that the greatest reliance should be put on the results of research.

Preview of Remaining Chapters

Chapter 2 describes some of the advantages of using desktop publishing to prepare instructional materials, and enumerates the differences between the usual applications of desktop publishing and desktop publishing for instructional purposes. It also distinguishes between two terms that are sometimes confused, instructional design and graphic design. It concludes with an overview of the various roles taken on by a desktop publisher that were formerly held by a number of people in the pre-desktop publishing industry.

Chapter 3 deals with making effective use of the power of the computer, whether in word processing or in page layout. It is very much a "how-to" chapter. Following the advice in it will shorten the process of getting from initial writing to a professional-looking final product.

Chapter 4 focuses on some of the very early decisions that need to be made: paper stock, margin size, and layout grids (including discussions of the number of columns to use, and whether or not the right margin of the text should be justified).

Chapter 5 describes the so-called "access structure" of the document. It deals with such topics as pagination, headers and footers, headings, paragraphs, lists, visual cuing, tables of content, and cross-references.

Chapter 6 is about fonts or typefaces. A number of technical distinctions are made, followed by a discussion about choosing the "right" font. Various characteristics of fonts (size, style, special effects) are described, and their potential uses delineated.

Chapter 7 deals with leading and kerning—the vertical and horizontal spacing of type, respectively. Different recommendations are given for text intended for adults and for children, and a number of technical matters related to leading and kerning are examined.

Chapter 8 enumerates several general principles of page layout, and highlights the use of white space on the page for a variety of purposes.

Chapter 9 is about tables—when to use them, how to plan and construct them, and where to put them. Special problems related to table construction are dealt with here, too.

Chapters 10 and 11 are not, strictly speaking, about text; rather, they are about illustrations. Illustrations, however, frequently accompany and augment text. Furthermore, illustrations often contain text.

Chapter 10 is about data graphics (graphs and charts). It deals with when they should and shouldn't be used, how to arrange information to be included, how they should be designed and presented, and where they should be placed in the instructional materials. The pros and cons of a number of types of graphs and charts are enumerated.

Chapter 11 deals with illustrations and other graphics—the different types and uses, how to design them, how to create them in a form useful for desktop publishing, and where to place them. It also deals with a few specialized categories of graphical material, such as borders, boxes, and rules, graphic organizers, and cartoons.

References for Chapter 1

Bove, T., and Rhodes, C. (1989). *Desktop publishing with PageMaker for the Macintosh.* Toronto: John Wiley and Sons.

Burns, D., Venit, S., and Hansen, R. (1988). *The electronic publisher.* New York: Brady.

Collier, D., and Cotton, B. (1989). *Basic desktop design and layout.* Cincinnati, OH: North Light Books.

Cowart, R., and Cummings, S. (1989). *The ABC's of Ventura.* San Francisco, CA: Sybex.

Davies, J. (1989). *Computing fundamentals: PageMaker.* Reading, MA: Addison-Wesley.

Davis, F. E., Barry, J., and Wiesenberg, M. (1986). *Desktop publishing.* Homewood, IL: Dow Jones-Irwin.

Felici, J., and Nace, T. (1987). *Desktop publishing skills: A primer for typesetting with computers and laser printers.* Reading, MA: Addison-Wesley.

Gregory, M., and Poulton, E. C. (1970). Even versus uneven right-hand margins and the rate of comprehension in reading. *Ergonomics, 13*(4), 427–434.

Hartley, J. (1978). *Designing instructional text.* London: Kogan Page.

Hartley, J., and Burnhill, P. (1977a). Fifty guidelines for improving instructional text. *Programmed Learning and Educational Technology, 14,* 65–73.

Hewson, D. (1988). *Introduction to desktop publishing.* San Francisco, CA: Chronicle Books.

Kleper, M. L. (1987). *The illustrated handbook of desktop publishing and typesetting.* Blue Ridge Summit, PA: Tab Books.

Lang, K. (1987). *The writer's guide to desktop publishing.* London: Academic Press.

Latif-Pembry, R. (1989). *Desktop publishing with WordPerfect.* Terra Cotta, ON: Norbry Publishing.

Lichty, T. (1989). *Design principles for desktop publishers.* Glenview, IL: Scott, Foresman and Co.

Miles, J. (1987). *Design for desktop publishing.* San Francisco: Chronicle Books.

Muncer, S. J., Gorman, B. S., Gorman, S., and Bibel, D. (1986). Right is wrong: An examination of the effect of right justification on reading. *British Journal of Educational Technology, 17,* 5–10.

Parker, R. C. (1988). *The Aldus guide to basic design* (2nd ed.). Seattle, WA: Aldus Corporation.

Printing layout and design. (1968). Albany, NY: Delmar Publishers.

Publish! (1989b). *101 best desktop publishing tips, vol. 2.* San Francisco, CA: PCW Communications.

Sans, J. C. (1988). *Handbook of desktop publishing.* Dallas, TX: Wordware Publishers.

Shushan, R., and Wright, D. (1989). *Desktop publishing by design.* Redmond, WA: Microsoft Press.

Swann, A. (1987). *How to understand and use design and layout.* Cincinnati, OH: North Light Books.

Tinker, M. A. (1963). *Legibility of print.* Ames, IA: Iowa State University Press.

Tinker, M. A. (1965). *Bases for effective reading.* Minneapolis: University of Minnesota Press.

Trollip, S. R., and Sales, G. (1986, January). *Readability of computer-generated fill-justified text.* Paper presented at the Annual Convention of the Association for Educational Communications and Technology, Las Vegas, NV.

Walker, P. (1990). A lesson in leading. *Aldus Magazine,* March/April, 45–47.

West, S. (1987). Design for desktop publishing. In The Waite Group (J. Stockford, Ed.), *Desktop publishing bible* (pp. 53–72). Indianapolis, IN: Howard W. Sams.

Zimmerman, B. B. (1989). *Working with WordPerfect* (3rd. ed.). Chicago, IL: Scott, Foresman.

Desktop Publishing
and Design

Why Desktop Publishing?

The primary reason educators should welcome DTP is the improved
legibility and aesthetic appearance of printed material. That statement
is not as simple as it sounds, however, as legibility and appearance are
inter-related through several other variables. It is true that xerographi-
cally reproduced material from a master done on an electric typewriter,
double spaced, is more than adequate as far as legibility goes, looks
reasonably good, and is a big improvement over the spirit-mastered or
mimeographed materials—often hand-written—universal in education
not too many years ago. However, typewriters are capable of printing
only 10 (pica) or 12 (elite) characters per inch, with a limited range of
vertical spacing, while typeset material can hold from 50% to 200%
more characters per inch (Kleper, 1987) and can have almost infinite

adjustment of vertical spacing. In an age when the consumption of paper is rapidly being recognized as a social problem, this is no small gain in efficiency.

Typeset materials look more polished and professional than the materials educators typically are able to produce. Typesetting, however, is normally out of the price range of reproducing instructional materials. That's where DTP comes in. While it is not exactly cheap, it is affordable in many educational situations. One of the major reasons for this affordability is that sophisticated software now incorporates much of the knowledge and capability previously held only by relatively highly-paid professionals—typographers, graphic designers, layout artists, illustrators, and the like.

The integration of text with graphics that the Macintosh pioneered also figures prominently in DTP, giving users with minimal artistic talent the ability to bring charts and graphs, clip-art line drawings, and perhaps even scanned photographs into their publications.

Planning, writing, and laying out a publication is a dynamic process. Although the three stages can be conceptualized independently, in reality there is a good deal of hopping back and forth between stages. The power of DTP comes into play when decisions made in one stage affect or are affected by decisions made in another stage. It is a great advantage to be able to edit and rewrite in response to what shows itself in layout. An author can usually quite easily shorten a chapter that is two sentences too long (too long, for example, in the sense that the two sentences end up on a separate right-hand page, necessitating a nearly blank page and another blank, left-hand, page before the start of the new chapter). The inclusion, exclusion, and even placement of diagrams and tables can be decided upon on the spot, in response to problems encountered during layout. Since it is the author making the decisions, there is no concern that the sense of the message will be altered by such an action. This is quite a contrast from pre-DTP procedures:

> Traditionally, there has been a distinct break between the writing/editing steps and the design process in producing any publication—the writer had no idea what the final pages would look like, and the designers didn't care what form the text and illustrations were delivered in, so long as they were complete and clear. The designer would then set up specifications for the page margins and type, and mark up the stack of typed pages and pencilled sketches for the typesetter and illustrator. The

> stages were distinct because the players and the tools used at each stage were different. Now it's possible for the writer to participate in the design and production if the design function is performed early enough in the cycle. Using the tools of electronic publishing, the distinction between the writing, design, and production phases is more of a concept than a matter of fact. If the writers know what the final design requires, they can insert tabs and carriage returns as appropriate while they are writing, and (optionally) perform other formatting operations. (Burns, Venit, and Hansen, 1988, p. 69)

Finally, the educator using a DTP system has a very good idea of what the finished product will look like, since the version on the computer screen closely matches the final printed version. This capability, often described as WYSIWYG (pronounced wissy-wig, and derived from "what you see is what you get"), makes it unnecessary for the user to have the graphic artist's skill of visualizing what a page layout will look like. As will be stressed throughout this book, it is important that educators make decisions, based on pedagogical criteria, about where certain elements should fall on the page.

Desktop Publishing vs. Desktop Publishing for Instruction

Different kinds of publications serve different purposes. Although lists of purposes vary, the one created by Shushan and Wright (1989, p. 7) is illustrative. They suggest that a publication may have as its primary purpose to:

- persuade (e.g., advertisements, posters, flyers);
- identify (e.g., business cards, certificates, stationery);
- inform (e.g., bulletins, brochures, magazines, newsletters);
- elicit responses (e.g., applications, order forms, surveys);
- provide reference (e.g., calendars, directories, schedules); and
- give how-to information (e.g., curriculum guides, instruction manuals, training guides).

Most DTP experts urge the would-be DTP publisher to consider the purpose or function of a publication carefully before embarking on any design decisions, as those decisions may vary according to the purpose (although they less frequently say *how* those design decisions differ). In this book, we concentrate on instructional materials—which probably fall into the last category identified by Shushan and Wright (with some spill-over into the second-last)—and ignore the other categories. Instructional materials include such things as class handouts, reading or lecture notes, laboratory manuals, individualized instruction packages, assembly or operating manuals, and even textbooks. The salient characteristic differentiating "regular" publishing (meaning all the other categories) from the subject-matter of this book is the intent—instruction—and it is a thesis of this book that the difference in intent should influence design decisions.

To facilitate discussion of design differences between the "regular" desktop publishers and educators doing desktop publishing, I will use the term DTP to denote the former, and DTPI (desktop publishing for instruction) to denote the latter.

Differences in Purpose of DTP and DTPI

The purpose underlying the preparation of any text is communication—getting a message from the originator to the reader, with as little distortion or loss as possible. Graphic designers and other DTP users will be quick to tell you that the purposes of their publications—no matter which of the categories above they fall into—are to communicate and to inform, and that there is little difference between their roles as communicators and that of an educator. I submit, however, that there are major differences between the information-providing and persuasion functions typical of DTP, and the instruction function of DTPI.

West implies that design is unrelated to purpose, by which she seems to mean content. She states that "specific purpose, beyond that of communication, is a secondary issue," and suggests that a well-designed brochure "...could be used to sell high-pressure gas valves or handbooks for housebreaking iguanas" (West, 1987, p. 60). Her point of view is a common one among graphic designers (Duchastel and Waller, 1979). If one were to generalize West's argument and place it into an educational context, one would come to the conclusion that a design for instructional materials in mathematics could be used effectively to teach English, or social studies, or philosophy; such a position would, in the minds of most educators, be quite untenable. Her statements almost epitomize the singular priority placed on the aesthetics of design by many DTP experts. DTP is generally much more concerned with how a document looks than with what it is that the document is supposed to do, and with how well it does it.

I believe that educators have a defensible right—indeed, perhaps an obligation—to change those priorities around, making aesthetics secondary to instructional considerations. Efficacy of learning is a more important criterion than is aesthetic appeal, in my judgment. In other words, in DTP form precedes function; in DTPI, form follows function. (This is not to say that instructional materials may or should be ugly, but merely that, when it comes to a choice between aesthetics and educational efficacy, the latter should dominate.)

Generally speaking, less persuasion (selling)—overt or subliminal—is done in DTPI materials than in many other kinds of publishing.

> The purpose of graphic design material is to communicate
> ideas, messages, visual statements and, occasionally, pure
> aesthetics. Most design work is geared to the sale or promotion
> of the product or service it is projecting...." (Swann, 1987, p. 63)

While it is true that instructional materials are, in a sense, persuading the learner to think and behave in certain ways, the persuasion is of a qualitatively different kind than that found in advertising, for example.

Linked to this notion of persuasion is motivation. Attention-getting and motivation play a larger role in DTP than in DTPI. This is not to say that attention-getting and motivation are not important in instruction, but merely that the teacher usually is available to perform at least part of that function, and the burden doesn't fall solely upon the text materials themselves. Shushan and Wright (1989) reflect the dominant assumption under which most DTP operates, when they say "In many cases the reader is at best indifferent and at worst resistant to the information you want to convey" (p. 7). Most educators, on the other hand, would feel a sense of personal failure if that were the case for the majority of their learners. By the time a learner approaches some instructional materials, he or she should have attained a certain level of motivation externally. "The eye is caught by the splashier elements of design—photos, graphics, colors, headlines—but the mind is often hooked by more low-key elements" (Felici and Nace, 1987, p. 7). It is concern for the mind, rather than the eye, that should dominate an educator's attention. Still, educators would do well to keep in mind Shushan and Wright's (1980) admonition: "You may have a target audience or even a captive audience, but you don't have a reader until you've involved that person through words or pictures or an overall impression" (p. 8). Some attention must be given to the motivational aspects of design and layout; however, the amount of effort involved, and the degree to which striking and unusual designs are necessary, is usually smaller in DTPI than in DTP.

In DTP, predictability implies boredom; variety is god. Designs are often made to be different as ends in themselves. On the other hand, predictability is a virtue in instructional materials, as it is in reference materials. Imagine a textbook which used a different way of displaying the instructional objectives of each chapter. Or a reference book that arranged things differently on every page. (This does not imply that educators should adopt a single page layout and use it for all their instructional materials, however. Different kinds of materials require different layouts.)

There are also major differences in the contents of instructional and non-instructional messages. An examination of some of the differences between text used for most other publishing purposes and text used for instruction shows that:

- Instructional materials typically make more frequent use of the following devices than do most other text materials:

  - "point form" or numbered points;

  - notes of explanation (e.g., footnotes or end-notes);

  - examples, which are often set out from the surrounding text in a special way, to make them easier to identify;

  - embedded questions;

  - graphic elements used as cuing devices (e.g., using boldface type to highlight new vocabulary, or using various symbols [e.g., ✓, ▲, ❏] to identify important points); and

- learner interactivity (e.g., blanks to be filled in; multiple-choice responses to be selected; paragraph-length answers to be constructed before proceeding with additional reading).

- Explicit reference to the structure of the subject-matter (e.g., the use of headings) is relatively more important in instructional materials than in many other kinds of published material.

- Germane illustrations with cross-references to them, as opposed to merely decorative or interest-generating illustrations, are more likely to be found in instructional materials than in other kinds. Frequently in non-instructional publications, graphics and devices such as pull quotes are used simply to fill the space available or to enhance the aesthetic appeal of the publication; in instructional materials, they must be germane to the presentation, and cross-referenced to the text, or they should not be used at all.

- Instructional materials often have more of a reference quality about them than many other published materials. That is, they are intended to be used for review of already-read material.

- Although the importance of the use of graphics is about the same in both instructional and non-instructional materials, it is usually the case that educational institutions do not have the facilities to create and modify graphics extensively, whereas in most other publishing efforts, such facilities are commonplace.

Think about the differences as you consider some of the reasons I will present later in this book for making layout decisions different from those advocated by members of the DTP industry.

The Design Environments of DTP and DTPI

In addition to the fundamental difference of purpose, there are other differences between DTP and DTPI. Consider the first four assumptions I laid out about your publishing environment (frequent revision of materials, limited print run, simple printing processes only, no color). While they are all realistic assumptions for DTPI, they are highly restrictive and not realistic for DTP.

Another factor in the design environments of DTP and DTPI is that of ownership of the work. Often, in DTP, one person—the designer or DTP expert—is doing the work for another—the client—as in pre-DTP days. The DTP expert often knows little or nothing about the content being manipulated and arranged. In DTPI, it is typical that the educator himself or herself is also doing the editing, typography, layout, and even printing of the master copy. This provides an advantage to DTPI, where informed decisions can be made regarding how editing of text, or different placement of illustrations and tables, may have significant effects on the efficacy of the instruction. (This added dimension of the content expert being involved in the layout of the work is new to the publishing industry, a result of the advent of DTP, and not yet universally accepted in the industry.)

The Design Priorities of DTP and DTPI

By and large, the graphic designer/layout person, whether using DTP or earlier, manual methods, is given a task that can be stated simply (if not carried out quite as simply): Given a relatively fixed amount of space (i.e., a certain number of pages), place given content onto it in such a way as to make it attractive, attention-getting, and readable. The designer must not waste space, of course, since space translates into extra paper which in turn translates into extra cost, but at the same time, space is a tool for the designer to use to make the work visually pleasing, attention-getting, and readable. The major emphasis in design in the majority of the publishing industry is aesthetic. Dramatic design attracts readers, and good design makes it easy for the reader to read, says conventional wisdom, and that is what the job is all about.

The educator, on the other hand, has different priorities—maximum instructional effectiveness is paramount, and aesthetics are second. This is not to say, of course, that aesthetics are not important; they are. But they are not as important as instructional effectiveness. This shift in priorities is made possible by the fact that the educator has a captive audience, in the best sense of the word. Since motivation to read the material is often largely external to the materials themselves, the same emphasis on attention-getting is not required. On the other hand, making it easy for the reader to read, and especially to learn, is an important concern for the educator.

Some might argue that designs of instructional materials should be bold and striking and fashionable and "now"—not "textbookish"—in order to attract and hold learners' attention, especially learners in their pre-teens and teens (a group traditionally felt to be difficult to motivate). If instructional materials looked like popular magazines, the argument goes, youngsters would be more likely to attend to them; educators have to compete with professional, commercial design by emulating it. However, research shows that there may be a danger in making instructional materials look too much like something other than what they are. Salomon (1984) found that learners perceived television as an "easy" medium and print materials a "tough" medium to learn from, and invested correspondingly different amounts of what he called invested mental effort. Sixth grade learners liked learning from television more, and felt they learned better from it, but actually learned more from print, even though (perhaps because?) they had to invest more mental effort to do so. Might it be that slick, contemporary (maybe even trendy) graphic design applied to instructional materials may create an effect similar to television, attracting learners more but helping them learn less because of the implied learners' perceptions? It's a research question waiting to be answered.

Fashion in Graphic Design

There is no doubt that certain elements of graphic design come into and go out of fashion (Collier and Cotton, 1989). To dispel any doubts, simply look at the layout and/or advertisements in a contemporary magazine, one from the seventies, and one from the fifties (your dentist's office should have at least one of each!). Staying in fashion is very important in DTP, but of almost no consequence in DTPI, in my opinion. The likelihood that fashionable graphic design will have a positive impact on instructional effectiveness is probably so small as to be negligible. If anything, it may have a negative effect, as hypothesized in the last paragraph.

Instructional Design vs. Graphic Design of Instructional Materials

What Does Instructional Design Include?

Instructional design (ID) is a systematic process used for producing instructional materials, which is now well established in educational theory and practice. It involves several distinct activities:

- clarifying educational needs and goals;

- deriving and specifying instructional objectives;

- analyzing the characteristics of the intended learners and the learning environment;

- analyzing the content to be taught;

- synthesizing the content in accordance with the analyses above and with established principles of instruction;

- exposing the learners to the instruction thus produced;

- collecting formative evaluation data on the effectiveness of the instruction; and

- revising any or all parts of the process to produce a second or subsequent version of the instructional materials.

Instructional design underlies the preparation of effective instructional materials, be they print, audiovisual, or computer-based (Clark, 1984), and instructional design should be applied to all the instructional materials you produce. However, instructional design is the subject matter for other books (e.g., Briggs, Gustafson, and Tillman, 1991; Dick and Carey, 1990; Gagné, 1987; Romiszowski, 1981), not this one.

The only reason I bring up the term *instructional design* now is that there is some potential for confusion. In this book I will talk about two kinds of design—instructional design and the design and layout of instructional materials—with an emphasis on the latter. My convention will be to use the full term instructional design or its common abbreviation, ID, when that is what I'm talking about. For the remainder of the time, design can safely be taken to mean graphic design, including layout (the way elements such as text and graphics are placed on a printed page).

Done well, both kinds of design are invisible. That is, the learner or reader will generally not notice either the instructional design or the graphic design when they are well done; they will be transparent. The learner/reader can then concentrate solely on the message being sent by the author. It is only when either or both the instructional design or the graphic design is poor that the learner/reader will notice that something is interfering with the reception of the message.

What Do Graphic Design and Layout Include?

Burns, Venit, and Hansen (1988, p. 89) identify the following design decisions as representative of those made in graphic design:

- selection of the typefaces, sizes, and styles for different elements within the text (including titles, headings, illustrations, and captions);

- specification of the basic format of the text (e.g., Will the paragraphs have a first line indent? What will be the space between paragraphs? Will the text be justified? Will headings be flush left or centered?);

- the basic page layout (or grid), including the page size, margins, orientation, and number of columns;

- determination of the final page count, or the range of pages expected to be filled. (Implicit is the notion of fitting the given text to the space available, a process called copy casting or copy fitting.)

To the above list could be added the enforcement of consistency in the use of type, graphics, and white space.

Layout includes "on the fly" decisions about placement of various elements (e.g., tables or figures in relation to the text referring to them), and sometimes even minor editing (as when a few words or lines must be deleted from a chapter so that they don't end up being the only thing printed on two whole pages, or so that a table or figure can be accommodated on the same page as the discussion pertaining to it).

Which Type of Design Is Most Important?

Although both kinds of design are important in the preparation of effective instructional materials, an edge can be given to the importance of instructional design. Clark (1984) has demonstrated that the use of principles of instructional design is more significant in determining effectiveness of instructional materials than the medium (e.g., television, computer-based instruction, print, etc.) chosen. Badly designed instruction cannot be salvaged by even the most creative visual treatment, but well-designed instruction will withstand considerable abuse in layout and design. It almost seems that learners don't necessarily expect good graphic design to be a part of instructional materials, and will often forgive its absence. Our goal, of course, should be to maximize both the instructional design and the visual design.

Which Type of Design Should Be Done First?

When DTP first began, the work flow model used was similar to that in the publishing industry at the time: writers produced text, which was then handed over to graphic designers for layout, then to printers. The model was familiar and reasonable; it worked well.

DTP, with its blurring of roles, however, had an effect on the model. Since the writer is sometimes also the person who does the layout, a more interactive model is developing. When a piece of work (or a line of text) is too long or too short to fit the layout nicely, it often gets rewritten on the spot. At the same time, newer generations of DTP software are responding to the changes in work model, and word processors are taking on more characteristics of layout software, while layout programs are beginning to build in many word processing features. The result is that today, much of what only DTP programs did a few years ago is also now being done by word processors, while DTP programs also have many word processing features. In fact, some high end word processors may offer sufficient DTP power to satisfy most educators' needs.

Still, your life will be simpler if you follow the original work model as much as possible. Try to create the content and do the instructional design before attending to the page design and layout. You will still have the facility to make minor corrections, and even major changes, right up until printing time, but sub-dividing the work this way will make it more manageable. To attempt to do the writing, the instructional design, and the page layout concomitantly will likely prove to be too much, at least until you've had some experience at those activities independently.

This means that your task starts with a word processor, and only when the instructional design and writing are finished do you begin to consider either formatting within your word processing software or transporting the text into a page layout program. Especially in the latter case, it is most efficient to strive for only minor revisions thereafter.

Roles in DTP

As noted in Chapter 1, DTP software builds in a good deal of specialized knowledge, but until much progress is made in the field of artificial intelligence, not all that is needed for the good design of instructional materials can be built in. When you, the educator, take on DTP, you are essentially taking on the roles of a number of highly trained people with varying functions (Burns, Venit, and Hansen, 1988; Hewson, 1988). You become a(n):

- author, whose function is to create the necessary content, with appropriate instructional design;

- editor, whose function is to make sure that materials of appropriate length are produced according to a specific time-line;

- sub-editor, whose function is to find and fix typographical, grammatical, and spelling errors;

- designer, whose function is to create a suitable visual "look" for the publication in question, including decisions about paper type and size, margins, and basic layout structure;

- typographer/compositor, whose function it is to choose the appropriate type and set it accurately;

- illustrator and photographer, whose function is to provide the graphics (line drawings and photographs);

- layout artist, whose function is to manually paste up bits of paper containing text and graphics, according to the specifications set down by the designer and typographer;

- expert reader, whose function is to find and fix substantive errors in the content; and

- proofreader, whose function it is to catch any errors that have crept in along the way.

Obviously, these roles encompass many skills. Don't be intimidated by the lengthy list; you have your DTP hardware and software to help you. And, as noted earlier, the function of this book is to bolster your skills primarily in the designer, typographer, layout artist, and partially in the illustrator, roles.

References for Chapter 2

Briggs, L. J., Gustafson, K. L., and Tillman, M. H. (Eds.) (1991). *Instructional design: Principles and applications* (2nd ed.). Englewood Cliffs, NJ: Educational Technology Publications.

Burns, D., Venit, S., and Hansen, R. (1988). *The electronic publisher*. New York: Brady.

Clark, R. E. (1984). Research on student thought processes during computer-based instruction. *Journal of Instructional Development, 7*(3), 2-5.

Collier, D., and Cotton, B. (1989). *Basic desktop design and layout*. Cincinnati, OH: North Light Books.

Dick, W., and Carey, L. (1990). *The systematic design of instruction* (3rd ed.). Glenview, IL: Scott, Foresman.

Duchastel, P. C. (1978). Illustrating instructional texts. *Educational Technology, 18*(11), 36–39.

Felici, J., and Nace, T. (1987). *Desktop publishing skills: A primer for typesetting with computers and laser printers*. Reading, MA: Addison-Wesley.

Gagné, R. M. (Ed.) (1987). *Instructional technology: Foundations.* Hillsdale, NJ: Lawrence Erlbaum Associates.

Hewson, D. (1988). *Introduction to desktop publishing.* San Francisco, CA: Chronicle Books.

Kleper, M. L. (1987). *The illustrated handbook of desktop publishing and typesetting.* Blue Ridge Summit, PA: Tab Books.

Romiszowski, A. J. (1981). *Designing instructional systems: Decision making in course planning.* London: Kogan Page.

Salomon, G. (1984). Television is "easy" and print is "tough": The differential investment of mental effort in learning as a function of perception and attributions. *Journal of Educational Psychology, 76,* 647–658.

Shushan, R., and Wright, D. (1989). *Desktop publishing by design.* Redmond, WA: Microsoft Press.

Swann, A. (1987). *How to understand and use design and layout.* Cincinnati, OH: North Light Books.

West, S. (1987). Design for desktop publishing. In The Waite Group (J. Stockford, Ed.), *Desktop publishing bible* (pp. 53–72). Indianapolis, IN: Howard W. Sams.

Using the Computer Wisely

This chapter doesn't fit here. But then it doesn't fit anywhere very well. It's not really about DTP, per se, and certainly not about DTP as it applies to instructional materials specifically. So why is it anywhere at all?

It's here because if you follow the advice given in this chapter, your job of page layout will be much easier than if you don't. This chapter really contains advice to the author, not to the designer or typographer or layout artist. Since you're as likely as not the author of your instructional materials (as well as all those other things), and since you will logically begin your publishing enterprise by writing something, the comments here need to be made before you begin writing. (You may choose to skip this chapter for now, if you are not going to be the author of documents. You should, however, read it eventually, as it contains information you will want to pass on to the author of documents you may be designing, in order to make your job easier.)

This chapter is about using your word processor as a word processor was intended to be used, rather than as a typewriter is used. Chances are you learned to keyboard (i.e., type) on a typewriter, and in so doing, probably picked up a number of bad habits—bad, that is, with respect to DTP. Too, word processors are capable of a number of things that typewriters aren't. Sometimes newcomers to word processing overlook these features, and end up doing a lot of unnecessary work as a consequence.

Word Processing and the Legacy of the Typewriter

The typewriter era spawned some operating procedures that are, in the context of word processing, not only obsolete, but often counter-productive in the sense that they have to be undone or re-done to match DTP requirements. Some of these are described below in a series of prescriptions and admonitions.

Single Spaces Between Sentences

The rule of not using the space bar twice consecutively applies equally at the end of a sentence, or following a colon. Most DTP guidelines state that only a single space should be used, since the double space we are accustomed to using on the typewriter leaves an aesthetically undesirable large space in typeset materials. If you have text created by someone who put a double space following the end of a sentence, use the global search and replace function (**Change...(⌘H)** in MS Word) to replace each of the following combinations with the combinations shown in Figure 3–1. (The symbol ƀ is used to denote a blank space made by pressing the space bar once.)

Replace this:	With this:
. ƀ ƀ	. ƀ
^? ƀ ƀ	^? ƀ
! ƀ ƀ	! ƀ
: ƀ ƀ	: ƀ

Figure 3–1. Sequence of MS Word global searches and replacements needed to eliminate double spaces between sentences. The caret (^) is produced with the Shift-6 key.

This sequence of replacements will have taken care of the vast majority of occurrences of unwanted blank spaces. Finally, to be sure you've got all the occurrences, do a **Find** to check for two consecutive spaces, making corrections where necessary.

In MS Word, you can use the space bar to type the ƀ right into the **Change...(⌘H)** boxes in the proper places. Other word processors may require you to use special codes to indicate a space; see their manuals for further advice.

"Curly" Quotation Marks and Apostrophes

A small thing that makes a significant difference in making a document look professional is the use of so-called "curly quotes" (" and " or ' and ') rather than the standard typewriter-like quotation marks (") and apostrophe ('), which should be reserved for the inch and foot abbreviations, respectively.

The Macintosh can make these special characters through the special keystrokes shown in Figures 3–2.

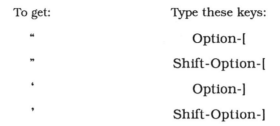

To get:	Type these keys:
"	Option-[
"	Shift-Option-[
'	Option-]
'	Shift-Option-]

Figure 3–2. "Curly" quotation marks and apostrophes can be made with special keystrokes on the Macintosh.

If using these key combinations is found awkward, the global search and replace using MS Word's **Change...(⌘H)** command can be used after a document is finished (Figure 3–3).

Replace this:	With this:
♭ "	♭ "
" ♭	" ♭
" .	" .
" ,	" ,
" ^ ?	" ^ ?

Figure 3–3. Sequence of MS Word global searches and replacements needed to replace typewriter-like quotation marks with "curly" quotation marks.

Repeat the sequence above with the ' , ', and ' characters. Finally, use **Find** to search for any more instances of " and ' , and adjust accordingly.

Alternatively, MS Word has a built-in feature called "Smart" Quotes, which correctly determines which curly quotation marks to use, even as text is being input or edited. If "Smart" Quotes is turned on (in the **Preferences** menu), you will not be able to use the " and ' characters from the keyboard to indicate inches and feet. Either turn off "Smart" Quotes when you need these symbols or place them into a glossary (described later in this chapter) for near-instant access whenever you need them.

"Before" and "After" Spacing
Rather Than Carriage Returns

It is common typewriter practice to create vertical space between, say, headings and bodies of text or between paragraphs by inserting extra carriage returns (i.e., pressing the Return key more than once). In word processing, this is not good practice. If you are not already in the habit of using only one carriage return at the end of a paragraph (or line), you should start now. If the extra carriage returns are left in a document, extra vertical space may appear at their locations once other format-ting steps, described later in this book, are carried out. Many word processors (at least the high-end ones) permit you to specify how much space is to be left before and/or after a line of text.

In MS Word, judicious use of the **Before** and **After** settings in the **Paragraph... (⌘M)** window eliminates the need for using more than one carriage return at the end of each paragraph.

A paragraph is operationally defined as anything followed by a carriage return. Thus a single line—indeed, a single word—may be a paragraph. The format for a paragraph is influenced by the settings made in the **Paragraph... (⌘M)** window (see Figure 3–4).

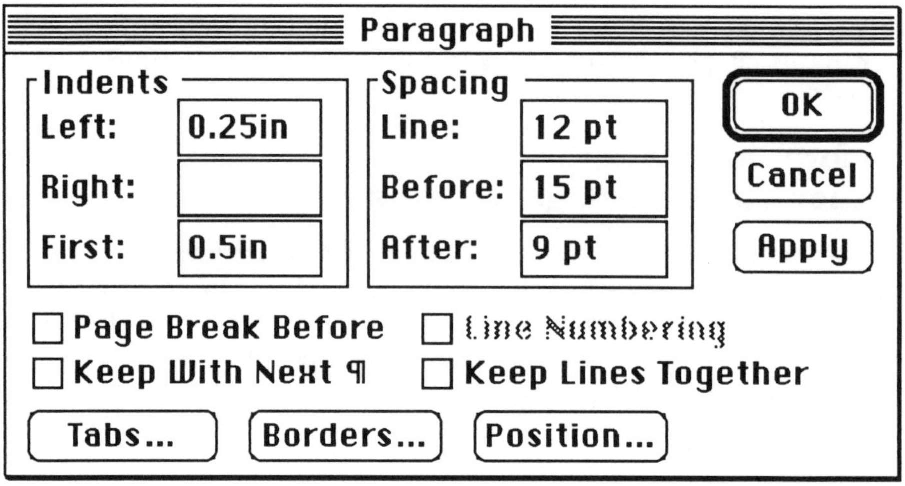

```
┌─────────────────────────────────────────────────────────┐
│ ≣≣≣≣≣≣≣≣≣≣≣≣≣≣≣≣≣ Paragraph ≣≣≣≣≣≣≣≣≣≣≣≣≣≣       │
│ ┌Indents ──────┐ ┌Spacing ──────┐  ╭──────────╮        │
│ │ Left:  │0.25in │ │ Line:  │12 pt │  │   OK     │       │
│ │                │ │                │  ╰──────────╯       │
│ │ Right: │       │ │ Before:│15 pt │  ╭──────────╮       │
│ │                │ │                │  │ Cancel   │       │
│ │ First: │0.5in  │ │ After: │9 pt  │  ╰──────────╯       │
│ └────────────────┘ └────────────────┘  ╭──────────╮     │
│                                         │ Apply    │     │
│   ☐ Page Break Before   ☐ Line Numbering  ╰──────────╯   │
│   ☐ Keep With Next ¶    ☐ Keep Lines Together           │
│   ╭── Tabs... ──╮  ╭── Borders... ──╮  ╭── Position... ──╮ │
└─────────────────────────────────────────────────────────┘
```

Figure 3–4. Settings in the **Paragraph... (⌘M)** window of MS Word.

In the **Spacing** section, you can specify the vertical spacing between lines (**Line**), the amount of space to be inserted before each paragraph (**Before**), and the amount of space to be inserted after each paragraph (**After**). The **Before** and **After** settings can, of course, be 0 if you simply want the same spacing between paragraphs as you have between lines within the paragraph. The spacing used in this book has a **Line** of 13 points and an **After** of 6 points. (A point is a unit of measurement used in the publishing industry. A more complete description of points is found in Chapter 6. Spaces **Before** and **After** can also be specified in terms of inches or centimeters.)

As the space after a given paragraph is normally the same space as the one before the paragraph following it, you typically would not have both **Before** and **After** spacing specified for normal text (or else you would end up with an inter-paragraph space equal to the sum of the two specifications). For headings, however, you might have spacing both **Before** and **After**. The heading immediately following, for example, has 18 points of spacing **Before** it and 6 points of spacing **After** it.

Dash Rather Than Two Hyphens

With typewriters, there was only one character available, the hyphen, so a dash had to be indicated by using two hyphens (--). The Macintosh will produce two different types of dashes, the em dash (—) and the en dash (–), as well as the hyphen (-). The em dash, which is as wide as the font size is high, is produced with Shift-Option-Hyphen and the en dash, which is half the width of an em dash, with Option-Hyphen.

The en dash is used:

- as a minus sign (e.g., Score – Mean Score);

- in dates (e.g., 10–Sept–89); and

- between numerals to indicate a range of page numbers (e.g., pp. 495–505).

When used as a minus sign, a space should precede and follow the en dash; otherwise there should be no space.

The em dash is used in other applications of a dash, such as the most common application, indicating a break in thought (e.g., Snyder and Taylor's work—although only a decade old—may not necessarily be relevant any longer.) There should be no space before or after the em dash.

Hyphens should only be used in compound words (e.g., trial-by-trial analysis).

No space should be used before or after a hyphen, or before or after an en or em dash.

Tabs Rather Than the Space Bar

In a similar manner, horizontal spacing should only be done through the use of tabs or the word wrapping margin—never with the space bar. It is important to use tabs rather than the space bar because, as is likely, if either the font type or the size of the font is changed, vertical mis-alignment will probably occur. In Figure 3–5a, the top and bottom paragraphs appear virtually identical. Turning on MS Word's **Show ¶ (⌘Y)** command in the **Edit** menu, however, reveals differences in the way the paragraphs were constructed (Figure 3–5b). The ➜ symbol represents a tab, while the dots (...) each represent space bars (i.e., the space bar was pressed three times to create the dots in the parentheses). Although the numerals and text line up properly in both paragraphs initially, they no longer do so when the font is changed from Bookman 9 (Figure 3–5a) to Times 9 (Figure 3–5c), or to Bookman 12 (Figure 3–5d).

1. Horizontal spacing should always be done with the tab key, never with the space bar. Failure to use the tab key almost always results in undesirable spacing.

1. Horizontal spacing should always be done with the tab key, never with the space bar. Failure to use the tab key almost always results in undesirable spacing.

(a)

➧ 1.➧Horizontal spacing should always be done with the tab key, never with the space bar. Failure to use the tab key almost always results in undesirable spacing.¶

...... 1....Horizontal spacing should always be done with the tab key, never with the space bar. Failure to use the tab key almost always results in undesirable spacing.¶

(b)

Figure 3–5. Using the space bar instead of the tab key can cause alignment problems if the font or the font size is subsequently changed. *(Figure continued on next page.)*

1. Horizontal spacing should always be done with the tab key, never with the space bar. Failure to use the tab key almost always results in undesirable spacing.

1. Horizontal spacing should always be done with the tab key, never with the space bar. Failure to use the tab key almost always results in undesirable spacing.

(c)

1. Horizontal spacing should always be done with the tab key, never with the space bar. Failure to use the tab key almost always results in undesirable spacing.

1. Horizontal spacing should always be done with the tab key, never with the space bar. Failure to use the tab key almost always results in undesirable spacing.

(d)

Figure 3–5. *(continued)*

The rule of thumb is: If you use the space bar two or more times consecutively, you are doing something wrong.

Word Wraps Rather Than the Space Bar or Tabs

When it is necessary to have outdented text (e.g., "point" form), the second and subsequent line(s) should be properly aligned through the use of the word wrap marker on the ruler rather than through use of either the space bar or tabs.

If you use tabs to form the left margin and carriage returns to form the right margin, instead of word wrapping, you will probably get undesirable effects if you have to change the margins later, or if you subsequently change either the font or the font size. Study the paragraphs in Figure 3–6. The paragraph in Figure 3–6a was done correctly, using word wraps, while the paragraph in Figure 3–6b was done incorrectly, using tabs at the left margin and carriage returns at the right. Although they will look virtually identical when printed, any changes made to the font, the font size, or the margin structure will yield detrimental effects on the incorrectly-done paragraph. These negative effects are exemplified in Figures 3–7, 3–8, and 3–9.

In Figures 3–6 through 3–9, margins are indicated by the arrows (↓), tab settings by the plus sign (+), and the word wrap setting by the double arrow (⇓).The ➜ symbol represents a tab, and the ¶ symbol represents a carriage return.

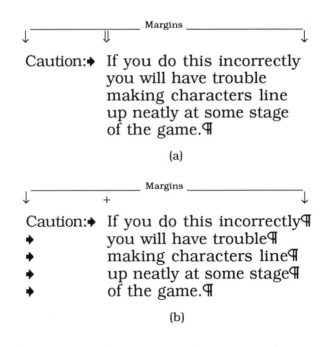

Figure 3–6. The paragraph in (a) was done correctly, with word wrap setting, while the paragraph in (b) was done incorrectly, with tabs at the left margin and carriage returns at the right margin.

Figure 3–7 shows what happens if you change the font size, while keeping the margins the same.

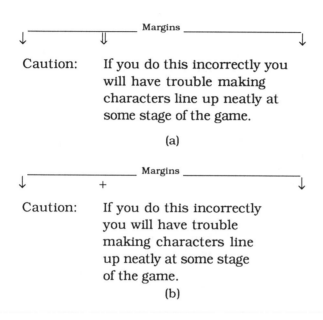

(a)

(b)

Figure 3–7. Changes in font size (from 12-point in Figure 3–6 to 10-point here), create unwanted formatting changes in (b), in which tabs were used at the left margin and carriage returns at the right margin. However, no unwanted changes occur in the correctly-done paragraph, (a).

Figure 3–8 shows what happens when the font itself is changed, although the font size is kept constant.

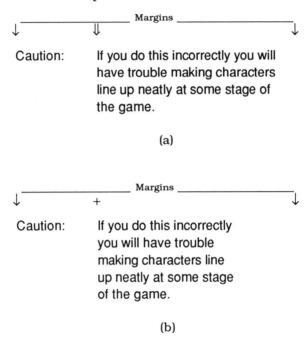

(a)

(b)

Figure 3–8. Changes in font (from Bookman in Figure 3–7 to Helvetica here), create unwanted formatting changes in (b), in which tabs were used at the left margin and carriage returns at the right margin. However, no unwanted changes occur in correctly-done paragraph (a).

Finally, Figure 3–9 shows what happens when the margins are changed. In all cases, the lines of text end up being shorter than they should be.

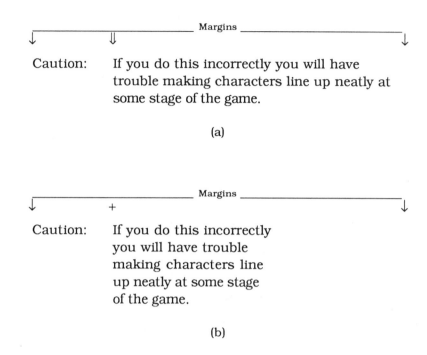

Figure 3–9. Changes in margins create unwanted formatting changes in (b), in which tabs were used at the left margin and carriage returns at the right margin. However, no unwanted changes occur in correctly-done paragraph (a).

"Hard" and "Soft" Carriage Returns

So-called "hard" carriage returns define the end of a paragraph whereas "soft" carriage returns cause subsequent text to fall on a new line, but it is still considered part of the same paragraph. In MS Word hard carriage returns (which show up on the screen as ¶ under the **Show ¶** (⌘Y) command) are created by pressing the Return key. Soft carriage returns (↵ under **Show ¶** (⌘Y)) are created by pressing Shift-Return. You would use a soft carriage return whenever you want to force text to a subsequent line without causing the normal end-of-paragraph happenings to occur. For example, you may normally have "space after" a heading to separate the heading from the body text. If you have an inordinately long heading, however, it may wrap at a logically inconvenient place, so you would use a soft carriage return to make the appropriate break.

The difference between a hard and a soft carriage return is best illustrated by an example (see Figure 3–10). The sense of the passage is better retained by the forced carriage return in (b) than by allowing normal word wrapping to occur as in (a); however, because additional "space after" is automatically placed at the end of a paragraph, the two lines of text in (b) appear to be too far apart vertically. A better solution is to use a soft carriage return, as in (c), which gives the desired effect.

Instructional Design vs. Design and Layout of Instructional Materials

(a)

Instructional Design vs.

Design and Layout of Instructional Materials

(b)

Instructional Design vs.
Design and Layout of Instructional Materials

(c)

Figure 3–10. Poorly wrapped heading in (a) has a better wrap but poorer vertical spacing when a hard carriage return is used in (b). Both the wrap and the vertical spacing are good when a soft carriage return is used (c).

Non-Breaking Spaces

Non-breaking (or "hard") spaces are the same as spaces created with the space bar, except that if they happen to be the last character in a line, they will not permit a wrap to occur. Another way of saying the same thing is that when two words are separated by a non-breaking space, they will always be kept on the same line, even though the first word might normally be on one line and the following word would—through normal word-wrapping—be on the next line. Although I am using the word *word* here, it could be any group of characters, like numerals. Indeed, it is with numerals that most instances occur when it would be wisest to use a non-breaking space.

For example, consider the pairs of arrangements of text in Figure 3–11. In the second case of each example, a hard space was used to keep the unit of measurement adjacent to the numerals, thereby enhancing the logical connection:

> It may be of interest to note that nearly 210 seconds passed before there was a reaction.

> It may be of interest to note that nearly 210 seconds passed before there was a reaction.

(a)

> The capital expenditures, now indicated on p. 456, are well in excess of estimates.

> The capital expenditures, now indicated on p. 456, are well in excess of estimates.

(b)

Figure 3–11. "Hard" spaces should be used to keep numerals and associated units contiguous, as they were in the second paragraphs of both examples (a) and (b).

Non-breaking spaces should be used whenever the meaning of the text might possibly be either distorted or made more difficult to discern by the first "word" being on one line and the second on a subsequent line. In the following list of circumstances when non-breaking spaces should be used, the non-breaking spaces are indicated with the symbol ⁒, which is MS Word's way of showing a non-breaking space on the screen when the **Show ¶ (⌘Y)** feature is turned on:

- between digits and units (e.g., 12⁒cm);

- between the time of day and *a.m.* or *p.m.* (e.g., 11:00⁒p.m.);

- between the time in numerals and the word *o'clock* (e.g., 5:00⁒o'clock);

- between the abbreviation for page and the page number (e.g., p.~26);

- between the word *Figure* and the figure number, or the word *Table* and the table number (e.g., see the data in Table~12);

- after abbreviations such as e.g. and i.e. (e.g.,~this work; i.e.,~whatever is necessary);

- in lists of enumerated items (e.g., (a)~letters, (b)~words, (c)~sentences; (1)~young women, (2)~young men, (3)~old women, (4)~old men);

- in mathematical equations which might unnecessarily fall onto two lines if non-breaking spaces are not used.

Proper Keys for Numerals, Ellipses, and Bullets

It is important to use the correct keys for certain characters. Two typical errors made by those who learned keyboarding on a typewriter are the substitution of an "l" (lowercase letter ell) for a "1" (numeral one) and the substitution of an "O" (uppercase letter oh) for a "0" (numeral zero). While these characters may sometimes appear to be very similar on the screen, they can look radically different when printed on a LaserWriter, especially if the font is changed.

An ellipsis (...) is normally used to indicate missing text, especially in a quotation. There is a special key combination on the Macintosh for an ellipsis, Option-;. It should be used rather than three periods because it is a single character. If an ellipsis should happen to fall at the end of a line of text, and it is improperly formed (i.e., made with periods), some of the periods can end up on a different line than the others. If the Option-; key combination is used, either all or none of the ellipsis will be on a given line.

Bullets (•) are made with the Option-8 key combination. They should be used with "point form" hanging indents, rather than using hyphens (-) or asterisks (*).

Creating Fill-in Blanks

Blanks to be filled in are typically created on the typewriter by using the underscore (_) character repeatedly. This method will work only sporadically in DTP, so it is better avoided.

In MS Word, for example, using the underscore will work fine with Times or Helvetica, but if the font is changed subsequently (say, to Bookman), the blanks may be replaced with broken (dashed) lines, which is generally undesirable aesthetically. Furthermore, the length of each blank will probably change when the font is changed. Finally, if the blanks are to be right-aligned (i.e., form an even right-hand margin), you will probably find that you cannot get them to align evenly when using the underscore character. Also, be aware that if an MS Word file is imported into a Macintosh environment from an MS-DOS environment, even though both machines are running compatible versions of MS Word, undesirable changes will probably occur.

A preferred way to create blanks is to use a tab with a line leader (see Figure 3–12 for the MS Word dialogue box to accomplish it). For blanks with words on either side of them, use a left (normal) tab set at the point where the blank should end. With the cursor at the point at which the blank should begin, simply press the tab key.

For blanks that should right-align, set a right-aligned tab where the blank should end, and press the tab key where the blank should begin: voilà, perfect blanks. MS Word seems to do some unexpected things with right alignment, too, depending upon which font is used, so you are well advised to make all your right-aligned blanks using the same font (which need be not be the same as the font used for words preceding the blank, of course).

Another good way to create blanks is to use the space bar as many times as is necessary to create the appropriate length of blank, then change the style of those spaces to underlined. Once again, this doesn't seem to produce an unbroken line consistently for all fonts, so experiment beforehand.

Rules (i.e., lines) drawn in page layout programs will also form adequate blanks.

Note that editing text ahead of blanks created by the methods described above will probably have undesired effects, so be sure your text is in final form before setting up the tabs.

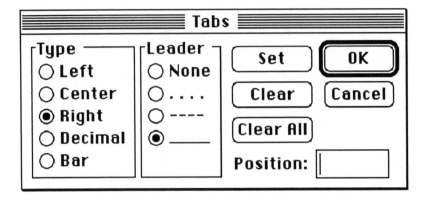

Figure 3–12. Using a right-aligned tab with a line leader to create fill-in blanks.

Extra Carriage Returns
in ASCII Documents

Documents produced on word processing systems other than the one you are using may be imported into your machine in a format called ASCII (pronounced ass-key). For all practical purposes, you can think of ASCII documents as consisting of only the characters *A–Z* (in upper and lower case), the numerals, and the punctuation marks normally found on a keyboard. (There are some "invisible" characters that form part of ASCII, too, but aside from a few such as carriage returns and tabs, they aren't relevant to this discussion.) ASCII documents therefore contain no formatting, font, or text style information.

When ASCII documents are imported to the Macintosh environment, they will usually have one of two forms. Either there will be carriage returns only at the ends of paragraphs, or there will be a carriage return at the end of each line of text, and probably two at the end of each paragraph. If there is only one at the end of each paragraph, well and good—that is what you want. If there are two, one of them is superfluous and must be eliminated. Similarly, if there are carriage returns at the end of each line, they must be deleted, along with the extra ones between paragraphs.

If the documents being imported are being created on a non-Mac machine, hopefully you can get the ASCII files to be produced without the extra carriage returns in the first place. If unwanted carriage returns are there, of course, you will have to remove them before you can format the document on the Mac. (The way to ascertain whether or not they are there is to get the formatting codes to show on the screen. In MS Word, this is accomplished by choosing **Show ¶ (⌘Y)** from the **Edit** menu.)

This removal is most easily accomplished by using the global search and replace feature of MS Word, called **Change... (⌘H)**. If it is only a matter of a document having a double carriage return at the end of each paragraph, the change is relatively straightforward. You simply replace a pair of carriage returns with a single one.

In MS Word, you must use a special pair of characters, ^P, in the **Change... (⌘H)** boxes to denote a carriage return. The caret (^) is produced with the Shift-6 key.

Replace this: With this:

^P^P   ^P

If, however, there are carriage returns at the end of each line, you must go through a series of steps. First you replace all the pairs of carriage returns with some other character that you don't expect to find in the text (e.g., §, created with Option-6). Then you replace each of the single carriage returns with a blank. Finally, you replace all the special characters with a carriage return (Figure 3–13).

Replace this:	With this:
^P^P	§
^P	ƀ
§	^P

Figure 3–13. Sequence of MS Word global searches and replacements needed to strip unwanted carriage returns from an ASCII document. The symbol ƀ denotes a blank.

If you have only a relatively small amount of memory (e.g., one megabyte on a Macintosh) or your document is lengthy (e.g., more than a dozen pages or so), it is wise to **Save** your document after each step in the replacement procedure above, so that you do not run short of memory in the middle of a conversion.

Following the sequence above will correctly convert most of the carriage returns, but perhaps not absolutely all. It works best in straight paragraphs of text. You may find a few surprises in headings and in tables, which you will have to correct manually.

The Word Processor's Glossary

Glossaries are collections of user-defined equivalencies that are most useful for difficult-to-type or oft-repeated prose (although graphics can also be used in MS Word glossaries). I have trouble typing the words *University of Saskatchewan* without making typographical errors. About half the time, it seems to turn out Univesrity of Saksatchewan; my fingers just can't seem to learn to do it right. By using the glossary, I "taught" MS Word that every time I type in the special code *uofs*, it should type out the words *University of Saskatchewan* in place of the code. By using only a few keystrokes, I can accomplish what would normally take many (troublesome) keystrokes. (I also taught it Mississippi and Massachusetts!)

Glossaries can typically hold lengthier text passages as well, so if there is a stock phrase or paragraph you use often (known as boiler-plate), it can be placed into a glossary, too. Glossaries can be great time-savers for complex collections of characters that are used repeatedly, like this one

$$x_{1,2} = \frac{-b \pm \sqrt{b^2 - 4ac}}{2a}$$

which I called up from my glossary by typing in *quad.* The only problem with glossaries is that you have to remember what your special little abbreviations are for each entry you have. Fortunately, some word processors (like MS Word) give you a menu from which you can choose if you forget, displaying the first part of the equivalent when you choose each abbreviation.

Word processors that do not have glossary functions may have macro functions which will permit essentially the same user-defined equivalencies.

The Scrapbook

The Macintosh has a special storage place in memory called the Scrapbook, which can be used to hold bits and pieces of text or graphics. You need only open the Scrapbook, copy the contents from one of its pages, close the Scrapbook, and paste what you copied into the document you are working on.

To place things in the Scrapbook, merely copy it (using the standard **Copy** command) from within whatever application program you are using (word processor, graphics programs, spreadsheet, etc.), open the Scrapbook, and **Paste** into the Scrapbook. When you close the Scrapbook, its contents are saved for you. To use them, open the Scrapbook, locate the "page" containing the item you want, and **Copy** it. Close the Scrapbook, and **Paste** the item into your word processing document.

To delete an item from the Scrapbook, simply **Cut** it out.

Store repetitively-used graphics or even lengthy passages of text in the Scrapbook for ready accessibility. By using a desk accessory such as SmartScrap™ and The Clipper™ you can even have multiple scrapbooks, with contents classified according to project or publication.

The Scrapbook is a particularly convenient way of transferring a number of graphics from a graphics program into a word processor, as its window can be kept open alongside the graphics program's window while copying the graphics, then alongside the word processor's window while pasting them.

Style Sheets

In pre-DTP days, style sheets were simply sheets of paper on which were enumerated all the information one needed to make a publication (or portions thereof) conform to a design. For example, a designer setting up the style sheet might specify that the "normal" text of a publication be a particular typeface in a certain size, with margins of such-and-such. Further, there should be so much space between paragraphs, and an additional certain amount of space before a major heading (title). The captions for figures should always begin with the word "Figure," followed by the number of the figure and a colon, and the description; the word "Figure" and the number and colon should be in boldface type, and the remainder of the caption should be in italic type. The whole caption should be a certain size of type. There should be a space of so many units between the top of a figure and the bottom of the text preceding it. And so on....

In DTP terms, a style sheet is an electronic equivalent of the older form. Using **Styles...** under the **Format** menu in MS Word, for example, you can set up a new document so that all major headings are a particular typeface and size, all text following the heading is a different typeface and size, etc. When writing at the keyboard, all the formatting decisions are made by the electronic style sheet, and the writer need not be concerned with what size the type should be for footnotes, figure captions, headings, etc. The writer simply types the heading, tells the word processor it is a heading by selecting from a menu, and continues typing the text that should follow the heading. The machine does all the work of making the text match the specifications, and produces much more consistent results than might obtain otherwise.

This is not the place to describe fully the capabilities and intricacies of styles; your word processor's manual does that. The point of raising the issue here is to encourage you to look into styles, since they will save you a lot of time and effort in the long run. Styles seem to be judged by many to be an esoteric tool, hence they are often overlooked. They shouldn't be. Although they may take some study and practice initially, they will pay off handsomely, especially if you will be producing a number of documents with similar layouts.

Hartley and Burnhill (1977b) extol the virtues of an educator pre-planning the layout of instructional materials, as well as the importance of communicating to printers the details of "...the required position on the page of every item of information to be typeset and printed" (p. 239). Style sheets allow you to perform both these functions very easily.

An interesting and very powerful feature of style sheets is that they can be set up relative to one another. That is, the styles for minor and major headings can be defined in terms of the style used for normal text. So can the style for, say, tables. Since style sheet information can include not only such things as typeface and size, but also the amount of space above, below, and to the right and left of the text, the specification of a style can be a very precise means of ensuring consistent placement of headings, tables, etc.

Furthermore, since styles can be set up relative to one another, a small change in one style can, at your option, bring about coincident changes in others. To illustrate, suppose that a document is completely laid out, using Bookman type as the "normal" type, but that the document also contains a number of other typefaces serving special functions. Suppose further that it is found necessary at the last minute to change the "normal" type to Times. While it is possible to easily change *all* the type in a document from Bookman to Times, using a word processor such as MS Word, doing that would cause you to have to go back and restore all the other fonts. Using style sheets, all you need do is change the specification for the "normal" font, and everything you wanted done—and none of what you didn't want done—happens automatically.

Template Documents

Template documents are "empty" documents that contain all the proper formatting information for the finished product. They are particularly useful when you are creating a number of documents all with the same format. That is, you can set up a document with appropriately-sized margins, font selection, leading, etc., but leave it devoid of content, or containing only the content that is common to all similar documents. When you open it, you can put in the new content, then save the document with a new name.

For a simple example, consider a memo. It will usually have the same format each time, with the title *MEMORANDUM*, and with *To:* and *From:* and *Date:* located somewhere on the page. To avoid repetitive typing of all those things (and perhaps more, like your name following the *From:* field), create a document containing just those bits of text, and save it, say with the name Memo Template. To use the template, click to set the cursor at the place(s) you want to type something in, and type in whatever else you want the memo to say. Then save the resulting document using the **Save As...** command, giving it a name that reflects its contents (e.g., Memo to Bill W.). The template document, Memo Template, will still exist in its original form, ready to be used again for the next memo, and you will have the other document (Memo to Bill W.) also stored on your disk.

On a Macintosh, if you want to protect yourself from accidentally saving some data in the template document, lock the template before using it, by clicking on the **Locked** box in the **Get Info...**(⌘I) window (see Figure 3–14). Then, if you accidentally try to **Save** the document instead of doing a **Save As...**, you will get a dialogue box requiring you to give the new (modified) document a new name.

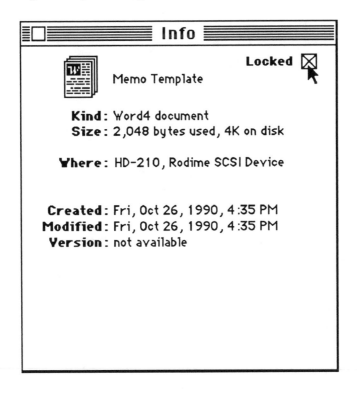

Figure 3–14. **Get Info…(⌘I)** window of a document, showing how to lock the document.

Newsletters, self-instructional modules, overhead transparencies, and worksheets are other documents for which template documents are ideal, as only their content, and not their basic structure, varies from one document to the next.

Outliners

Outliners are separate programs (or portions of a word-processing program) that are designed to assist in the creation and manipulation of outlines. Outlines, as you have undoubtedly been told—somewhere, sometime, probably by an English teacher—are powerful tools for writers.

When I had to submit outlines with my essays in English 101, I always waited until I had finished writing the essay to construct the outline. (Otherwise, how would I know what to put in, and in what order? I had to find out what I said before I could tell you what I was planning to say, didn't I?)

If your approach to writing is like mine was, you'll be tempted to ignore an outliner. My advice to you is: don't ignore it. Although I had used MS Word for years, I had never really bothered to find out much about the outliner portion of the program. When writing this book, I decided finally to invest a half hour to learn how to use it.

It's wonderful!

It allows me to bounce immediately from word processor to outliner mode with a single keystroke. While in outliner mode, I can rearrange headings in the outline until their order seems to make sense. Sub-headings can be collapsed or expanded in view, so that I can see only the level of detail that I want at that time. When I go back into word processor mode, all the text attached to those rearranged headlines has also been moved along with the headings, just as I wanted it.

I don't think I could ever consider approaching a writing task again without making use of it. It isn't useful only for major writing tasks, either; I even find myself using it for small writing tasks such as composing business letters and memos that are a little on the complex side. It really does help organize your thoughts. As Lang (1987) puts it, "...I haven't yet met a writer who has stopped using an outliner after giving it a fair try..." (p. 58). She points out a major strength of outliners: You can see the structure of the entire document, which gives rise to a more logical flow of ideas. Of course, it is instantly manipulable, so the structure can be experimented with until it seems just right. It also offers an interesting side-effect in that writer's block ceases to be as much of a problem. Because you can tinker with the structure and its supporting text interchangeably, you can begin work at either level and bounce back and forth until the creative juices start flowing again of their own accord.

Instructional materials, especially, can benefit from the use of outliners. No matter how careful our task and content analyses are, it is inevitable that, even at the writing stage, we will have to change at least some of the order of presentation of the material. An outliner—

especially one so thoroughly integrated with a word processor as the one in MS Word—makes these changes easy.

Spelling Checkers

Spelling checkers are built into many word processing and/or page layout programs, or are available as adjuncts to them. They are invaluable for finding letter transpositions and other typographic errors, and for assisting poor spellers. They also are extremely objective, in that they cannot use context to aid interpretation, hence do not inadvertently gloss over misspellings and typos as humans sometimes do. They are not infallible, however, even if the dictionaries they come with are large and complete. Their major shortcoming is the opposite side to their objectivity: They are not capable of determining the appropriateness of a given word in its context. As luck would have it, when I first typed the initial sentence of this paragraph, it ended with the words *adjuncts to hem*, which would have been perfectly acceptable to a spelling checker, of course, but not to a human reader. The bottom line is that spelling checkers are valuable aids for finding both blatant typos and those typos that you can read right past no matter how many times you re-read your work, but they cannot substitute for a good proofreader. Use both.

Hyphenation

Hyphenation is used in two different cases:

- when required by correct spelling and grammar as defined by dictionaries or style guides (e.g., American Psychological Association, 1983; Gibaldi and Achtert, 1988; *The Chicago Manual of Style*, 1982; Turabian, 1976); and

- when used to provide a smoother-looking or justified right margin (i.e., a right margin in which all the text lines up vertically).

Hyphenation should always be used in the former case; the comments in this section pertain only to the latter case. I will discuss justification of text more fully in the next chapter; it must be mentioned here, however, because part of the process of producing right-justified text usually involves using hyphens liberally. As I will demonstrate during the discussion of justification, there is reason to believe that the use of hyphens, in most circumstances, is a poor idea from an instructional point of view, as it has been hypothesized to slow reading and to interfere with comprehension.

Many word processors and page layout programs provide for automatic hyphenation. By providing algorithms that hyphenate, or by providing dictionaries against which hyphenation can be checked, these programs frequently hyphenate better than people do, but they still often make errors.

A number of designers admit that hyphenation compromises readability (e.g., Lichty, 1989; White, 1983), but the practice is still widespread. If your word processor or page layout program is one that has automatic hyphenation, I suggest you find out how to turn it off.

If you leave text completely unhyphenated, there will probably be a few places where the right margin is unacceptably choppy. Polysyllabic language typical of higher education, especially, can cause wildly varying right margins. It seems to me reasonable that the most extreme problems be taken care of through judicious hyphenation, but that in general, hyphenation be avoided if possible. In this book, I hyphenated normally-unhyphenated words very sparingly, and only when unacceptably-large white spaces appeared at the ends of lines of text. I also checked carefully that no hyphenated word could be confusing.

Guidelines for Hyphenation

If you decide to hyphenate despite the caveats above, you would be well advised to follow these guidelines gleaned from a number of sources:

- Do not hyphenate names or other words which begin with a capital letter (Hewson, 1988).

- Do not hyphenate display sections of text—such as headlines or titles—or captions (Bove and Rhodes, 1989; Burns, Venit, and Hansen, 1988; Hewson, 1988; Shushan and Wright, 1989).

- Do not hyphenate words to leave only a few letters before or after the hyphen. (Burns, Venit, and Hansen, 1988, say two letters; Hewson, 1988, says three; but in my opinion, anything less than five is too little.)

- Do not hyphenate words to produce breaks which create either new meaning (e.g., far-thing) or ambiguity (e.g., propos-als, or reap-pear) on either side of the hyphen, or break the construction of the word (Hewson, 1988).

- Do not hyphenate numbers (Burns, Venit, and Hansen, 1988).

- Do not hyphenate words of one syllable (Burns, Venit, and Hansen, 1988).

- Do not permit more than two (some writers say three) hyphens in a row along the right-hand margin (Burns, Venit, and Hansen, 1988; Shushan and Wright, 1989).

- Do not hyphenate an already hyphenated word.

- Hyphenate on a double consonant, unless the word's root ends with a double consonant (e.g., miss-ing, not mis-sing) (Burns, Venit, and Hansen, 1988).

"Hard" and "Soft" Hyphens

Most word processing programs allow you to use three different kinds of hyphens, all of which look the same but act differently with respect to word wrapping. A normal hyphen in a word always appears as a hyphen, no matter where the word containing it is located relative to the right margin. When the word is at the right margin, wrapping will occur at the hyphen if that action will make the line the proper length. The normal hyphen should be used most of the time; exceptions are listed below.

A "hard" or non-breaking hyphen also always appears as a hyphen, no matter where the word containing it is located. It will not permit wrapping, however, even though the conditions are right for wrapping.

You should use a hard hyphen in telephone numbers, for example, to keep both parts of the number together on the same line, or to keep together a phrase such as *12-inch diameter.*

A "soft" or optional hyphen is a hyphen that is embedded in a word in such a way that it is not normally visible. It automatically becomes visible (and effects a wrap at that point) if and when the location of the word containing it falls into the wrapping range. If subsequent editing changes the location of the word, the soft hyphen again disappears from view. If you use a soft hyphen at all, it would usually be in an exceptionally long word that stands a chance of ending up near the right margin after editing text prior to the word.

In MS Word, the different kinds of hyphens are created with the special key combinations shown in Figure 3–15.

To get a:	Type these keys:
normal hyphen	-
hard hyphen	⌘ ~
soft hyphen	⌘ -

Figure 3–15. MS Word key combinations to achieve different kinds of hyphens.

Managing Files

Newcomers to desktop publishing may inadvertently cause themselves difficulties with file management that can be avoided with a little planning and a modicum of diligence. Following are a few tips that will help you avoid these problems.

Keep Files Relatively Small

The fact that your word processor or page-layout program *can* handle huge files doesn't mean that it *should* be made to do so. There are benefits to keeping the files sizes small:

- Moving around (scrolling) inside the document is generally much faster in a small document than in a larger one.

- Doing a **Save** generally takes less time with smaller documents than with larger ones.

- Making backup copies of documents takes less time and they fit onto floppy disks better when files are small, which may encourage you to do it more often.

- One person can be working on one portion of the document while another is working on a different one. (If you find yourself doing this, take extra pains to do lots of **Save As...**, giving the newly created files unique names or version numbers. It's all too easy to accidentally trash a file you subsequently need. Also, pay attention to the document modification time [Last Modified] that shows when windows in the Finder are put into the **by Name** mode of the **View** menu. This will help to avoid confusion about which version is the most recent.)

There is a lower limit beyond which it becomes dysfunctional to make file sizes smaller, of course. File sizes of 20–30K are quite easy to handle; even 40–50K are not too difficult. In lengthy documents (e.g., books), it is probably best to allocate each chapter to a separate file. Try to keep the divisions logical (i.e., don't break a document in two arbitrarily; what you gain in speed of accessing portions of it may be more than lost in confusion). If you need frequent access to several chapters at once, keep them open and simply move from one to the next via the **Window** menu.

Saving Files and Making Backups

Saving and backing up files is such a fundamental part of using a computer that it shouldn't need to be mentioned here. Nevertheless, I have seen too many users—even experienced ones—lose important work through lack of attention to these simple acts. I simply can't over-state the importance of making regular and frequent backup copies of all your documents. While writing, editing, or laying out a document, you should allow no more than 10–15 minutes to pass without doing a **Save**. If you are doing critical, trying work, you should save even more frequently. Don't do any more work between **Save**s than you are prepared to lose completely if there is a power failure or other disruption of normal operation.

Backups (copies of your original file, on a different disk than the original) should also be made quite frequently, although generally not as frequently as **Save**s. Once again, you can use the criticality of your work as a guide: the more catastrophic a loss would be, the more frequently you should make backups. For most people and most projects, making backups about once per hour seems a reasonable compromise.

Naming and Cross-Referencing Files

Use names for files that will communicate their contents (which is much easier to do in the Macintosh world, where names can be up to 32 characters long, than in the PC-DOS world, where the length of names is severely limited). Alternatively, keep a separate document cross-referring file names and file contents (a much more troublesome procedure, and risky since it is error-prone).

Be consistent in the use of names. Don't call one document "Chapter 2" and the next one "Ch. III." When more than one person is involved, it is especially important to set up a file-naming convention right at the start of the project.

Pay special attention to the naming of graphics files or separate files containing tables, which will be inserted into the document at a later time. Names for these files must be absolutely unique, so that the wrong graphic doesn't get inserted. It is not a good idea to name these files "Figure 1," "Table 5," etc., since the insertion or deletion of a figure or table as writing and editing proceed will ultimately cause confusion. Rather, give them (short) descriptive names.

Within the text document, it is a good idea to insert the actual file name of the graphic, and perhaps a description of its location within a folder or on a particular disk. When it finally comes time to integrate the text document with the graphics files, the procedure is more likely to be straightforward.

Handling Graphics and Large Tables

Keep graphics and large tables out of the text document until the last moment to speed scrolling while writing and editing. The larger and more complicated graphics are, the longer it takes to display them on the screen. Scrolling through a graphics-laden document can seem to take forever, especially when you have to bounce back and forth across them repeatedly. Large tables (especially those created with MS Word's **Insert Table...** command) also take a very long time to scroll through. It is preferable to create these graphics and tables as separate files and store them elsewhere until all the text has been completed and edited.

Create easily distinguishable place-holders (e.g., #@* INSERT FIGURE "CLASSIC MARGIN PROPORTIONS" HERE —ON DISK "FIGURES and TABLES") to mark their intended locations within the text, and insert the graphics or tables just prior to layout. If you use a unique string of characters as part of the place-holder (e.g., #@* in the example above), you can use the search and replace feature of your word processor to locate all the places where graphics need to be inserted when it comes time to do so. If your naming system has been well thought out, the placement will proceed rapidly and error-free. Do a careful final proofreading, however, to ensure that the right graphic or table ends up in the right place.

Incidentally, holding off on the insertion of graphics and large tables helps keep file sizes manageable, as graphics files are typically quite large compared to text files.

If you find that you must do a good deal of scrolling around in a document after you have inserted the graphics and large tables, use MS Word's **Preferences...** menu under the **Edit** menu. If you click the **Use Picture Placeholders** box, the graphics in the document will be temporarily replaced by gray boxes, greatly speeding scrolling. When all editing is finished, un-check the box, and the graphics reappear. (By the way, it is not necessary to un-check the box in order to print the document.)

Manual vs. Electronic Paste-Up

DTP, particularly on the Macintosh, makes it so easy to integrate graphics with text that one can get carried away with the opportunity. Occasionally you will find a graphic that is just too large, or of the wrong file format, or otherwise truculent to work with in the usual manner electronically. At times like that, you must weigh the relative advantages and disadvantages of investing the time necessary to make the system work the way it is supposed to. It may just be simpler and easier to revert to "old-fashioned," manual methods (leaving a blank space in the document, and cutting and pasting bits of paper after printing to fill that space) to accomplish what needs to be done. This is especially true if the material surrounding the graphic is not likely to have to be revised frequently; if it is likely to need to be revised soon, perhaps it may be worth the extra effort to cut and paste electronically.

References for Chapter 3

American Psychological Association. (1983). *Publication manual of the American Psychological Association* (3rd ed.). Washington, DC: The Association.

Bove, T., and Rhodes, C. (1989). *Desktop publishing with PageMaker for the Macintosh.* Toronto: John Wiley and Sons.

Burns, D., Venit, S., and Hansen, R. (1988). *The electronic publisher.* New York: Brady.

Gibaldi, J., and Achtert, W. S. (1988). *MLA handbook for writers of research papers* (3rd ed.). New York: Modern Language Association of America.

Hartley, J., and Burnhill, P. (1977b). Understanding instructional text: Typography, layout and design. In M. J. A. Howe (Ed.), *Adult learning* (pp. 223–247). London: John Wiley and Sons.

Hewson, D. (1988). *Introduction to desktop publishing.* San Francisco, CA: Chronicle Books.

Lang, K. (1987). *The writer's guide to desktop publishing.* London: Academic Press.

Lichty, T. (1989). *Design principles for desktop publishers.* Glenview, IL: Scott, Foresman and Co.

Shushan, R., and Wright, D. (1989). *Desktop publishing by design.* Redmond, WA: Microsoft Press.

The Chicago manual of style (13th ed.). (1982). Chicago: University of Chicago Press.

Turabian, K. L. (1976). Student's guide for writing college papers (3rd ed.). Chicago: University of Chicago Press.

White, J. V. (1983). *Mastering graphics.* New York: Bowker.

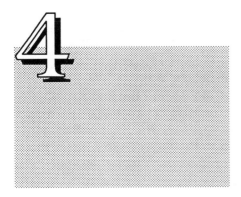

Initial Design Considerations

There are a number of preliminary design concerns that may influence how your work proceeds, and are therefore best addressed early in the project. Although final decisions on many of these matters may be postponed somewhat, at least initial consideration ought to be given early, so that all options are kept viable. Among these are paper selection (including whether or not both sides of the page will be printed), margin sizes, the number of columns of text to be used per page, and whether text will be right-justified or ragged. (Binding methods should also be considered at this stage, as they relate to some of these questions, but they are beyond the scope of this book. If you need more information about binding possibilities, consult with your printing agency.)

Paper Stock

A very fundamental consideration is the selection of paper you will use to print your work. There are many things to consider when selecting a paper: grain, bulk and thickness, brightness, shininess, opacity, weight, color, and finish (Burns, Venit, and Hansen, 1988; White, 1983). For special printing jobs, you would be wise to contact your printer for consultation before beginning the design of the publication. Such design characteristics as the type of font and the kinds of illustrations used may affect or be affected by the kind of paper selected. Very fine lines (either in illustrations or in serifs on small type sizes) may require a harder, smoother finish to the paper than coarser lines and larger type do. The method of reproduction (e.g., xerography, offset) will also affect the type of paper needed.

The most common sizes of paper used in education in the USA and Canada are the so-called letter size (8 $1/2$" × 11") and legal size (8 $1/2$" × 14"), although some jurisdictions have adopted the international A4 size, which measures 210 mm × 297 mm. Most educational institutions make use of the standard xerographic paper for a variety of purposes, and we will assume that the majority of your desktop publications will be done on that kind of paper. (You should be aware that paper is available with a special surface optimized for laser printing. If you need to eke out every last bit of quality available from your laser printer, look into using it, but be forewarned that it is more expensive than standard xerographic paper.)

A decision which will have a major impact on your subsequent design decisions is whether you want to print on both sides or only one side of the page. As noted above, most copy centers in educational institutions routinely stock paper designed to be printed on one side only, because that is what is usually asked of them. That paper is not suitable for printing on both sides because it is not sufficiently opaque, and the print on one side interferes with the readability of the print on the other side. However, most copy centers can also provide—upon request— a more opaque paper designed to be printed on both sides.

Here are some considerations that may enter into your decision:

- **Cost**. There are several dimensions to the question of cost. The actual cost per page of paper is often only marginally higher for the more opaque paper, which will accept print on both sides, as compared to the less opaque paper, which is suitable only for print on one side. Rarely, if ever, is the more opaque paper twice the cost of the other, making double-sided printing more economical, on a per-page basis. Since the two-sided pages occupy only half the space of one-sided pages, there is the potential for savings in storage costs, too. Shipping costs may figure into this consideration, as well. However, paper and shipping represent only part of the potential cost. Design costs for revisions may also be a consideration.

- **Volatility of content**. Some materials may need frequent revisions, either as a result of formative evaluation data or as a result of rapidly-changing content. If the revisions are such that they can typically be made without occupying significantly more page space than the original, individual pages can be printed and distributed to update the publication. Given an appropriate choice of binding, as well (e.g., ring binder), the initial choice of single-sided printing may be most cost-effective if content is volatile. Additional pages may be inserted between existing ones, and given subsidiary numbers (e.g., p. 12a or p. 12.1). At worst, an entire chapter might have to be revised and inserted between two others that remained intact.

  Very stable content can be printed on both sides.

- **Nature of content**. If the content is exclusively text (i.e., no illustrations or other unusual features), double-sided printing may be a good choice. However, if there are many figures or tables in the text, single-sided printing may make it easier to keep the relevant text proximate to the referents. (It is always awkward, from an instructional point of view, when a learner has to repeatedly turn a page to view the figure being described by the text.) That same criterion may work in the other direction, however: Sometimes a full spread (i.e., a two-page arrangement) is required to provide enough space to keep all the elements proximate. Inclusion of exceptionally large figures of tables may also necessitate two-page treatment.

- **Learner responses**. Instructional materials frequently require the learner to write on them, by filling in blanks, circling multiple-choice responses, writing paragraph-length answers, etc. With most paper commonly available to educators, writing (especially with ball-point pens or pencils with hard lead) will cause deformation of the page surface, making any text printed on the other side very difficult to read.

  In some instructional materials, learners are required to remove certain pages (e.g., to turn in assignments). It would be unwise to have material that is not intended for submission printed on the back of material that is.

- **Color coding**. If color coding of pages is used to indicate different kinds of learning activities (e.g., mail-in exercises, self-tests, auxiliary reading material, etc.), single-sided printing is likely to be more efficient than double-sided. The use of color-coded pages always introduces some wastage of space, but having text printed on two sides will usually increase the amount of wasted space.

- **Complexity of printing and binding**. The sophistication of the printing and binding processes available to you may have an influence on your decision, as well. Some presses and processes will be capable of handling varying sizes of signatures (printed sheets containing 4, 8, or 16 pages of the publication, laid out in such a manner that when the sheet is appropriately folded and cut, the pages appear in consecutive order); others will not. Check with your print shop.

As an aside, it should be noted here that the decision to print the final document as either single-sided or double-sided has nothing at all to do with printing the page proofs or master pages of camera-ready copy on a laser printer. Laser printers typically print only on one side of the page (although there are some exceptions); only after laser printing would the individual pages be arranged appropriately by the (human) printer to yield the final single-sided or double-sided product.

Margin Size

This very basic design element appears to have quite a mixture of tradition, rationalization, and aesthetic purpose associated with it, as well as widely varying advice.

Margins, according to some (Hartley, 1978; Lichty, 1989), should occupy about 50% of the page. (If that seems a large space devoted to margins, consider that a default MS Word page—one inch top and bottom margins, 1.25 inch each side—provides for text to cover only about 58% of the page.) Indeed, some traditional guidelines for establishing margins call for larger margins, yielding only about 45% or 33% of the page devoted to text (Burns, Venit, and Hansen, 1988; *Printing layout and design*, 1968).

Margins comprising half the page seem to be quite common, historically. A study done in the early 1930's examined the margins of 400 textbooks, and found that, on the average, very nearly 50% of the page was devoted to margins. However, it found that most readers tended to overestimate the amount of space devoted to print: 90% of readers tended to believe that 60% or more of the total page was devoted to print (Tinker, 1963).

Additional studies showed that material on a flat page having no margins at all was as legible as material having margins of the usual size (Tinker, 1963). Tinker argued, on the basis of his results, that margins (especially wide ones) could be done away with, yielding no loss except perhaps in aesthetic terms.

A variety of reasons are given for the relatively wide margins called for by traditional guidelines. Hartley (1978) attributes wide margins to earlier days, when books were purchased unfinished, then trimmed and bound to match the other volumes of the buyer's library. Wide margins were necessary to allow for the variety of sizes of books in different individuals' collections. Others point to the precedents set by Gutenberg's Bible and early books by the fifteenth-century printer Aldus Manutius (Lichty, 1978). Still others defend their formulas on the basis of binding demands and perceptual considerations (Lang, 1987), and on the functions of the printed materials (i.e., novels, texts, and reference books should differ in the sizes of their margins because they are used in different ways) (Collier and Cotton, 1989).

A time-honored (albeit somewhat complicated) method of deciding the appropriate sizes for margins involves some geometry:

☐ On a two-page spread, draw a diagonal from the lower left of the left-hand page to the upper right of the right-hand page.

☐ Draw another diagonal from the lower right of the right-hand page to the upper left of the right-hand page.

☐ Where the two lines cross, construct a perpendicular to the top of the right-hand page.

☐ Draw a line from the point where the perpendicular meets the top of the page, down to the lower left corner of the left-hand page. The point at which that line meets the second line drawn establishes the upper left corner of the text block on the right-hand page.

☐ From this point, extend lines parallel to both page edges to establish the top and left-hand margins.

☐ From the point where the top margin intersects the first diagonal drawn, extend a line downward, parallel to the right edge of the page to establish the right-hand margin.

☐ From the point where the right-hand margin cuts the second diagonal drawn, construct a horizontal line to establish the bottom margin (Burns, Venit, and Hansen, 1988; *Printing layout and design*, 1968).

As can be seen from Figure 4–1, however, this creates very large margins, with the text covering only one-third of the page. West (1987) calls this proportion "ideal" and "classic" (p. 55).

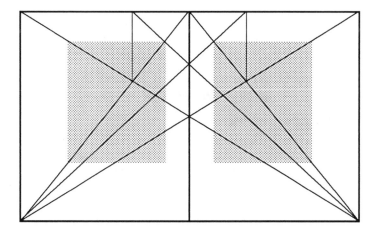

Figure 4–1. Geometrically-derived, "classic" margins.

A simpler, also well-established rule of thumb for book page margins (see Figure 4–2) suggests the inner margin (gutter) should be one-eighth the width of the page, as should the top margin. The outer margin should be the same as the head plus one-third of the gutter (the gutter

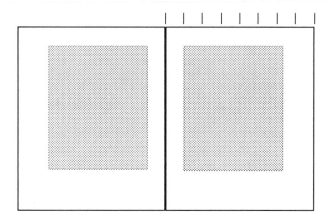

Figure 4–2. One rule of thumb for margins, based on one-eighth of the page size.

being double the inner margin). The bottom should be equal to the outside margin plus 2 picas ($^1/_3$") (*Printing layout and design,* 1968).

Margin size is at least in part related to line length, which in turn has been shown by research to be intimately related to font size; both these variables will be discussed more fully in subsequent chapters.

The typical arrangement of margins used in books is to have a mirror-image spread across two facing pages (see Figure 4–3).

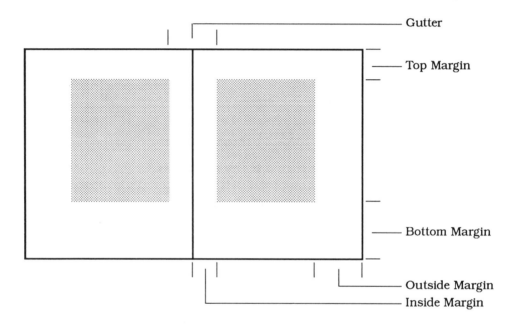

Figure 4–3. A typical two-page spread with mirror image margins.

Although its very typicality may be reason enough to emulate this margin arrangement, there are also good reasons to stay away from it. They will be discussed more completely in the section on layout in Chapter 8.

Tinker (1957) did some research which bears on the size of the gutter margin. He examined the difference in legibility of text on a flat surface and on a curved surface (such as would be produced by a small inner margin in a bound volume), and found that legibility was impaired by the curved surface. He recommended the use of much wider gutter margins to counteract this effect (Tinker, 1965).

In summary, it would appear that although wide margins may not be necessary for legibility, most readers have come to expect them to occupy 40–50% of the page. (It might also be worth noting here that many laser printers require margins of at least $^1/_2$".)

Whatever margins you choose to use, the established advice would appear to be to keep them the same throughout the whole document. While graphic designers may consider it sacrilege, I suggest that educators can and should break this rule in two situations:

- when graphics, tables, illustrations, or examples need to be wider than the conventional margins, possibly because it would be prohibitively expensive to re-size them to fit within the margins; and

- when creating a smaller or larger bottom margin makes for a more reasonable construction in terms of content. This point will be discussed in greater detail in Chapter 8.

Grids

The use of a grid for design and layout has become virtually standard in the publishing industry over the past several decades. In pre-DTP days, the grid was usually printed in non-repro blue (a color that would not photograph on the films used in the printing industry, hence would not be reproduced) on layout sheets. Layout artists then pasted various bits of printed paper onto the grid, using the grid lines to aid alignment and spacing.

With the advent of DTP, page layout programs generally emulate the grid electronically. Since electronic grids are infinitely adjustable, designers can manipulate them as they like. Grids can usually be maintained across all pages (master grids) or for selected pages only (page grids). Their function in layout programs is the same as it was when paper was used: to aid spacing and alignment. Figure 4–4 shows an electronic grid from the popular page layout program PageMaker.

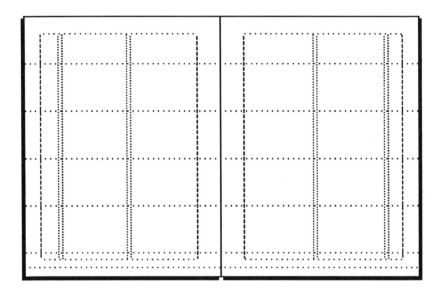

Figure 4–4. Sample grid from a page layout program, PageMaker.

The greatest claimed benefit of the grid is consistency. By using the grid, a layout artist ensures that all pages of a multi-page publication have exactly the same shape—that specified by the designer who established the grid. It is considered permissible, under certain constrained circumstances, to change the grid to accommodate necessity. Thus a grid which starts out as a two-column grid may, on certain pages, become a three-column grid. But almost never is the external boundary of the grid (i.e., the margins) allowed to change.

> Certain types of publications—especially magazines and newsletters—can have different styles of layout to reflect the content of different editorial sections. To cope with this intended variety of layout within their pages the designer produces a grid that can be used in several different ways—a mixed grid. (Collier and Cotton, p. 30)

Considerable effort is spent in DTP books convincing the reader that the grid is essential for the placement of not only all text, but graphics as well. The first choice is usually to custom-make the graphics of an appropriate size to fit the grid (a choice not usually open to the educator, for time and cost reasons): "Make elements fit completely into one or more grid fields when possible. If you create your grid before you create your visuals, you can format charts and diagrams to match" (West,

1987, p. 68). Second best is to place off-size graphics on the page in such a way that the grid structure still makes itself felt: "When visuals don't fit the grid fields exactly—for instance, if a photo needs to be wider than a single field but not as wide as two—try to make it end in the center of a field, and align it top and left" (West, 1987, p. 68).

To my educator's eye, the value of a grid may be overstated in some of the DTP literature. I say this for the following reasons:

- Although it is true that from an instructional point of view, consistency of placement of text and graphical elements is highly desirable so that the learner doesn't have to search for things (Hartley and Burnhill, 1977b), layout of instructional materials isn't usually approached in the same order as layout of non-instructional DTP materials. More specifically, DTP often places illustrations before text; DTPI usually places text before illustrations (this point will be elaborated in Chapter 8).

- For most instructional materials, a single layout usually suffices for the entire publication. Unlike the case of a magazine, where the layouts of advertisements and even articles will change literally from one page to the next, instructional materials are typically quite consistent throughout the entire publication, as Hartley and Burnhill claim they should be.

- The use of other means of ensuring consistency of placement (e.g., style sheets) generally provides as good, or better, layout for instructional materials as does the use of a grid.

- Educators frequently find themselves in a position of having either to violate a grid or change their content, and in choosing the lesser of the evils they will generally violate the grid, so why bother having one? For example, an educator using DTPI to prepare instructional materials may encounter an existing illustration which perfectly addresses a point being made in the text (and for which copyright clearance has been obtained!). If that illustration is too large to fit the grid, conventional DTP wisdom says, the educator should either reduce the illustration's size (probably photographically) or not use it. Since the likelihood of having the facilities, time, and money to do the former is small in educational environments, the choice really comes down to violating the grid or not using the illustration. Most educators—and properly so, in my opinion—would choose to violate the grid.

Case in point: When I designed Table 9–2 (p. 193), I tried to make it just wide enough to fit into the margins established for this book. However, MS Word's table-construction sub-program wouldn't let me put tab settings any closer together than they currently are in that table, at least with the type size I used. Although I wanted to, I couldn't make the table narrower. I was forced to consider various alternatives for dealing with the problem, including modifying the table, which would have been an easy "out." In normal publishing practice, the publisher would simply have photographed the table and reduced it slightly to fit. Most educators, however, don't have the facilities to do that, so I asked that the table be allowed to remain slightly oversize to illustrate the point that its instructional effectiveness is not diminished by its violation of the margins. Fortunately, the publisher agreed to humor me.

To be sure, it is in nobody's best interests to produce text publications which have wildly and arbitrarily varying margins or spacing, but the accomplishment of that aim really requires only common sense and diligence, not necessarily a grid. Perfectly adequate layout for instructional materials can be accomplished with a word processor which doesn't employ a grid—at least not a physical grid—particularly if "before" and "after" spacing is employed with headings and elements such as figures and tables and their captions. Still, the underlying structure of a document has to be conceptualized somehow, and the grid is a useful metaphor.

As noted earlier, the decision to print on one or both sides of the page requires considerable thought. One consideration related to that decision is that if single-sided printing is selected, the visual unit for layout is a single page (see Figure 4–5a).

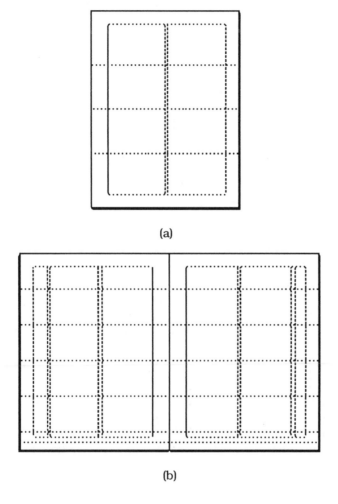

Figure 4–5. (a) Single page and (b) two-page spreads.

If both sides of the page will be printed, the visual unit for layout is the two-page spread. In the latter case, all design must be done relative to *both* pages that will be seen by the reader at the same time.

There are many possible combinations for underlying grids on a two-page spread. One is the mirror-image spread, commonly used in textbooks (Figure 4–5b). Figure 4–6 shows two other possibilities.

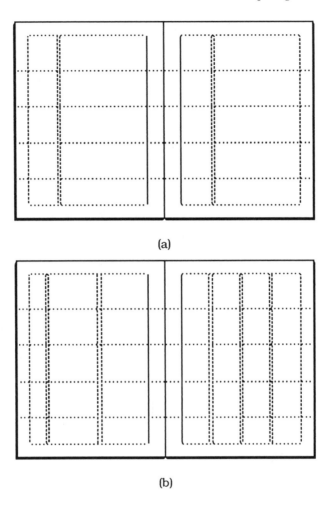

(a)

(b)

Figure 4–6. Other two-page spread grids: (a) one-page layout on a two-page spread, and (b) a two-page layout.

Some designers admit that the mirror image (Figure 4–5b) is difficult to work with if there are any last-minute changes (Burns, Venit, and Hansen, 1988). Hence this design is probably best left to textbooks and other publications where the copy will not be undergoing frequent revision. A one-page layout can be effectively used even in a two-page spread (Figure 4–6a). This is similar to the layout often used for business reports and proposals, and should work well for most instructional materials. The artistic layout employed in Figure 4–6b is not likely to be very functional if used throughout a document for instructional materials; it would likely require forced truncation or extension of the content to fit the layout.

Columns

As noted earlier, the page size and the margin size are intimately related to the question of how many columns of text will be used, and how wide they will be. One cannot make a decision about margins without considering columns, and vice versa.

To complicate matters, there is an intimate and powerful relationship between line length (i.e., column width) and optimum font size, as well as leading (vertical spacing between lines). All these matters will be discussed in greater depth in subsequent chapters. For now, we will simply examine a few generalizations about the types and purposes of columns, the number of columns, and column widths.

Types of Columns

There are two general classes of columns, snaking and side-by-side (see Figure 4–7), and different word processing and layout programs may handle them differently. MS Word, for example, has provision for both kinds; PageMaker has provision only for snaking columns automatically but makes it easy to create side-by-side columns.

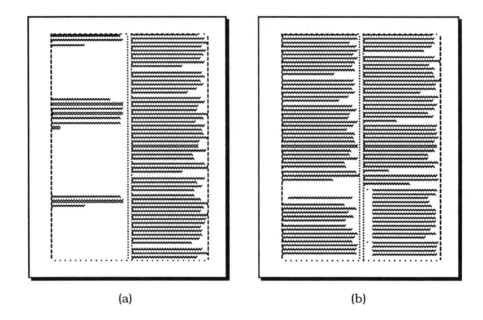

(a)   (b)

Figure 4–7. Two types of columns: (a) side-by-side and (b) snaking.

The difference between the two types lies in the manner in which text is placed into them, and the way they are intended to be used (Figure 4–8).

Side-by-side columns generally relate to one another across the gap separating them. They are designed to be used by reading some of the contents of the left column, then some of the contents of the right column, then some of the contents of the left column, etc. (Figure 4–8a). That is, a heading may be in the left-most column, and the text pertaining to that heading may be in the right-most column. Or a terse set of instructions may be in the left column, with a more elaborated set in the right column. A diagram, or even something as simple as a set of numbers, can occupy the left column while the steps identified by those numbers occupy the right column (e.g., outdented "point" form is a simple example of side-by-side columns).

Snaking text, on the other hand, is text that merely fills up a column, then continues flowing into the next column, etc., until all columns are full (in PageMaker) or takes all the text within a section and "folds" it into the specified number of columns of approximately equal length (in

MS Word). Snaking text is designed to be read from top to bottom within a column, then from top to bottom of the next column to the right, etc. (Figure 4–8b). PageMaker "pours" text into consecutive columns in this manner when you use the **Place** command, and MS Word does the equivalent when you specify **Columns Number** = 2 (or more) under the **Section** command. Snaking columns treat all text—body and heading— equally, stringing it out serially. That is, headings normally fall within the columns, rather than spanning them. (Actually headings can be placed to span two or more columns in PageMaker, but that requires that the heading be taken out of the file that contains the text. In MS Word, the same effect can also be achieved, by putting the heading into a different section than the body text.)

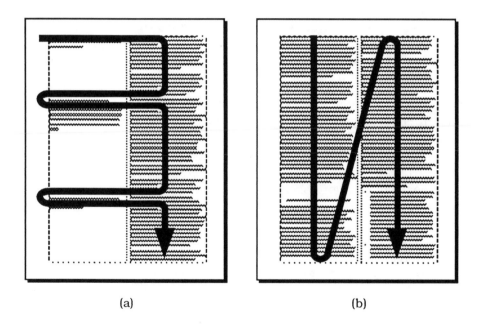

(a)   (b)

Figure 4–8. Normal reading paths of text in (a) side-by-side and (b) snaking columns.

Side-by-side columns can be effected in PageMaker by creating two separate text columns, side by side, then placing the appropriate text in each, and aligning it vertically manually. This necessitates that two separate text files—one for each column—be created, or else a good deal of cutting, pasting, and scrolling must be done from a single text file. In MS Word, the two columns of text are actually created one above the other (in the same file), and only appear side by side when the **Print Preview (⌘I)** mode or **Page View (⌘B)** is used.

Width of Columns

The topic of column widths is not very different from many others in DTP: Everyone seems to have a different rule for what is right. As mentioned in Chapter 1, a quick glance at the variety of advice available simply leaves one confused: Some authors say that a column of text should be 35–40 characters long (West, 1987), while others will permit as many as 75 characters (*Publish!*, 1989b). The entire range between those figures is also well represented as "the Truth." Lang (1987) states that "the evidence suggests that lines should be between four and five inches wide, with 4.5 inches being the optimum" (p. 165), and Lichty (1989) suggests that the "proper" column width is 1.5 lower-case alphabets (*a–z,a–m*), "give or take a pica or two" (p. 53).

There seems to be consensus that different kinds of publications call for different column widths. Newspapers, for example, traditionally have many very narrow columns per page (especially in the want ads, which are only used for reference, not for sustained reading), while books may have two or only one. Clearly, consideration does have to be given to the purposes to which the publication will be put, and compromises may have to be made:

> ...narrow columns tend to break up the structure of sentences and force a lot of word breaks and hyphenation, both of which tend to interfere with smooth readability and comprehension. On the other hand, wide columns tire the eye and make it difficult to find the start of the next line. (White, 1983, p. 62)

Readers tend to dislike both very short and very long line lengths, research has shown (Tinker, 1965, p. 147).

Number of Columns

As suggested earlier, consideration of the function of the publication is one of the first things mentioned by most DTP experts. Most DTP books spend a number of pages discussing and illustrating different columnar arrangements for a wide variety of publications—brochures, newsletters, magazines, newspapers, pamphlets, and business reports—which are beyond the scope of this book. We will avoid discussion of these non-instructional publications, and concentrate our efforts solely on instructional materials.

Single column. There seems to be a good deal of sympathy among DTP experts for the simple, single-column format, particularly for the category of print materials which would include instructional materials.

> Most commercial magazines use a large size and two or three columns across the page. The evidence from reading research suggests that the line lengths which result are much shorter than the optimum for comfortable reading. In addition, to print several columns of text side by side is itself apparently unhelpful to the reader, since the eye can become confused as its scan moves from one line to the next. This practice was adopted originally when pages were printed using hot metal, and it was necessary to allow many people to check their own sections of the paper simultaneously. It may not be possible to convince the newspaper and magazine barons that they no longer need to follow these outdated conventions, but at least you can avoid following in their footsteps! (Lang, 1987, p. 165)

> [The wide-margin one-column] format is especially well suited for single-sided documents that are either stapled or intended for three-ring binders. Use the left side of the page for the wide margin so that the space will look planned. (If you use the right side, it may look as though you ran out of copy and couldn't fill the page.) (Shushan and Wright, 1989, p. 48)

> The fewer the columns, the easier a grid is to work with. A simple one-column format requires relatively little planning and allows you to place text quickly. When done well, this format has an unstudied, straightforward look in which the hand of the designer is relatively invisible. That lack of "fuss" suggests a serious purpose that is appropriate for business plans, reports, proposals, press releases, announcements, simple manuals, and various forms on internal communications. [I would suggest that the list could be expanded to include virtually all instructional materials.] (Shushan and Wright, 1989, p. 46)

> A one-column grid with a wide margin is perhaps the most useful of all the designs in this book for internal reports, press

releases, proposals, prospectuses, and other documents that
have unadorned running text and need to be read fast. You may
be tempted, with desktop publishing, to take something you
used to distribute as a typewritten page and turn it into a
multicolumn format, simply because you can. The danger is
that you'll devote time to layout that would be better spent on
content. (Shushan and Wright, 1989, p. 48)

The chief advantage of a single-column design is that it is easy to work
with, both in the first instance and when editing—no small consideration when materials may have to be revised frequently.

The obvious disadvantage of a single-column design, especially for the
8 $1/_2$" × 11" format typically used by educators, is that the line length
becomes very long, making reading difficult. This problem can be
circumvented by making the text column relatively narrower than the
page, leaving a column of white space. The extra white space can give the
page an open, uncrowded, and inviting feeling (see Figure 4–9).

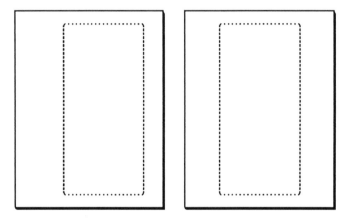

Figure 4–9. Two variations of a single-column format.

To be effective, says Miles (1987), the width of the text column in a wide-
margin, one-column format should be perceptibly narrower than the
page. Like others (e.g., Shushan and Wright, 1989; West, 1987), he
advises that the white space be on the left of a single page. If the publication is a two-page spread, the blank space should be toward the inner
margins. Keeping the blank space on the left, whether the publication is
a single page or a two-page spread, has the advantage that the blank

space can be used for side headings, illustrations, icons, pull quotes, or other forms of marginalia. Even if these features are not built into the design, the so-called "wasted" space engendered by the wide margin is not really wasted. Learners may use it to make notes for themselves.

Some designers also think of this design as boring or stodgy. However, learners are quite accustomed to this format, and shouldn't find it unusual.

On the basis of research on tables in text, Burnhill, Hartley, and Young (1976) conclude that

> ...if comprehension and reading ease are thought to outweigh minor increases in paper costs, then a single-column layout is to be preferred for the presentation of complex instructional materials, provided that the interline spacing is adequate and that line spacing is used to denote paragraphs. (p. 17)

Multiple columns. Davis, Barry, and Wiesenberg (1986) suggest that one, two, or three columns per 8 $1/2$" × 11" page are reasonable for reports, papers, and other similar documents (presumably instructional materials would also fit into this category). It is my belief, however, that three columns on a page of that size are too many, and that the negative effects of so many columns (very short lines, making for choppy phrasing or requiring hyphenation) will far outweigh any advantages. Indeed, even using two columns has some serious disadvantages:

- Instructional materials frequently employ an outdented "point form," which tends to look very choppy in columns, especially in narrow columns. Many times, there will be sub-points under major points, further exacerbating the problem.

- Headings can become a problem. If the headings are long, they may occupy several lines in a narrow-column layout; they will not only look odd, but will likely be difficult to read, as well. Formatting headings across columns (i.e., headings spanning columns) is a possible solution, but one that necessitates considerable extra work—work which may have to be re-done if any revisions or editing are necessary. Furthermore, having headings span several columns may cause the reader to be confused about where to look next (Spiegelman, 1987).

- It may be difficult to fit graphics and tables into the multi-columnar format, at least without considerable effort in preparing graphics of appropriate size or re-sizing them photographically.

- A multi-columnar format makes it difficult, if not impossible, to use many of the cuing devices (arrows, icons, or other methods of identifying location) that form a fundamental part of the access structure of many instructional materials.

- Interactivity devices such as blanks or spaces left for students' responses may become so narrow as to be dysfunctional.

I must stress that all the opinions in this section are based on the assumption that the two or three columns are equal width, and filled with the same kind of content (i.e., they are snaking columns). Side-by-side columns, of course, can be used to great instructional advantage in some situations, and if they can be, perhaps they should be. Because of the way they are constructed and laid out, the criticisms in the points above simply do not apply to them (except perhaps for the first).

Research conducted by Paterson and Tinker in 1940 with college students, using material from a psychological journal, found that 60% of the students preferred a two-column format over a one-column format (Tinker, 1965). (Of course, journal articles are not subject to revision.)

Lang (1987) discourages the use of multiple columns but suggests that if you must use them, you should separate adjacent columns with a vertical line, or rule. Lichty (1989) states that a space of $1/6$" or more ($1/3$" for two-column 8 $1/2$" × 11" pages) will serve the same function. Paterson and Tinker experimented with various combinations of spaces and rules, and found no significant differences in speed of reading (Tinker, 1965).

Justification of Text

Justification of text is causing it to line up at either or both of the left and right margins to form a straight vertical line. The opposite of justified text is ragged text (see Figure 4–10). Figure 4–10a shows what is technically called left justified, right ragged text (also known as flush left text). Because it is very rare that the left edge is unjustified (an exception may be poetry), it is common to call this type of justification simply *ragged right*, or more commonly, *unjustified* text. Figure 4–10b is, strictly speaking, called right justified, left ragged text. Also known as flush right text, it is—and should be—rarely used in instructional materials. A more common name for it is *ragged left* text.

Figure 4–10c shows fully justified (or left- and right-justified) text, which is also referred to simply as *justified* text.

A number of practices in the publishing industry are simply traditions. According to Kleper (1987), the tradition of having text right-justified (i.e., text forming a straight edge down the page at the right margin) originated with the scribes who copied text by hand before the invention of movable type.

(a)

A number of practices in the publishing industry are simply traditions. According to Kleper (1987), the tradition of having text right-justified (i.e., text forming a straight edge down the page at the right margin) originated with the scribes who copied text by hand before the invention of movable type.

(b)

A number of practices in the publishing industry are simply traditions. According to Kleper (1987), the tradition of having text right-justified (i.e., text forming a straight edge down the page at the right margin) originated with the scribes who copied text by hand before the invention of movable type.

(c)

Figure 4–10. Varieties of justified text: (a) left justified, right ragged; (b) right justified, left ragged; (c) fully justified; and (d) centered. *(Figure continued on next page.)*

A number of practices in the publishing
industry are simply traditions. According to
Kleper (1987), the tradition of having text right-
justified (i.e., text forming a straight edge down
the page at the right margin) originated with
the scribes who copied text by hand before the
invention of movable type.

(d)

Figure 4–10. *(Continued.)*

Figure 4–10d shows centered text, also uncommon in instructional
materials, except for headings.

Most word processors and layout programs will provide for the easy
conversion of text to any one of the formats shown in Figure 4–10.
Whether or not one *should* do it is another matter. Once again, we can
turn to DTP experts for advice.

There are several arguments presented for right justified text:

> The desirability of justifying text to both margins is another
> source of hot debate. My own feeling is that the balance is
> firmly on the side of justification. The reasons are partly
> aesthetic, but right justification also serves to define the right
> margin in a way that makes it more useful to the reader—both
> visually and practically. And since it is so widely used in
> conventionally printed books, it is therefore familiar to the
> reader. The major argument against it is the strange results you
> get with short lines and conservative hyphenation. But then,
> the evidence is that short lines are harder for readers, so I don't
> have much sympathy with that line of reasoning. (Lang, 1987,
> p. 169)

> There is...little doubt that text in which all lines are of similar
> lengths is easier to read than lines with markedly varying right-
> hand ends, hence the importance of good hyphenation. (Lang,
> 1987, p. 82)

> *Justified text* is familiar and predictable. Some say that it is the
> easiest to read. It most certainly is the norm: For over 500 years
> printers, with the evident support of their readers, have
> determined that the sense of orderliness conveyed by justified
> type is preferable to consistent word spacing and ragged right
> margins. Regardless of arguments to the contrary, justified text

> is preferred for long works that require continuous reading and
> concentration: texts, novels, newspapers, and magazines.
> (Lichty, 1989, p. 63)

Lang's arguments are clearly fallacious. In reading, the left margin
serves as a decidedly necessary landmark as the eye sweeps back to
begin another line, but the right margin serves no comparable function.
(In concurrence, White suggests that "in long blocks of type...it is unwise
to use ragged left setting, because a neat left-hand margin is a far easier
reference point to which the eye can return in the process of reading"
[White, 1983, p. 62].) Thus while it may be functional for the left margin
to be justified (which it virtually always is), it is difficult to understand
how the right margin functions analogously. The fact that right-
justified text is widely used and familiar, of course, does not make it
right. Even the counter-argument Lang presents against not using it—
line length—is completely spurious. Line length is not the issue, except
possibly for the very last line of each paragraph. Her claim of little
doubt in the second quotation is open to question, as she offers no
evidence to support it.

Lichty's argument, similar to Lang's second one—everybody's doing it—
is not really an argument at all, hence requires no further comment.

Both White (1983) and Burns, Venit, and Hansen (1988) claim that text
with a ragged right margin takes more space than text with a fully
justified right margin. This claim simply does not make sense. It is not
the justification per se that reduces the space occupied but the
hyphenation that often accompanies right justification: In order to
keep the inter-word spaces relatively small, long words near the ends of
lines must be hyphenated. If the same words in a given passage of text
were hyphenated in the same way, both ragged right text and right-
justified text would require the same number of column inches.

There are also those who take positions against right-justified text.
White (1983, p. 62–63) suggests using ragged right margins, giving as
support for his argument exactly the same point—popularity of right-
justification—that Lang and Lichty give for not using them. Ragged right
margins, he suggests, look different and are therefore more interesting.
He also states that ragged right margins read better, since words, which
are perceived as groups of letters, are more consistently presented
together (again, because hyphenation is not required as frequently).
White expands on the argument by saying that the irregular inter-word

and perhaps even inter-letter spacing caused by full justification "...makes the eye stumble," and "...makes reading tiring and more like work" (p. 63).

Spiegelman (1987) also strongly supports the use of ragged right margins, claiming that legibility is maximized when letter spacing and word spacing are kept constant. Davis, Barry, and Wiesenberg (1986) suggest that ragged right margins help make the document look less formal and are valuable when the text is liable to be revised frequently, both of which would appear to be typical of instructional materials. Kleper (1987) says that ragged right text is easier to read, and helps avoid the "rivers of white" problem that invariably crops up with fully justified text (Figure 4–11). Since it takes extra work to get rid of them, and an increased use of hyphens (Lichty, 1989), they can be viewed as a reason for not using right justification.

> Right justification is especially awkward with multiple columns; the more columns there are, the worse the problem is, as the narrower the columns are. Right justification should especially be avoided with narrow columns (Davis, Barry, and Wiesenberg, 1986). Burns, Venit, and Hansen (1988) say that short lines (less than 60 characters) should not be justified.

Figure 4–11. The evenness of text can be disrupted by so-called "rivers of white" caused by right justification. If they are not immediately visible to you, try squinting as you view the text.

Another argument for ragged right margins is that symmetrical, formally balanced layouts are usually considered static and boring (Miles, 1987). A desirable degree of asymmetry is induced by using unjustified (i.e., ragged right) text. Miles (1987) suggests that the choice to justify or not justify is a matter of personal preference, and firmly states his own preference not to justify. Justified text can appear very ponderous, he says, especially in double columns, whereas unjustified text makes the page lighter by increasing the amount of white space.

Right justification is especially awkward with multiple columns; the more columns there are, the narrower the columns are and the worse the problem is. Right justification should be avoided with narrow columns (Davis, Barry, and Wiesenberg, 1986). Burns, Venit, and Hansen (1988) say that short lines (less than 60 characters) should not be justified.

Turning to research, Muncer, Gorman, Gorman, and Bibel (1986) had college students read right-justified and ragged right text passages, and found that they performed significantly worse on right-justified text. (Interestingly, good readers were more adversely affected than were poor readers.) Trollip and Sales (1986) also investigated the effects of right-justified text on both recall and recognition, also using college students. They found that right-justified text significantly reduced reading speed; however, comprehension was not affected. It should be noted that both the Muncer, Gorman, Gorman, and Bibel, and the Trollip and Sales studies used daisy-wheel printers, so the justification was accomplished only by inserting extra (whole) non-proportional spaces between words.

To my mind, there are no good arguments for using right-justified text, the practices of the ancient scribes notwithstanding. There may be some good reasons for not using it, however. I believe it would be prudent simply not to use right-justified text.

References for Chapter 4

Burnhill, P., Hartley, J., and Young, M. (1976). Tables in text. *Applied Ergonomics, 7*(1), 13–18.

Burns, D., Venit, S., and Hansen, R. (1988). *The electronic publisher.* New York: Brady.

Collier, D., and Cotton, B. (1989). *Basic desktop design and layout.* Cincinnati, OH: North Light Books.

Davis, F. E., Barry, J., and Wiesenberg, M. (1986). *Desktop publishing.* Homewood, IL: Dow Jones-Irwin.

Hartley, J. (1978). *Designing instructional text*. London: Kogan Page.

Hartley, J., and Burnhill, P. (1977b). Understanding instructional text: Typography, layout and design. In M. J. A. Howe (Ed.), *Adult learning* (pp. 223–247). London: John Wiley and Sons.

Kleper, M. L. (1987). *The illustrated handbook of desktop publishing and typesetting*. Blue Ridge Summit, PA: Tab Books.

Lang, K. (1987). *The writer's guide to desktop publishing*. London: Academic Press.

Lichty, T. (1989). *Design principles for desktop publishers*. Glenview, IL: Scott, Foresman and Co.

Miles, J. (1987). *Design for desktop publishing*. San Francisco: Chronicle Books.

Muncer, S. J., Gorman, B. S., Gorman, S., and Bibel, D. (1986). Right is wrong: An examination of the effect of right justification on reading. *British Journal of Educational Technology, 17,* 5–10.

Printing layout and design. (1968). Albany, NY: Delmar Publishers.

Publish! (1989b). *101 best desktop publishing tips, vol. 2*. San Francisco, CA: PCW Communications.

Shushan, R., and Wright, D. (1989). *Desktop publishing by design*. Redmond, WA: Microsoft Press.

Spiegelman, M. (1987). Interior design for documents. *PC World*, March, 178–185.

Tinker, M. A. (1957). Effect of curved text upon readability of print. *Journal of Applied Psychology, 41,* 218–221.

Tinker, M. A. (1963). *Legibility of print*. Ames, IA: Iowa State University Press.

Tinker, M. A. (1965). *Bases for effective reading*. Minneapolis: University of Minnesota Press.

Trollip, S. R., and Sales, G. (1986, January). *Readability of computer-generated fill-justified text*. Paper presented at the Annual Convention of the Association for Educational Communications and Technology, Las Vegas, NV.

West, S. (1987). Design for desktop publishing. In The Waite Group (J. Stockford, Ed.), *Desktop publishing bible* (pp. 53–72). Indianapolis, IN: Howard W. Sams.

White, J. V. (1983). *Mastering graphics*. New York: Bowker.

Access Structure and Orienting Devices

Access structure is the "...co-ordinated use of typographically signalled structural cues that help students to read texts using selective sampling strategies" (Waller, 1979, p. 175). Waller's thesis is that learners read instructional materials selectively. They rarely, if ever, begin at the beginning and read straight through to the end, as one might a novel. Rather, they exercise a combination of browsing, reading certain parts carefully, skimming others, and skipping still others entirely. Recognition and acceptance of the existence of this behavior, and design to accommodate it, can assist learners in their efforts.

Waller (cited in Marland and Store, 1982, p. 98) has suggested that there are three functions of text presentation: transactional (legible type, ergonomics of handling and storage, orthography), stylistic (decorative illustration, quality of paper and binding), and structural. The structural function is sub-divided into global and local functions. Included in global functions are such features as contents lists, study guides, introductions, objectives, instructions, and indexes; local functions include text headings, running heads, section numbers, page numbers, abstracts, and in-text descriptors (e.g., "essential reading"). This chapter focuses on those elements comprising both the global and local structural functions: pagination, headers and footers, headings, pull quotes and variations, paragraphs and indention, lists and outdention, color coding of pages, icons as orienting devices, tables of contents, indexes, and cross-references. Some of these features are useful only for longer pieces of instruction, others are useful for all lengths; some are useful primarily for textbooks, others are useful primarily for individualized instruction packages.

Pagination

Any document of more than two pages should have page numbers. Even the shortest document, if un-paginated, risks confusion when one individual tries to communicate reference to a certain passage to another individual.

Traditionally, title pages (and frequently, initial pages of a chapter, which are by custom printed as right-hand pages) do not have page numbers printed on them, but are counted in the sequence of pagination. Also traditionally, preliminary pages (e.g., title page, copyright notice, table of contents, list of illustrations, preface or introduction, etc.) are numbered in lower-case Roman numerals, whereas the remainder of the book is numbered in Arabic numerals. From the point of view of optimizing access structure, these practices appear adequate, although one is tempted to argue that putting page numbers on even the first pages of chapters would assist accessibility: If a learner is looking for a particular page number, and encounters the first page of a new chapter, he or she must flip another page to determine the location—a small, but unnecessary, inconvenience. Thus, in this book the first page of each chapter contains a page number, located right where all the others are.

Type of Numerals Used

Tinker's (1963) research clearly suggests that Arabic numerals should be used wherever possible, since they are read significantly faster and more accurately than Roman numerals. Indeed, Tinker recommended that Roman numerals not be used for most printing. As noted above, however, there seems to be little likelihood of a problem with using lower-case Roman numerals for the preliminary pages.

Serial vs. Chapter-by-Chapter Numeration

Instructional materials can be either numbered serially or chapter-by-chapter. In serial numeration, you begin with page 1 and keep going. In chapter-by-chapter numeration, you re-start from page 1 at the beginning of each chapter. In order not to confuse the reader completely, you include a prefix to the page number which denotes the chapter or section (e.g., page 4–3 indicates the third page in the fourth chapter or section; it is preceded by page 4–2 and followed by page 4–4). There are advantages and disadvantages to both systems.

Serial numeration is straightforward and common, and therefore likely to be less confusing than chapter-by-chapter numeration. It works best when there is no likelihood of having to re-paginate or supplement an existing document. For example, when a book is printed and bound, there is little likelihood that additional pages will subsequently be printed for inclusion in that book. Once the master copy of the book comes off the laser printer, that's it; the job is done.

Not all instructional materials are as stable as books, however. Many types of manuals and self-instructional packages presume that changing content or evolving instructional design will necessitate changes, which may require either replacement of pages, addition of pages, or deletion of pages. In such situations, it makes more sense to paginate chapter-by-chapter, since only the necessary portions of the document can be printed up on the laser printer and substituted into the master copy of the existing document. You only need consider an extreme case to see the efficiency: What if you had to re-print the master copy of a 200-page document because you deleted page 9, which happened to be the second-last page of the first chapter? On the other hand, the chapter-by-chapter numeration system is not all that common, and may cause confusion for some readers. If using the chapter-by-chapter numeration system, it is wise to take pains to explain it early in the publication.

When chapter-by-chapter numeration is used and there is more than one appendix, there may be advantages to providing each appendix with its own sequence (e.g., A–1...A–*n*; B–1...B–*n*, etc.).

Headers and Footers

Headers (also known as running heads) are text that appears at the top of every page of a document, or, alternatively, at the top of every page of a section of a document. For example, it is common practice in books to have the name of the book in the header of every left-hand page, and the name of the chapter in the header of every right-hand page.

Footers are the same as headers, except that they appear at the bottom of every page.

Headers or footers also usually carry the page number. In keeping with the notion of maximizing accessibility, headers and/or footers should be made as useful as possible (i.e., they should provide, insofar as is possible, information that will help the learner navigate through the document).

Headings

Headings in instructional materials serve a similar function to headlines in magazines and newspapers. The purposes of headlines, say Shushan and Wright (1989), are to:

- attract readers' attention;
- make the subject-matter readily apparent; and
- indicate the relative importance of items.

The purposes of a heading are all those things, plus to make plain the structure of the knowledge being taught, by indicating where the upcoming information fits in the grand scheme of things, and how the various bits of text relate to one another. A system of headings can also break up long passages of text and make it seem less forbidding (Miles, 1987).

Headings help communicate the structure of the subject matter to the learner. A useful tool for teasing out the structure of a collection of subject-matter is an outline; a useful tool for communicating the structure to the learner is the translation of the outline into a system of headings.

Headings are also useful to learners in their function as markers or sign-posts (the accessing and orienting function). In other words, they help learners locate certain content after they have first encountered it, thereby acting as part of the access structure of the document (Waller, 1977; 1982).

Research on Headings

There has been considerable research done on the effectiveness of headings (Brooks, Danserau, Spurlin, and Holley, 1983; Hartley and Jonassen, 1985; Hartley and Trueman, 1983, 1985). Some of the more important generalizations to come from that research are that in terms of recall of information, search for information, and retrieval of information:

- the use of headings is better than the lack of headings, particularly for long-term learning (delayed post-tests);

- embedded headings (see Figure 5–1) are as effective as marginal headings; and

- headings in the form of statements are as effective as headings in the form of questions.

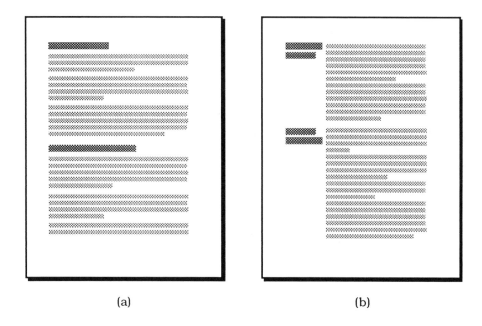

(a)   (b)

Figure 5–1. Two types of headings: (a) embedded headings; (b) marginal headings. The dark shading indicates a heading while the light shading indicates body text.

The overall impact of headings, as determined by meta-analysis of a number of studies, is somewhere between one-quarter and one-half standard deviation (Hartley and Jonassen, 1985). There appears to be a developmental process associated with the use of headings, although children as young as 10 have benefitted from the use of headings, and there is some evidence that the existence of headings is most beneficial to young, less capable learners.

Learners do not necessarily know intuitively how to use headings (Hartley and Jonassen, 1985). For that reason, an explanation of the heading system, and how it relates to the structure of the content, should be included early in the instructional materials. Research by Brooks, Danserau, Spurlin, and Holley (1983) showed that learners who were instructed in how to use headings as study aids did better than learners not given such instruction.

Heading Terminology

To facilitate discussion of the various levels of headings, the following sample outline of content will be used. In it, left-to-right spacing has been used to indicate which items are subordinate to others.

Types of Doughnuts Available

Sugared Doughnuts

Glazed Doughnuts

Chocolate Glazed Doughnuts

Dark Chocolate

Light Chocolate

Caramel Glazed Doughnuts

Cake Doughnuts

The History of Doughnuts

The Sex Life of Doughnuts

Male Doughnuts

Female Doughnuts

For purposes of this discussion, *Types of Doughnuts Available, The History of Doughnuts*, and *The Sex Life of Doughnuts* are called Level One Headings (i.e., the superordinate level). *Sugared Doughnuts, Glazed Doughnuts, Cake Doughnuts, Male Doughnuts*, and *Female Doughnuts* are referred to as Level Two Headings. They are subordinate to Level One Headings, but superordinate to the next level—Level Three Headings— which consist of *Chocolate Glazed Doughnuts* and *Caramel Glazed Doughnuts. Dark Chocolate* and *Light Chocolate* are called Level Four Headings.

Number of Levels of Headings

Wherever possible, the number of levels of headings should be kept to three or fewer (Lang, 1987; Miles, 1987), as learners are liable to have difficulty deciphering and following the structure of the text if more levels of headings are used. Four levels of headings are described here to account for the extreme case (e.g., a long book); more than four levels should generally not be used. Instead, the content should be re-structured.

As a general rule, a heading should be used at any level if and only if there are two or more headings at the same level. For example, suppose the entire content of a module could be represented by the following outline.

An Introduction to Today's Inner Tubes

The Shape of Inner Tubes

The Composition of Inner Tubes

Artificial Materials

Synthetic Rubber

Rubberized Synthetics

Natural Materials

The Uses of Inner Tubes

In this case, *An Introduction to Today's Inner Tubes* should be dropped as a heading, and the content re-arranged as necessary to make *The Shape of Inner Tubes*, *The Composition of Inner Tubes*, and *The Uses of Inner Tubes* the superordinate headings in the module. The reason *An Introduction to Today's Inner Tubes* should be removed is that there is no second heading that is parallel to (i.e., at the same level as) *An Introduction to Today's Inner Tubes*.

If, on the other hand, the following outline represents the structure of the content, it is legitimate to use *An Introduction to Today's Inner Tubes* and *Inner Tubes of the Future* as superordinate headings, even though *Inner Tubes of the Future* has no subordinate levels. It is important, however, to ensure that *Inner Tubes of the Future* really is at the same conceptual level as *An Introduction to Today's Inner Tubes*; the mere mechanical act of assigning the level to an item is, by itself, insufficient.

An Introduction to Today's Inner Tubes

The Shape of Inner Tubes

The Composition of Inner Tubes

Artificial Materials

Synthetic Rubber

Rubberized Synthetics

Natural Materials

The Uses of Inner Tubes

Inner Tubes of the Future

Nested Section Numbering

With highly structured content (e.g., a technical manual), nested section numbering might be appropriate (Lang, 1987). Nested section numbering (example below) can be forbidding and overwhelming to the uninitiated, however, so it should be used judiciously, and only when necessary. If there is any chance that some learners are not familiar with the numbering scheme, pains should be taken to explain it, early in the instructional sequence.

1.0 An Introduction to Today's Inner Tubes

1.1 The Shape of Inner Tubes

1.2 The Composition of Inner Tubes

1.2.1. Artificial Materials

1.2.1.1 Synthetic Rubber

1.2.1.2 Rubberized Synthetics

1.2.2 Natural Materials

1.3 The Uses of Inner Tubes

2.0 Inner Tubes of the Future

Figure 5–2. Nested section numbering.

Location of Headings

Some DTP experts recommend that headlines be placed in the upper left corner of the page, on the basis that reading proceeds from left to right and top to bottom (White, 1983); there is also some research that shows that readers indeed scan pages in this manner (Johnsey, Wheat, and Morrison, 1990). Others recommend that main headings are "...ranged right at the top of a right-hand (i.e., facing) page" (Lang, 1987, p. 157). As already noted, Hartley's research has shown that there is no difference between embedded and marginal headings (Hartley and Jonassen, 1985; Hartley and Trueman, 1983, 1985).

The important thing would seem to be that one level of heading is clearly differentiated from another level. That differentiation can be based on any combination of typeface, type size, type style (bold, italic, or plain) white space before and/or after the heading, and location of the heading (left-ranging, centered, or right-ranging; embedded or marginal). This should not be interpreted as meaning that a great variety of these factors should be used to help the differentiation. Indeed, just the opposite should be your goal. Vary as few of these factors as possible while making the differences between levels of headings immediately obvious to the learner, or you will end up with a busy, over-done look to your pages.

A scheme as simple as the one employed in this book is adequate. (Obviously, it's not the only acceptable one, but it might be instructive to consider it.) The first order of heading (chapter names) is right-justified 24-point bold Helvetica, with 45 points of white space before and 12 points after the heading. The second order of heading is 18-point bold Bookman (the same typeface as the body text), centered, with 36 points of white space before and 9 points after. Third-order headings are left-justified 14-point bold Bookman, with 18 points before and 6 points after, and fourth-order headings (which are used only occasionally) are 10-point bold, italic Bookman set into the paragraph and separated from the body text by a period. As simple as this scheme is, the headings are readily differentiated from one another, yet are similar enough to give coherence to the total document.

Headings and White Space

As exemplified by the data in the last paragraph, it is a good idea to leave extra white space before and after headings to help readers differentiate headings from body type. There is no apparent rule of thumb about how much space to leave, but you should assign less space between the heading and what follows it than between the heading and what precedes it. Miles (1987) suggests what appears to be a common-sense rule—the amount of space placed before and after a heading should reflect its importance in the hierarchy. Thus you would place more white space around a level one heading than around a level two heading, which in turn would have more white space surrounding it than a level three heading, etc.

Capitalization

As will be demonstrated in Chapter 6, there is research evidence showing that the use of all capital letters makes reading slower, and hence should be avoided, even in headings. White (1983) agrees that type set in all caps is harder to read, but suggests that a few words set in all caps is no problem. He also presents an argument against the common practice of capitalizing major words in a heading:

> The Up-And-Down Style of typesetting [i.e., caps and lower-case in headlines] to this writer's thinking at least, seems illogical and a hangover from the past that is accepted somewhat unthinkingly. It was invented as a makeshift solution to overcome shortages of capital letters when newspaper headlines were set all cap. Such shortages are no longer with us, and headlines are set large and bold to distin-guish them from the body copy anyway. So such extra added differentiation as capitalizing the first letter of every important word (which is what this style entails) becomes excessive. Not only does it lead to arguments as to which words are important and deserve such treatment, but it also decreases the words' legibility because it is an unnatural way of presenting them. Furthermore, it decreases the distinguishing features of proper names in headline by making everything look like proper names with initial capitalization. Why is it still done? Because of habit.... (White, 1983, p. 69)

Other DTP experts acknowledge that there are differences of opinion about which words should and shouldn't be capitalized in headings; the rule of thumb is that only major words should be capitalized, but there seems to be no agreement as to what constitutes a major word. No research appears to have been done on this point.

Word Wrapping

While it is always a good idea to keep headings as short as possible, occasionally headings will necessarily be longer than the column width permits. In such cases, you should go beyond simply letting the word-wrapping feature of your word processor or page layout program determine where the line change should occur. Place a soft carriage return into the heading at a place which will minimize the possibility of distortion or interruption of the thought underlying the heading. In other words, use the carriage returns in such a way as to maximize the sense of the message. (Hyphenation of headings should be avoided.)

Having said that, wherever possible within the advice of allowing sense to prevail, allow the text to form a triangle with the apex pointing downward, leading the eye to the body text that follows it (*Printing layout and design*, 1968).

In Figure 5–3a, the sense of the heading is interrupted by a carriage return, although the desired triangular shape exists. In Figure 5–3b, the sense is improved, but the triangular shape pointing away from the text that follows the heading is counterproductive. In Figure 5–3c, both the sense of the heading and the shape are optimized.

Prose-Relevant Pictures and Older Learners' Recall of Written Prose

(a)

Prose-Relevant Pictures and Older Learners' Recall of Written Prose

(b)

Prose-Relevant Pictures and Older Learners' Recall of Written Prose

(c)

Figure 5–3. Multi-line headings should be constructed to maximize the sense of the heading, and to create a triangular shape pointing to the text that follows.

Paragraphs and Indention

The paragraph is sometimes referred to as the basic unit of composition. Properly written, a paragraph should consist of one or more sentences that develop a single idea. The end of a paragraph signals the beginning of a new idea.

It is common practice to delineate the beginnings of paragraphs by either indenting the first line of the paragraph or by allowing extra space between paragraphs. The purpose of these two devices, of course, is the same as the purpose of paragraphs themselves—to help the reader identify when a change of thought is occurring.

Tinker's research showed that indenting the first line of a paragraph increased legibility (Tinker, 1963). Although no similar research was found for providing space between paragraphs, it seems likely that such a device would likewise increase legibility. Indeed, one could speculate that space between paragraphs may have an even more salutary effect than indention, because of the more open, airy appearance of the page. Hartley and Burnhill (1977a) argue that using white space rather than indention more readily illustrates the underlying structure of the text, particularly when short paragraphs are involved.

Several rules of thumb appear for how much indention should occur. Bove and Rhodes (1989) say that the indent should be equal to the leading. Miles (1987) suggests a double space. Collier and Cotton (1989) recommend that the indent be a multiple of the leading (e.g., 24 or 36 points for 12-point leading), and Lichty (1989) suggests a 2 pica indent (about $^3/_8$" or 1 cm). Kleper (1987) ties the indention to the line length, suggesting that for lines up to 3" long, the indention should be 1 em space (i.e., the space should be as long as the font is high); for line lengths between 3 and 4", the indention should be 1 $^1/_2$ em spaces, and for line lengths of 4 to 5", the indention should be 2 em spaces.

Miles (1987) makes the point that indention plus unjustified right margins make for a very ragged look to the text, and suggests that it is therefore preferable to use white space to indicate paragraphs. Lichty (1989) recommends a 6-point gap between paragraphs.

Using the "space after" parameter in MS Word provides a convenient way of achieving the desired inter-paragraph gap automatically whenever a carriage return occurs (see Figure 5–4).

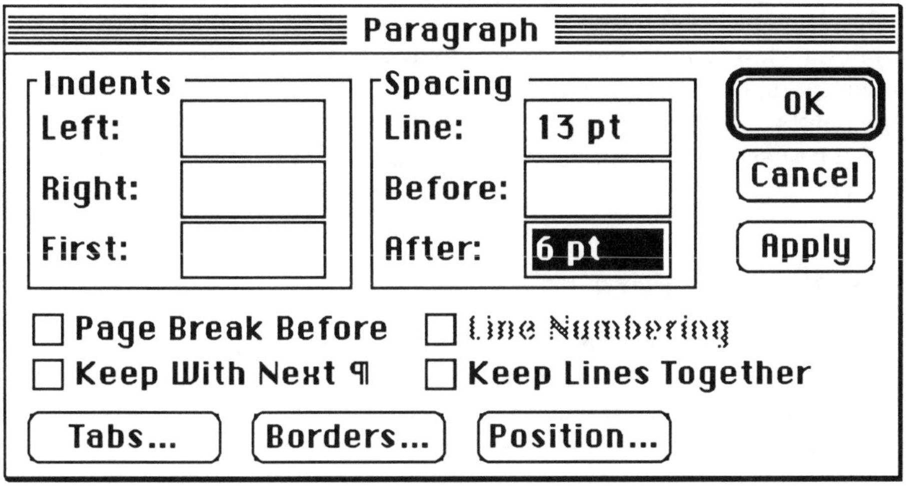

```
┌─────────────────────────────────────────────────────┐
│ ▓▓▓▓▓▓▓▓▓▓▓▓▓▓▓▓▓  Paragraph  ▓▓▓▓▓▓▓▓▓▓▓▓▓▓▓▓▓      │
│ ┌─Indents──────────┐ ┌─Spacing──────────┐ ┌────────┐ │
│ │ Left:   [      ] │ │ Line:   [13 pt ] │ │   OK   │ │
│ │                  │ │                  │ └────────┘ │
│ │ Right:  [      ] │ │ Before: [      ] │ ┌────────┐ │
│ │                  │ │                  │ │ Cancel │ │
│ │ First:  [      ] │ │ After:  [6 pt  ] │ └────────┘ │
│ └──────────────────┘ └──────────────────┘ ┌────────┐ │
│                                            │ Apply  │ │
│  ☐ Page Break Before   ☐ Line Numbering   └────────┘ │
│  ☐ Keep With Next ¶    ☐ Keep Lines Together         │
│  ( Tabs... )   ( Borders... )   ( Position... )      │
└─────────────────────────────────────────────────────┘
```

Figure 5–4. Inter-paragraph spacing can be easily accomplished with the "space after" setting in MS Word.

Lists and Outdention

Outdention is simply reverse indention: the first line begins to the left of the point at which the remaining lines in the paragraph begin. Another way of saying this is that the wrap point on the word processor's ruler is set to the left of the left margin. Outdention is also know as a hanging indent.

Outdention can be used as an attention-getting way to arrange regular text. It is also commonly used for vertical lists ("point form"). The use of this format while using spatial cues makes multiple items easier to access and review, and learners prefer them (Frase and Schwartz, 1979). Whenever there is a series of two or more related items in the body of text, consideration should be given to placing them in point form, one above the other.

Each successive point should begin with a point identifier, which is most commonly a bullet (•), created on the Macintosh by the keystroke Option-8. Usually, bullets are preferable to numerals (Miles, 1987); however, in cases where points will have to be referred to later by number, numerals can be used instead of bullets as point identifiers. A hyphen (-), often used as a point identifier in typewritten manuscript, should not be used. If it is intended that the learner check off the points in turn as they are read or dealt with, then a check box (□) can be used. It is made with the Zapf Dingbats character for "n", done in Outline style.

Subordinate Points

If points must be "stacked" (i.e., points must be listed under points), then the subordinate points should begin with the point identifier about $^1/_8$" to the right of the wrap point of the superior point, and should use the same amount of indention. For example:

- This is the first point. It stands alone.

- This is the second point. In order to show you where this point should wrap to, I will make it extra-long, even though it is nonsensical. It has three sub-points, namely:

  - Sub-point one, which just happens to be one that is long enough to be able to show you where it should wrap.

  - This is sub-point two.

    - This is sub-sub-point one.

    - This is sub-sub-point two.

  - Sub-point three is here.

- Point three begins here.

Numbered Points

If the points must be numbered (i.e., if you need to refer to specific items later), Arabic numerals should be used, as Tinkers (1963) research showed them to be more easily read than Roman numerals. The numerals may be followed by a period, but one certainly isn't required. You may also choose to use either a right parenthesis after the numeral, or a pair of parentheses surrounding it:

1 The first alternative;

2. The second alternative;

3) The third alternative; and

(4) The fourth alternative.

Some technical subjects may require a numeration system similar to the nested section numbering shown earlier in Figure 5–2. Military and government documents seem to favor this system. The same cautions apply to this system of numbering points as to nested section numbering of headings: it can be intimidating and confusing to the learner who is not familiar with it. My advice would be to avoid this scheme of numeration unless it is absolutely required. Then, take extra pains to explain the system to the learner, the first time it is encountered in the text.

Introducing Headings

Point form is an effective way of introducing subsequent headings and showing the structure of upcoming content. That is, you can provide an overview of what is coming up, then list the major points in point form. The major points can then also be used as headings for the subsequent sections which expand the information available.

Visual Cuing

Visual cues of various kinds can be built into instructional materials to help the learner. Sometimes certain words or passages of text are set in boldface type or italic type; other times dingbats (e.g., ▲, ★) or icons may be used to designate certain kinds of activities; color (either as a highlight or as a background) may also be used. The location of text (e.g., set off in the margin, or inserted as a pull quote, a segment of text set off from the rest of the body text, serving as an enticement) may also be used systematically to cue learners to important items.

Foster's (1979) assessment of the research literature on visual cuing is that though some negative findings have been reported, there is a considerable amount of research that shows that cuing can have positive effects on post-test scores (especially immediate post-tests). Foster used capitalization as a visual cue in his research, and found that effective reading of core content was enhanced, without any evidence of reading speed being retarded by the cues. In an earlier study, which also involved various kinds of pre-test conditions, Foster and Coles (1977) had found that cuing with either capital letters or bold text was more effective than no cuing when there was no pre-test. They concluded that "...when readers have been given a clear indication of the material to be found, bold type is a better means of visually distinguishing it than capitals" (p. 64).

Rickards and August (1975) failed to find an effect on immediately post-tested material when they used underlining as the cue, even though Crouse and Idstein (1972) had found such an effect when a fairly lengthy text (6000 words) was used. Coles and Foster (1975) also found an effect, but only when specific instructions were given to attend to underlined material, a particular method of studying the text (SQ3R) was used, and comprehension tests referred only to the cued material.

Research shows that the use of bold or italic characters for emphasis and for cuing is useful, providing that they are not used too frequently (Glynn, Britton, and Tillman, 1985). On the basis of several research studies, Hartley and Burnhill (1977b) concluded that typographic cuing is likely to have little effect unless the learner is specifically informed of the function of the cuing, and instructed on how to deal with it.

Color Coding as an Orienting Device

Foster and Coles (1977) noted that while many current textbooks (particularly psychology texts) used color typographic cuing, they were unable to discern any evaluative research done to determine its effectiveness.

Hartley and Burnhill (1977a) advised that using color as a typographic cue is often unnecessary, and that using color excessively can create problems for learners. If color cuing is used, it should be used sparingly, with full explanation to the learner of how and why it is being used.

Color coding of pages is sometimes done in instructional materials that are ring-bound, for the purpose of differentiating the types of information they contain. For example, actual instruction may be on white paper, while assignments that must be turned in may be on pink paper. This kind of color coding is done on the presumption that it helps orient learners to the tasks at hand, but apparently no research has actually been done regarding its effectiveness for that purpose.

Icons as Orienting Devices

Icons are pictorial or graphic signs that possess the properties of an object, an action, or an idea that they represent. In the context of instructional materials, icons could be graphic representations of various learning activities. They can be included in instructional materials primarily to act as what Waller calls "orienting" devices, part of the access structure of the document (Waller, 1977, 1982). In other words, they act as highly visible reference points, or sign-posts, indicating the location of certain kinds of material.

Icons used in instructional materials should always be explained in the introduction to the materials. Obviously, their use should be consistent within a given package of materials (i.e., a given icon should mean the same thing across different portions of the instructional package); it is highly desirable that the icons be given at least approximately the same meaning across different packages of instructional materials, as well. Just as the first symbol on the right means "Women's Washroom" and the second symbol means "Airport" internationally, the third symbol could be given the meaning "Read in the Textbook" and the fourth symbol could be given the meaning "Mail in the Assignment."

Some samples of other icons, and suggested meanings, are given in Figure 5–5.

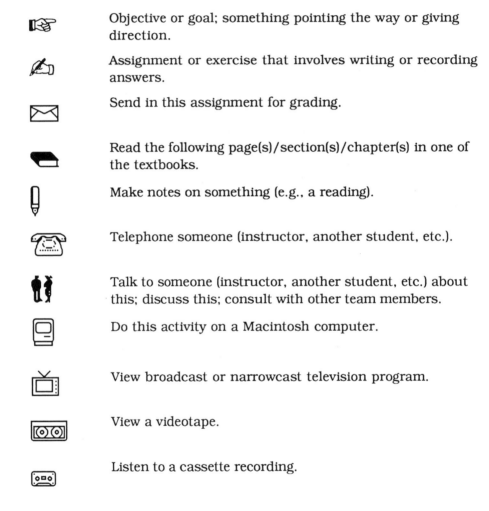

Objective or goal; something pointing the way or giving direction.

Assignment or exercise that involves writing or recording answers.

Send in this assignment for grading.

Read the following page(s)/section(s)/chapter(s) in one of the textbooks.

Make notes on something (e.g., a reading).

Telephone someone (instructor, another student, etc.).

Talk to someone (instructor, another student, etc.) about this; discuss this; consult with other team members.

Do this activity on a Macintosh computer.

View broadcast or narrowcast television program.

View a videotape.

Listen to a cassette recording.

Figure 5–5. Some icons that could be used with instructional materials, and suggested meanings.

Table of Contents

> The purpose of the table of contents is twofold: its principal
> purpose is to enable people to find major topics directly, while
> a subsidiary aim is to provide an overview of the nature and
> coverage of the book, magazine or report. (Lang, 1987, p. 160)

Waller (1982) suggests that the purpose of a table of contents is to
display the structure of the document; he regards it as an important
element of the access structure which learners use to locate whatever
they are looking for quickly and easily. All instructional materials
that employ headings should have tables of contents. The table of
contents should list the headings used, in the order they appear, and
with page numbers attached. The table of contents should list all orders
of headings used, and subordinate headings should be differentiated
from superordinate headings by indention and/or font size.

Common sense dictates that considerable vertical white space should be
used in tables of contents, in order to facilitate rapid location of the
information desired. However, if the table of contents is very lengthy,
this approach may have to be compromised somewhat. One layout of
tables of contents that has been used in order to overcome length is the
run-in style (see Figure 5–6a). It differs from the more conventional
nested style (Figure 5–6b) by embedding page numbers amongst
headings. To my eye, this makes for a very confusing and difficult-to-
use table of contents. I was unable to locate any research that assessed
its effectiveness vis-à-vis the more conventional style. However, my
bias is to avoid the run-in style in tables of contents.

With unusually long entries in the table of contents (i.e., those taking
more than one line), ensure that all lines of the entry stop well to the
left of the page numbers. Do this by using a soft carriage return (Shift-
Return) at an appropriate spot. If you allow the normal word-wrapping
to occur, words will frequently appear too close to the page numbers,
making it difficult to pick out the numbers from amongst the words.

A lengthy or complex table of contents (i.e., one with a large number of
subheadings), or one that has relatively short headings but a relatively
wide column should employ leader lines (the dotted lines between the
headings and the page numbers shown in Figure 5–6b). Leader lines

Chapter 1: Teachers and Typographers, Professors and Printers 1
Is This Book for You? 3; Why Was This Book Necessary? 5; Research vs. "Trusting Your Tummy" 6; Discrepancies in Advice 7; Unspecified "Evidence" 8; Questionable Advice (...at Least from a Pedagogical Point of View) 9; Backgrounds and Perspectives 11; Sources of Information 12; Preview of Remaining Chapters 12.

(a)

Chapter 1: Teachers and Typographers, Professors and Printers 1

Is This Book for You?..3
Why Was This Book Necessary?..5
Research vs. "Trusting Your Tummy"..6
Discrepancies in Advice..7
Unspecified "Evidence"..8
Questionable Advice (...at Least from an Educator's
Point of View)..9
Backgrounds and Perspectives..11
Sources of Information..12
Preview of Remaining Chapters..13

(b)

Figure 5–6. Two arrangements of tables of contents: (a) run-in; (b) nested.

should not be made with repeated period keys; rather, the right-aligned tab for the page number should have a leader line attached to it. In MS Word, this is done through the Tabs dialogue box (Figure 5–7).

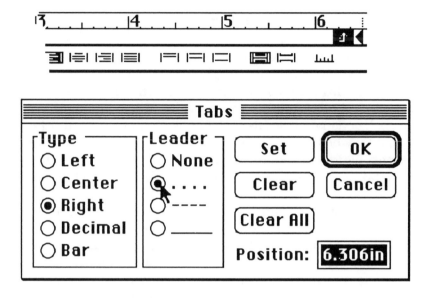

Figure 5–7. MS Word's Tab dialogue box, showing how the leader lines are associated with the selected tab settings.

If the table of contents is very short, and white space can be used to separate entries sufficiently that no confusion is likely, the leader lines may be dispensed with.

MS Word has an automatic table of contents construction feature. If headings are constructed using **Styles**, or if they are manually coded, MS Word will build your table of contents for you.

Indexes

Creating indexes is a specialized job whose description is beyond the scope of this book. I want only to point out that occasionally one sees indexes constructed in a style similar to the run-in style of tables of contents. This arrangement for an index conserves space, no doubt, but is, like the run-in table of contents, very confusing (at least to my eye). I recommend avoiding it.

Cross-References

Cross-referencing within a lengthy document can be a problem, particularly when the document undergoes revision. The usual method for cross-referencing is to write something (say on page 114) such as "see *Dealing with Cross-References* on page 22," or "see Figure 5, page 99." Because instructional materials are often likely to be revised between printings, it may be found necessary, say, to include additional text or an additional figure just before the figure being referred to. That new figure then takes the number 5, and, because of its size, probably causes the original Figure 5 to appear now on page 100. For the single cross-reference, then, both the figure number and the page number have to be revised. Unfortunately, most existing word processing and page layout programs do not do updating of cross-references automatically; one hopes that they might do so in future versions. Until they do, however, the only way to update cross-reference changes is to use the search and replace feature of the word processor to locate every instance of every figure or table or section name that must be changed—a tedious job at best, and one that can be very error-prone. It is wise to maintain an index of the names and numbers of the tables and figures (both original and revised), as well as a table of contents listing the headings, when doing a final proofreading of the document, to ensure that all cross-references have been correctly updated.

An alternative which is easier for the educator, but is probably more difficult for the learner, is to eliminate the cross-reference to page numbers, and simply refer to the heading of the section by name, or to the figure or table number.

Style manuals usually insist that tables and figures should each be numbered (e.g., American Psychological Association, 1983; *The Chicago Manual of Style*, 1969), but with independent series of numbers. This numeration scheme sometimes causes much page-flipping when a table or figure is cross-referenced in the text well after it appears. To avoid the confusion engendered by having separate series of sequential numbers for tables and figures which may not always correspond (i.e., Table 5 may come before Figure 3), it may be a good idea to use the same series of numbers for both figures and tables, but retain the names Table and Figure, as appropriate (Lang, 1987). Thus a typical sequence might be Figure 1, Figure 2, Table 3, Figure 4, Table 5, Table 6.

If that nomenclature seems too radical, perhaps both figures and tables could be re-named *Displays*, and numbered sequentially.

References for Chapter 5

American Psychological Association. (1983). *Publication manual of the American Psychological Association* (3rd ed.). Washington, DC: The Association.

Bove, T., and Rhodes, C. (1989). *Desktop publishing with PageMaker for the Macintosh.* Toronto: John Wiley and Sons.

Brooks, L. W., Danserau, D. F., Spurlin, J. E., and Holley, C. D. (1983). Effects of headings on text processing. *Journal of Educational Psychology, 75,* 292–302.

Coles, P., and Foster, J. (1975). Typographic cueing as an aid to learning from typewritten text. *Programmed Learning and Educational Technology, 12,* 102–108.

Collier, D., and Cotton, B. (1989). *Basic desktop design and layout.* Cincinnati, OH: North Light Books.

Crouse, J. H., and Idstein, P. (1972). Effects of encoding cues on prose learning. *Journal of Educational Psychology, 63,* 309–313.

Foster, J. J. (1979). The use of visual cues in text. In P. A. Kolers, M. E. Wrolstad, and H. Bouma (Eds.), *Processing of visible language* (Vol. 1, pp. 189–203). New York: Plenum Press.

Foster, J., and Coles, P. (1977). An experimental study of typographic cueing in printed text. *Ergonomics, 20*(1), 57–66.

Frase, L. T., and Schwartz, B. J. (1979). Typographical cues that facilitate comprehension. *Journal of Educational Psychology, 71,* 197–206.

Glynn, S. M., Britton, B. K., and Tillman, M. H. (1985). Typographical cues in text: Management of the reader's attention. In D. H. Jonassen (Ed.), *The technology of text (volume two): Principles for structuring, designing, and displaying text* (pp. 192–209). Englewood Cliffs, NJ: Educational Technology Publications.

Hartley, J., and Burnhill, P. (1977a). Fifty guidelines for improving instructional text. *Programmed Learning and Educational Technology, 14,* 65–73.

Hartley, J., and Burnhill, P. (1977b). Understanding instructional text: Typography, layout and design. In M. J. A. Howe (Ed.), *Adult learning* (pp. 223–247). London: John Wiley and Sons.

Hartley, J., and Jonassen, D. H. (1985). The role of headings in printed and electronic text. In D. H. Jonassen (Ed.), *The technology of text (volume two): Principles for structuring, designing, and displaying text* (pp. 237–263). Englewood Cliffs, NJ: Educational Technology Publications.

Hartley, J., and Trueman, M. (1983). The effects of headings in text on recall, search and retrieval. *British Journal of Educational Psychology, 53,* 205–214.

Hartley, J., and Trueman, M. (1985). A research strategy for text designers: The role of headings. *Instructional Science, 14,* 95–155.

Johnsey, A. L., Wheat, N. H., and Morrison, G. R. (1990, January-February). *Layout design making: The placement of illustrations.* Paper presented at the Annual Convention of the Association for Educational Communications and Technology, Anaheim, CA.

Kleper, M. L. (1987). *The illustrated handbook of desktop publishing and typesetting.* Blue Ridge Summit, PA: Tab Books.

Lang, K. (1987). *The writer's guide to desktop publishing.* London: Academic Press.

Lichty, T. (1989). *Design principles for desktop publishers.* Glenview, IL: Scott, Foresman and Co.

Marland, P. W., and Store, R. E. (1982). Some instructional strategies for improved learning from distance education materials. *Distance Education, 3*(1), 72–106.

Miles, J. (1987). *Design for desktop publishing.* San Francisco: Chronicle Books.

Printing layout and design. (1968). Albany, NY: Delmar Publishers.

Rickards, J. P., and August, G. J. (1974). Generative underlining strategies in prose recall. *Journal of Educational Psychology, 67*(6), 860–865.

Shushan, R., and Wright, D. (1989). *Desktop publishing by design.* Redmond, WA: Microsoft Press.

The Chicago manual of style (13th ed.). (1982). Chicago: University of Chicago Press.

Tinker, M. A. (1963). *Legibility of print.* Ames, IA: Iowa State University Press.

Waller, R. (1977). *Three functions of text presentation.* (Notes on transforming, 2). Milton Keynes, England: Institute of Educational Technology, The Open University, mimeograph. Cited by Marland, P. W., and Store, R. E. (1982). Some instructional strategies for improved learning from distance teaching materials. *Distance Education, 3*(1), 72–106.

Waller, R. (1982). Text as diagram: Using typography to improve access and understanding. In D. H. Jonassen (Ed.), *The technology of text: Principles for structuring, designing, and displaying text* (pp. 137–166). Englewood Cliffs, NJ: Educational Technology Publications.

White, J. V. (1983). *Mastering graphics.* New York: Bowker.

Fonts and Type

Strictly speaking, a font is the collection of all characters making up a particular combination of typeface, typestyle, and size (Burns, Venit, and Hansen, 1988; Davis, Barry, and Wiesenberg, 1986; Lichty, 1989). Typeface refers to the general outline or shape of the characters. Examples of typefaces are Times, Helvetica, Bookman, and New Century Schoolbook (Figure 6–1). There are thousands of others, as well. Typestyle refers to variations on the basic typeface. Examples of typestyles are plain (often called roman), bold, italic, and bold italic. Thus (again, strictly speaking) the Courier 12 italic font is different from the Courier 12 bold font, and Palatino 12 italic is a different font than Palatino 14 italic.

Macintosh users, however, have taken some liberties with the terminology, and typically use the word *font* to refer to the typeface, appending a **Style** description to it to specify the typestyle, and a numerical value to specify the size in points. I will continue that practice in this book, using the terms *font* and *typeface* interchangeably.

This is Times.

This is Helvetica.

This is Bookman.

This is New Century Schoolbook.

This is Courier.

This is Palatino.

This is Avant Garde.

Figure 6–1. Various typefaces or fonts.

Despite my suggestion in Chapter 1 that it is unnecessary for you to learn about the processes and vocabularies endemic to the publishing industry, there is one term relating to measurement of type that you will have to know in order to follow some of the upcoming discussion.

A fundamental unit of measurement in printing is the point. There are about 72 points in an inch (i.e., a point is 0.0138 inches, or approximately $1/72''$) (Kleper, 1987). Type sizes are measured in points. Typical type sizes are 10-point and 12-point (see Figure 6–2). Type smaller than about 8-point is too small for most people to read with ease, while type sizes of 14 points and above are generally reserved for special uses, such as headings or titles. This practice is in keeping with Paterson and Tinker's (1940) research, which showed that 6-, 8-, and 14-point type were read considerably more slowly than 9-, 10-, 11-, and 12-point type. The latter sizes were all equally legible when properly used (Tinker, 1965).

This is Times 9.	This is Times 10.	This is Times 12.
This is Helvetica 9.	This is Helvetica 10.	This is Helvetica 12.
This is Bookman 9.	This is Bookman 10.	This is Bookman 12.

Figure 6–2. Various fonts in three sizes.

Type sizes are determined by measuring the vertical distance between a point on a character and the same point on the same character on the line below the first, when the lines are set with minimum vertical spacing. In the days of lead type, it was the size of the block of lead on which the character was cast that was measured, not necessarily the height of the character, and that tradition has continued. Consequently, although the distance between the baselines of characters on two successive lines is always equal to the type size (expressed in points), there can be considerable variation in the actual size of characters from two different fonts of the same size (Figure 6–3).

Figure 6–3. 24-point Bookman, Avant Garde, and Times. Note that the characters in the Times and Avant Garde fonts are smaller and larger, respectively, than the corresponding characters in the Bookman font.

Fonts are the stuff of typography, which concerns itself with selecting an appropriate typeface for a particular purpose, and specifying how the type should be used in a particular publication. Typographers make decisions about how to use type to differentiate among the various elements of a publication (Burns, Venit, and Hansen, 1988, p. 90):

- chapter titles or feature article headlines;
- various levels of headings or headlines;
- headers and footers;
- body copy;
- figure captions;
- labels within figures;
- tables;
- footnotes; and
- special sections, such as sidebars or summaries.

In DTP, as in publishing in pre-DTP days, much emphasis is placed on the selection of an appropriate font or fonts for particular uses. Most DTP books spend many pages discussing different fonts, assessing their "personalities," and recommending their use for certain applications but not others. Before examining some of these pronouncements, a few definitions and distinctions are necessary.

Body Text vs. Display Text

Typefaces can be classified into categories according to function. The number and names of functional categories of typefaces vary from one DTP expert to the next, but Burns, Venit, and Hansen's (1988) typology is typical. They suggest that there are five categories of faces:

- body (or body text or body copy);
- display;
- decorative;
- script or cursive; and
- special.

The categories are somewhat loosely defined, and a particular font might arguably be placed in more than one category.

The distinction between body and display faces is primarily one of size. Fonts whose sizes are in the 9–12 point range are usually considered suitable for large amounts—the body—of the text, hence are called body typefaces. Fonts larger than that are typically used for headings, headlines, or display ads, and thus are called display faces. Some typographers suggest that certain fonts should only be used for body or displays, never for the other purpose, but others are more relaxed about the differentiation.

Decorative typefaces are usually ornate and eye-catching, and should be used in very limited amounts, if at all, in instructional materials. Script or cursive faces are made to resemble handwriting; their use is typically limited to such things as announcements. Special typefaces include unusual symbols or characters, such as mathematical symbols or dingbats (see Figure 6–4).

This is Avante Garde.   𝕿𝖍𝖎𝖘 𝖎𝖘 𝕷𝖔𝖓𝖉𝖔𝖓.
This is Palatino.   *This is Ravenna.*
This is Zapf Chancery.   Σψμβολ ≡∝©≅↔.
This is Helvetica.   Тьис ис Киев.
        ✳❄✿▲ ❄▲ ✺●□❄ ♣❄■✳❂❂▼▲✎

Figure 6–4. Samples of different typefaces.

Serifs

Another way of classifying fonts is to put them into one of two categories—those with serifs and those without. Serifs are the perpendicular finishing strokes at the ends of lines forming the letter (see Figure 6–5).

      (a)   (b)

Figure 6–5. Characters without serifs, (a), and with serifs, (b).

Sans-serif fonts (those without serifs) generally are thought to have a cleaner, more modern look, but are claimed by some to be more difficult to read. The contention is that the serifs aid the eye in interpreting what the character is, and a common "proof" for that contention is showing only the top half of some text; presumably the font with serifs is easier to interpret than the sans-serif font (see Figure 6–6).

Illitoracy   Illitoracy

Figure 6–6. When only the top half of a word is seen, the one with serifs (right) seems to communicate more information than the one without serifs. (After Lichty, 1989, p. 30)

"Evidence about the readability of different typefaces is inconclusive in deciding between the relative merits of serif and sans-serif faces" says Lang (1987, p. 167), even though Tinker (1963, 1965) describes studies which show clearly that there is no difference in legibility between serif and sans-serif fonts. Serifs "...aid the eye to move along from left to right..." and so are good, says White (1983, p. 58), but he also admits that tests have shown that legibility is equal between serif and sans-serif fonts.

Hartley (1987) recapitulates and dismisses another contention:

> Some investigators have argued that serifs in printed text increase the spacing between the letters slightly, and that this makes the text easier to read, but there does not seem to be any conclusive proof for such assumptions. (p. 8)

In any case, it is widely recommended that a serif font be used for body text, and that, in general, sans-serif fonts be reserved for headings, headlines, or other special uses. Collier and Cotton (1989) claim that Helvetica, a sans-serif font, is the most popular typeface in the world (p. 34). By that, they must mean the most-used typeface rather than the most-liked, because some research has shown that learners do not particularly like it, ranking it below Bookman, New Century School-book, and even Courier as a font they think it would be most easy to read and study from (Misanchuk, 1989). However, sans-serif fonts are generally considered to be more legible in smaller sizes (e.g., 6–8 point) than fonts with serifs. Therefore, Collier and Cotton's suggestion, that sans-serif fonts are better suited than fonts with serifs for short bodies of text or text not intended for continuous reading (e.g., reference works, tables, catalogs, etc.), seems reasonable.

Bit-Mapped vs. Outline Fonts

There are currently two main methods of representing text on a computer, whether the text is ultimately displayed on a screen or printed on paper: bit-mapped fonts and outline fonts.

Bit-Mapped Fonts

Bit-mapped fonts are made up of a series of square "dots" on an invisible grid arranged in such a way that together, they present the shape of the character. Each dot is called a pixel, and represents the finest (smallest) unit possible on the display of the DTP system. On a computer screen, each pixel is either illuminated (on) or not illuminated (off), to produce the shape of the character. On a dot-matrix printer, each corresponding pixel is either printed (on) or not printed (off). The series of instructions defining a character is represented within the DTP system as a series of ON's or OFF's (actually, 1's and 0's), corresponding to whether or not the individual pixel is illuminated (or printed) or not (see Figure 6–7).

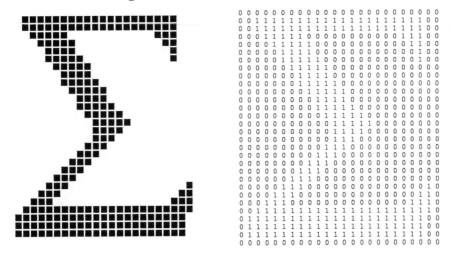

Figure 6–7. (a) Bit-mapped character Sigma displayed as pixels on a screen; (b) a computer's internal representation of a bit-mapped character.

You can see that storing the information defining each character takes many bits (1's and 0's) of space.

When bit-mapped fonts are used, each font (in each size) must be resident in the system (either in the computer or in the printer attached to the computer) in order to give the highest-quality results. Since most word processing and page layout programs permit a variety of font sizes (4-point to 127-point is quite common; some programs permit an even wider range), you can see that a very large number of fonts must be available to the printer in order to print high-quality versions of every possibility. Because each font occupies a considerable chunk of computer storage space, it is simply not cost-effective to have all sizes of all typefaces available to a printer. Instead, if a particular font is not resident in the printer, the printer will generally make use of a smaller version of the same font, simply scaling it up to make it the larger size. In performing this scaling, relatively smaller dots are just made larger. The result is that the scaled-up character has a relatively rough outline. Compare the characters in Figure 6–8. The character on the left is 10-point size (the image in the figure is magnified, of course). The middle character is the result of simply scaling up the 10-point bit-map character to 20-point size. The character on the far right is a true 20-point bit-map character. To get an idea of what they would look like printed at true size, squint at the figure below; notice how the right-most character appears much smoother.

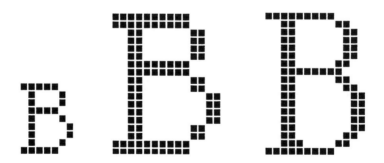

Figure 6–8. Scaled-up vs. actual-size bit-mapped characters.

In general, bit-mapped fonts (especially in larger sizes) will tend to look rougher and more jagged—no matter what the resolution of the printer used—than outline fonts, because of the way they are enlarged.

Outline Fonts

Outline fonts are defined as mathematical curves, rather than as a series of points. Although this is an over-simplification, imagine a printer that uses an imaginary pen, moving a unit at a time, to create shapes in a space large enough for one character. A character may be defined by the following instructions:

> Define one unit as equal to two points
> Raise the pen
> Move the pen to the upper left corner
> Lower the pen
> Drag the pen down ten units
> Drag the pen right seven units
> Drag the pen up one unit
> Drag the pen left six units
> Drag the pen up nine units
> Drag the pen left one unit
> Raise the pen

The pen would trace out the outline of a simple, non-serifed L.

Now suppose you wanted to make a version of the character that was twice as large. You could tell the printer to make one "new" unit equal to four points, and the rest of the instructions would remain the same.

Although this sounds like a lot of instruction to be providing the printer for each character, in fact it is much more economical than the instructions necessary for bit-mapped fonts, where each pixel making up the character has to be identified as being either on or off. Notice that only 1 of the 11 instructions describing the letter *L* must be changed to make another, larger, version.

Characters composed of curves are more complex, of course, but any curve can be described in terms of a mathematical function. (Figure 6–9 has the outline representation of the bit-mapped character Σ from Figure 6–7.) Because that function can be scaled up or down quite handily by a computer, as in the analogy described above for the letter *L*, it is unnecessary for a printer to have more than one size of a font available.

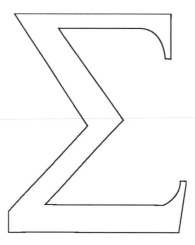

Figure 6–9. Outline font character.

PostScript® is a page-display language developed by Adobe Systems Inc., that is quite widely used in laser printers; indeed, it is considered the current industry standard. In particular, it is currently universally used in Apple® LaserWriter printers, where a number of PostScript fonts are built into the machines. (As this is being written, Apple is introducing a new outline font system called TrueType®. It is different from PostScript, but compatible with it. There will likely continue to be a mixture of PostScript and TrueType fonts in use for many years.)

Outline fonts, therefore, give the best resolution over a range of sizes of a font, when a laser printer is used. For that reason, it makes sense to use a PostScript or TrueType font if you are doing DTP.

Unfortunately, you can't tell for sure whether or not a font is a PostScript or TrueType font, by looking at the name of the font. Apple did establish a convention that uses the names of cities for bit-mapped fonts and other names for PostScript and TrueType fonts, but the naming system is not foolproof. In the MS-DOS world, you simply have to find out some other way (i.e., from the producer of the font) whether or not it is a PostScript font. The situation is being further complicated by the facts that several companies have managed to produce compatible clones of PostScript (i.e., they work the same as PostScript fonts, but they are not true PostScript) and that different companies sometimes give different names to the same font.

Proportional Fonts vs. Non-Proportional Fonts

In a proportional font, the width of a character varies according to what character it is: The horizontal space devoted to the letter *i* is less than the space devoted to the letter *m*. Non-proportional fonts, like those found on typewriters, devote the same amount of space to each character (Figure 6–10).

Proportional fonts allow more text to be printed in a given amount of space than do non-proportional fonts. They also manage to do that without looking crowded. (This font is Times 10.)

```
Proportional fonts allow
more text to be printed in
a given amount of space
than do non-proportional
fonts. They also manage to
do that without looking
crowded. (This font is
Courier 10.)
```

(a)   (b)

Figure 6–10. Samples of a proportional font, (a), and a non-proportional font, (b).

Both bit-mapped and outline fonts can be either proportionally spaced or non-proportionally spaced; however, most outline fonts are proportionally spaced. Courier is the primary non-proportional outline font in use. It emulates the look produced by an IBM® Selectric® typewriter Courier ball.

Proportional fonts not only look more appealing, but also permit more text in the same amount of space, relative to non-proportional fonts;

they are therefore preferred for DTP applications. Some writers (e.g., Miles, 1987) feel that proportional fonts are more legible and less tiring to read than non-proportional fonts, because the inter-letter distances are kept constant. There is a greater number of proportional fonts available in DTP than non-proportional, and they usually lend an air of authority and formality to a document. However, a font like Courier may be used to create a somewhat more informal look, as is sometimes desirable in business letters, for example.

Resident Fonts vs. Down-Loadable Fonts

Resident fonts are those that are "built in" to the printer's memory, hence are always available. On the Apple LaserWriter printer, the resident PostScript fonts are: Times, Helvetica, Courier, and Symbol. The Apple LaserWriter II printer has all the fonts named earlier, plus Avant Garde, Bookman, Narrow Helvetica, New Century Schoolbook, Palatino, Zapf Chancery, and Zapf Dingbats (see Figure 6–11).

Times	Bookman
Helvetica	Narrow Helvetica
Courier	New Century Schoolbook
Σψμβολ (Symbol)	Palatino
Avant Garde	*Zapf Chancery*

■❂□❀ ❀❖■✳❂❀▼▲ (Zapf Dingbats)

Figure 6–11. Samples of all current resident fonts in Apple LaserWriters.

Down-loadable fonts are supplied by one of a number of specialty software houses. These fonts, produced under license from the font's copyright holders, are available in a wide variety of popular typefaces (literally thousands). They are designed so that the computer sends the necessary font information to the printer just before the document is printed; when the job is finished printing, the font information is flushed from the printer. Generally, suppliers of down-loadable fonts provide the necessary ancillary software and instructions on their use when you purchase the fonts.

It is up to you to determine whether the font you want to use is available on the printer accessible to you (a point especially germane if you are having a typesetting shop provide you with very high quality output or if you will be printing your final copy with someone else's computer). If it is not, you may have to make special arrangements to get it down-loaded to the printer. For this reason, it is usually safest to stick with the standard Apple fonts shown in Figure 6–11.

Choosing the "Right" Font

More than any other element, body text can whisper or shout, look old or look new, relax the reader, startle the reader, or send the reader away after two paragraphs, never to return....
[Typeface] may be the single most important decision of your entire publication...and it can make or break your design.
(Lichty, 1989, p. 25)

By a conservative estimate, there are more than 5000 typefaces in common use (Kleper, 1987). Of course, not all of them are yet available on DTP systems, but there are thousands of fonts available to DTP now (Shushan and Wright, 1989), and more coming available each month. The variety is truly staggering, and the very existence of so many makes it difficult for the novice to choose an appropriate font for his or her publication. Even if Lichty's admonition is taken with a grain of salt, there is common agreement among DTP experts that choosing the typeface for a publication is an important decision. Shushan and Wright (1989) suggest that "typography...gives a page a certain personality...and an overall feeling" (p. 14).

We noted earlier that the consensus is that body type should have serifs. Given the financial circumstances of most educational environments, it seems reasonable to assume that, in the light of compelling reasons to the contrary, it would be wise to use one of the fonts resident in the laser printer rather than purchase an additional, down-loadable font. How should one go about choosing a particular typeface, then, given that it should probably have serifs? Which of the LaserWriter's fonts would best serve the purpose?

The Aesthetics of Typefaces

Presumably one should be able to get advice about what typeface to choose from the DTP experts who write on the subject of typography and design. When one tries that approach, however, one again finds a lack of agreement among the experts, as well as an abundance of artistic language justifying the choice of what seems to be essentially personal favorites. Here's a sampling of advice, with a particular focus on Bookman as one of the eligible faces:

> Generally speaking, the typefaces in common use are equally legible, so even the inexperienced user runs little risk of selecting a text typeface that is terribly inappropriate. Readers seem to prefer a typeface that is neither light nor bold, but approaches boldness. Readers also prefer a serif to a sans serif typeface, although there is no difference in reading speed between the two. (Kleper, 1987, p. 30)

Bookman qualifies under these guidelines, but then, so do others, like New Century Schoolbook and Times.

"The display faces of Bookman, Avant Garde, and Helvetica Narrow, will be principally reserved for headlines and display boxes of text" (Hewson, 1988, p. 81). Hewson's implication appears to be that Bookman should not be used as a body text.

Burns, Venit, and Hansen (1988) call Bookman "sturdy" and "readable" (p. 101), and say that it has become more popular since it became one of the standard Apple LaserWriter fonts.

"A report that suggests the writer has big shoulders would work well in Bookman. It's a sturdy, highly legible typeface, used in many newspapers and often described as a workhorse because it's so versatile" (Shushan and Wright, 1989, p. 28).

"Caslon, Bookman, Binny Old Style and Ronaldson are types that may be used on all jobs quite successfully" (*Printing layout and design*, 1968, p. 135).

Lichty (1989) says:

> Bookman is fat and round, its o is almost a circle. This
> stretches the printed line and makes it almost too easy to read.
> The eye can absorb more than Bookman has to offer in a single
> line, giving this typeface a distinctly "Dick and Jane" personal-
> ity... (p. 33)

Unfortunately, the picture is no more clear when one reads the various
prescriptions of when to use or not use Times, New Century Schoolbook,
and a variety of other fonts. Thus the range of opinions as to which
typeface constitutes the best choice for a particular publication is quite
broad, depending upon which expert is consulted. Perhaps this is a
question that can best be answered by reference to research.

Research on Typefaces

Tinker (1963, 1965) provides very comprehensive reviews of research
into typography and legibility that he and his colleagues—primarily
Paterson—did, covering literally dozens of studies spanning several
decades and involving tens of thousands of subjects. Among the many
variables investigated was typeface.

Much of the research on differences in legibility among fonts was done
in the late 1920's and early 1930's. Although many—perhaps most—of
the specific typefaces investigated at that time are no longer as widely
used as they were then, the findings are probably generalizable:

- There is no appreciable difference in legibility among a wide
  range of fonts (Tinker, 1963, 1965; Paterson and Tinker, 1932),
  but readers are likely to have strong preferences about which
  typeface they like to read. (Obviously, the generalization about
  equal legibility does not extend into very ornate or unusual
  fonts.)

- Readers tend to find more legible those fonts with a serif (as
  opposed to a non-serif font) and one that has a heavy stroke
  (bordering on boldface), clearly distinguishing characteristics
  between letters, considerable white space within letters, and
  substantial width to the letters (Tinker, 1963).

Regarding typeface choices, Dreyfus (1985) states:

> The outcome of many experiments indicates there is no
> statistically significant difference between the legibility of a
> wide variety of text types, even between serifed and unserifed
> types. On the other hand, differences of real statistical
> significance were detected when readers were asked which
> styles of type they preferred....This finding ought to be studied
> by those who decide in what types to compose the vast amount
> of printed matter that is intended to attract or to persuade, but
> which nobody is *obliged* to read. (p. 18)

Dreyfus, of course, was speaking primarily to those in mass media,
rather than to educators, but his suggestion ought not to be dismissed
lightly. Although learners in a school setting are usually captive, they
still have the choice of devoting their full attention to reading
something, or not doing so. Educators have traditionally focused their
research efforts primarily or solely on the attainment of cognitive
outcomes, because that is what they are best able to measure, given the
state of the art of measurement and evaluation technology. But what of
the affective outcomes?

Hooper and Hannafin (1986) argue that text that is "pleasant to look at"
may have positive transfer to learning, even though the measurable
effect of some of the variables involved may be minimal. (Although
Hooper and Hannafin were talking about text on a cathode-ray tube,
rather than on the printed page, perhaps the same argument could be
made in the other circumstance.) In other words, the argument goes, if
no detriment to learning can be attributed to font choice, why not
provide learners with what they believe is most appealing, on the
expectation that positive affective reaction is generally beneficial to
learning? To be sure, there is some suggestion in the literature that
what learners prefer is not always what they learn best from (e.g., see
Clark, 1984), but so long as learner preferences do not actually hamper
learning, perhaps they should be taken into consideration.

Tinker's generalizations seem to match the findings of a recent study of
learner/reader preferences (Misanchuk, 1989), undertaken with
Dreyfus' advice in mind. The study asked learners to compare samples
of text made up of all possible combinations of the fonts Bookman,
Courier, Helvetica, New Century Schoolbook, and Times, all in 10-point
size. They were asked to make their judgments based on the question,
"Which of these two pages of text do you think it would be most easy to

read and study from?" The order of preference was Bookman (most preferred), New Century Schoolbook, and Courier. Helvetica and Times were least preferred.

That various typefaces connote different meaning has been proclaimed by a number of typographers and DTP experts, almost invariably without any supporting evidence. There is a little research available on the topic, however. Morrison (1986) investigated the emotional connotations of various typefaces, after having found only six earlier studies on the topic, all of which he claimed used stimulus materials of a questionable nature. He found that different typefaces evoked similar emotional reactions from different groups of people (instructional technology students, student typographers, and naive college students), that italic faces were perceived as more active than roman, that bold typefaces were seen as forceful and vigorous, and that sans-serif faces were viewed as more potent than seriffed ones. However, since Morrison used typefaces in his study that are not commonly available to desktop publishing, in a size about twice that of normal body text (24 point), it is difficult to determine how applicable his findings are to the current discussion.

Choice of Font and Length of Publication

Throughout this book there has been a consistent message: efficacy of learning is more important than aesthetics. Activities such as copy fitting have been downplayed in importance. Still, it is worth recognizing that in certain circumstances, the length of the final product may be an important consideration. The choice of typeface can have a marked effect on length. Some fonts are more compact than others, given the same font size. Times, for example, is much more compact than Bookman or New Century Schoolbook (perhaps that is why it is not particularly well liked by readers). Figure 6–12 compares the amount of space taken by three different fonts, all 9-point.

With respect to instructional materials, it is my belief that efficacy of learning is a more important criterion than is aesthetic appeal. This is not to say that instructional materials can or should be ugly, but merely that, when it comes to a choice between aesthetics and educational efficacy, the latter should dominate.

(a)

With respect to instructional materials, it is my belief that efficacy of learning is a more important criterion than is aesthetic appeal. This is not to say that instructional materials can or should be ugly, but merely that, when it comes to a choice between aesthetics and educational efficacy, the latter should dominate.

(b)

With respect to instructional materials, it is my belief that efficacy of learning is a more important criterion than is aesthetic appeal. This is not to say that instructional materials can or should be ugly, but merely that, when it comes to a choice between aesthetics and educational efficacy, the latter should dominate.

(c)

Figure 6–12. Amount of space taken by the same passage printed in different fonts: (a) Bookman, (b) Palatino, (c) Times. Leading and font size remain the same in all cases.

Limit the Number of Fonts Used

"The worse excess of the neophyte is to use too many typefaces in one document" (Simonsen, 1985, p. 59).

Whatever the choice of font used for the body text, Lang (1987) offers advice universally echoed by DTP experts: Keep it simple. With so many fonts to choose from, a novice is liable to decide to use a number of them within one document, or worse yet, on one page. That would be a mistake.

There is widespread agreement that the number of fonts used should be strictly limited; the only disagreement comes as to whether the maximum number is two or three, and whether the styles (e.g., italic and bold) are included in that limit or not (Bove and Rhodes, 1989; Davis, Barry, and Wiesenberg, 1986; Lang, 1987). An oft-repeated rule of thumb is to limit font choices to two—one serifed for body type, and one sans-serif for headings and/or figure labels and captions (Burns, Venit, and Hansen, 1988; Lichty, 1989)—and to use different sizes and styles (italic, bold) to indicate levels of headings. Lichty also suggests that similar-looking fonts not be used together on the same page (or indeed, within the same publication) for different purposes (e.g., Bookman and New Century Schoolbook, or Helvetica and Avant Garde).

Font Size

As noted at the beginning of this chapter, research has shown that the optimum sizes for body text are in the 9–12 point range. Since some fonts appear to be larger than others, for a given font size, this range should be regarded as approximate.

When different sizes of the same font are used for different purposes (e.g., to indicate headings, as footnotes, etc.), it is important to recognize that most people cannot differentiate a single point size (e.g., the difference between 9-point and 10-point) (Spiegelman, 1987). West (1987) points out that subtle changes in typography may confuse the reader. Therefore, if you change the size of a font used for one purpose, in order to use it for another purpose, make sure the change in size is sufficiently great to be recognizable. When the purposes to which only slightly different sized text is put are quite different, there should not be a problem. For example, using 10-point text for body text and 9-point text for footnotes should not be confusing, since footnotes, by virtue of their location, are not likely to be confused with body text.

There is a rule of thumb called the Rule of X's which can be used to determine what font size should be used for headings. It states that the height of the upper-case *X* of the smaller font should be the same as the height of the lower-case *x* of the larger font. Thus the lower-case *x* of a heading should be as high as an upper-case *X* of the body text that follows the heading (or of the text forming the next-lower order of heading in the case of multiple levels of headings). Figure 6–13 illustrates the Rule of X's for a particular combination of font and sizes:

Major headings are in 20-point Bookman, minor headings are in 14-point, and body text is 10-point.

Major Heading Xx Xx Minor Heading Xx Xx Body Text

Figure 6–13. The Rule of X's is illustrated by these three font sizes.

Font Styles

Word processing and page layout programs generally provide the opportunity to print any font (in any size) in a number of variations, or font styles. Among these are plain, bold, italic, outline, shadow, caps, small caps, and combinations of those (Figure 6–14). Some page layout programs (e.g., PageMaker) also offer reverse style (i.e., white letters on a black background); it is also possible to create reverse lettering in MS Word by using embedded PostScript commands.

Variations	plain
Variations	bold
Variations	italic
Variations	bold italic
Variations	outline
Variations	bold outline
Variations	shadow
Variations	shadow italic
VARIATIONS	all caps
VARIATIONS	small caps
Variations	reverse

Figure 6–14. Some font styles available.

With so many options available, one is liable to want to make use of many, if not all, of them.

Resist the temptation.

In particular, for instructional materials, eschew the outline and shadow styles, reserving them for title pages if you must use them, and make very sparing use of caps, either full size or small caps. What you are left with, then, is the opportunity to use either bold letters or italics. That hardly limits you, however, since you are free to use different type sizes, as well.

Bold or Italic Characters

Different disciplines, and indeed different style manuals within disciplines, may well have different recommendations for when italic and bold type should and shouldn't be used. My recommendations below are based on the APA style manual (American Psychological

Association, 1983), Felici and Nace (1987), and common sense. I suggest that italics should be used for:

- introducing a technical or key term. The term should be italicized only the first time it is used;

- titles of books, periodicals, films, etc.;

- characters, words, or phrases cited as a linguistic example (e.g., the letter *a* and the word *word* were written on the chalkboard);

- specialized applications (e.g., genera, species, and varieties in biology; statistical symbols; some test scores and scales);

- identifying foreign words or phrases not commonly used in English (e.g., The *lingua franca* of trade is money);

- distinguishing speakers in a question-and-answer style of writing, as in an interview; and

- distinguishing introductory material or editorial commentary from the main text.

Italics should not be used for:

- foreign words and abbreviations common in English (e.g., ad lib, et al., e.g., i.e., etc.); and

- mere emphasis. (I feel this rule may be broken if confusion is likely to result without some indication of emphasis, but in general, restructuring of the sentence to provide the emphasis should be attempted first. If more than one or two words on one or two pages are italicized for emphasis, the device is probably being over-used.)

If your discipline demands the use of a different style manual, which specifies different uses for italics, by all means follow it.

Research shows that the use of bold or italic characters for emphasis and for cuing is useful, providing that they are not used too frequently (Glynn, Britton, and Tillman, 1985). If the intention is to emphasize by making the word(s) look different, then they must, in fact, look different. Over-use of bolding or italics leads to saturation and no emphasis is inferred by the learner.

In general, bold type is preferred for emphasis, rather than italics. However, if bold is being used as a cuing device for another purpose (e.g., to indicate technical terms or words found in a glossary), italics may be used for emphasis, subject to the constraints described above regarding over-use.

Tinker's studies (Paterson and Tinker, 1940; Tinker, 1963, 1965) showed that while boldface type is read just as quickly as plain type, some 70% of readers prefer plain type, judging boldface to be relatively illegible. While boldface may be used for emphasis without sacrificing legibility, long passages of it should be avoided, since readers don't like it.

Italic print, on the other hand, is read more slowly than plain type, and is disliked by even more readers: 94–96% of readers prefer plain type to italic (Paterson and Tinker, 1940; Tinker, 1955; Tinker and Paterson, 1928). In fact, Tinker's recommendation is that "...*the use of italics should be limited largely to those rare occasions when added emphasis is desired or to brief headings in textual material* [italics his]" (Tinker, 1965, p. 135).

Underlining

Underlining of words, phrases, or sentences should generally not be used in DTP. In typewriter mode, underlining was a signal to the typesetter that whatever was underlined was to be set in italic type. Since DTP provides italic type, underlining is redundant, and lends an aura of amateurism to printed copy. Avoid it.

Shadow and Outline Letters

Shadow and outline letters should also be avoided, not only because they are difficult to read, but also because they are ordinarily unnecessary, given the range of font sizes available, and the ability to use bold and italic styles.

All Capital Letters

Research shows that phrases all printed in capital letters are read nearly 12% more slowly than the same phrases printed in capitals and lower-case (Tinker, 1965; Tinker and Paterson, 1928), and 90% of readers consider all-capital type to be less legible than lower-case. Therefore, the use of all-capital type should also be avoided for virtually all applications, including continuous reading text and headings and titles (Tinker, 1965, p. 138). Rather, use larger font sizes and bold or italic type (or even a different font) to provide the different look required of titles and the like. Tinker (1965) decries as "unfortunate" the practice of using all caps within a paragraph of lower-case text to set off certain words, phrases, or sentences. "Such material is read significantly slower than Roman lower case and is considered relatively illegible and unpleasant by readers" (p. 138).

Bullets, Boxes, and Dingbats

Bullets (•) , Boxes (□), and dingbats (☞✔✍◆▲✎❂✄) are special characters available in DTP. (Strictly speaking, both bullets and boxes are also classified as dingbats, but because they are more commonplace, I speak of them as different.) On the Mac, bullets are made by the keystroke Option-8 in all fonts. The box shown was made by using Outline style on the black square formed by the character *n* in the Zapf Dingbats font. The other dingbats shown, and many more, are also characters in the Zapf Dingbats font.

When used in moderation, bullets, boxes, and dingbats can be valuable additions to your text, but the key word here is *moderation*. Using too many in one document (especially using too many different ones) will make the document look busy and possibly confusing.

Bullets are most frequently used in conjunction with "point form," where they look better than periods, hyphens, or asterisks. Boxes, of course, are used in questionnaires or in lists of activities which need to be checked off. Dingbats can be used for a variety of purposes, such as separating sections of text (where one, two, or three dingbats are centered in the column between the two sections of text that you want to separate, as in the example below). They can also mark specific activities, and are frequently used in instructional materials to signal important points, review points, instructional objectives, and other similar devices.

❧   ❧   ❧

Since dingbats come from a font of their own, you may have to change their point sizes to match the height of the text they accompany. That is, you may find that 14-point or even 16-point dingbats of a certain kind look best with 10-point body text. (Since Zapf Dingbats is a PostScript font, the characters will look good when printed at any size; they can look pretty crude on the screen, however, in larger sizes.) Experiment with different combinations before deciding which looks best.

Even bullets sometimes look too small when set near text of the same point size; you may want to use a larger size bullet to give it more emphasis. Burns, Venit, and Hansen (1988) suggest that bullets and boxes should be as close to the x-height (i.e., the height of a lower-case letter x) as possible, or else they should be centered vertically in that size space, if they are not. To get larger, more dramatic bullets (for a given font size), you should use Avante Garde, New Century Schoolbook, Bookman, or Palatino bullets with Helvetica, Times, or Courier body type (*Publish!*, 1989a). However, do not make the bullets larger than the capital letters of the text that follows them (Miles, 1987).

Typographic Effects

Drop Caps and Raised Initial Letters

In medieval times, calligraphers spent hours lavishly illustrating the initial letter of each chapter of a book, often using gold leaf and all manner of colors. We might well admire their efforts as works of art, and wonder at their dedication in doing such work, but not many would suggest emulating their behavior today. Yet, increasingly, word processors and layout programs identify as a big selling feature the ability to create "drop caps" and raised initial letters (see Figure 6–15).

D idijice cgmdgibe pedhc ecebc dg cbeide
   cecdge ihhdicidignc gidpged immo hbgobieeino. Dpic cpihdeb jeoinc gidp i cdeh-jy-cdeh ix "gidcdpbgeop" gm pgg i lidijice hiccioe ic ecel dg cbeide in cch ihhdicidign mgb ceehino denind midec.

D idijice cgmdgibe pedhc ecebc dg cbeide cecdge
 ihhdicidignc gidpged immo hbgobieeino.
   Dpic cpihdeb jeoinc gidp i cdeh-jy-cdeh ix "gidcdpbgeop" gm pgg i lidijice hiccioe ic ecel dg cbeide in cch ihhdicidign mgb ceehino denind midec.

D idijice cgmdgibe pedhc ecebc dg cbeide cecdge ihhdicidignc gidpged immo hbgobieeino. Dpic cpihdeb jeoinc gidp i cdeh-jy-cdeh ix "gidcdpbgeop" gm pgg i lidijice hiccioe ic ecel dg cbeide in cch ihhdicidign mgb ceehino denind midec.

Figure 6–15. Examples of drop caps and raised initial letters.

Fancy initial letters—at least as far as educators are concerned—are likely to do little to help readers attend to the task at hand; indeed, the fancier they are, the bigger distraction they provide. Despite software programmers' best efforts, drop caps and raised initial letters still require more work to use than ordinary characters, and the time spent creating them would be better spent attending to the quality of instructional design and of the message being presented.

My advice about drop caps? Forget them.

Distorted Text Styles

Sometimes graphic designers deliberately distort text, by stretching or compressing it, or by applying a slant or perspective to it. This treatment is most often applied to text in graphics; the intention usually is dramatic effect. However, research shows that text thus distorted is simply harder to read (Tinker, 1963, 1965).

Avoid using distorted text.

References for Chapter 6

American Psychological Association. (1983). *Publication manual of the American Psychological Association* (3rd ed.). Washington, DC: The Association.

Bove, T., and Rhodes, C. (1989). *Desktop publishing with PageMaker for the Macintosh.* Toronto: John Wiley and Sons.

Burns, D., Venit, S., and Hansen, R. (1988). *The electronic publisher.* New York: Brady.

Clark, R. E. (1984). Research on student thought processes during computer-based instruction. *Journal of Instructional Development, 7*(3), 2-5.

Collier, D., and Cotton, B. (1989). *Basic desktop design and layout.* Cincinnati, OH: North Light Books.

Davis, F. E., Barry, J., and Wiesenberg, M. (1986). *Desktop publishing.* Homewood, IL: Dow Jones-Irwin.

Dreyfus, J. (1985). A turning point in type design. *Visible Language, 19*(1), 11–22.

Felici, J., and Nace, T. (1987). *Desktop publishing skills: A primer for typesetting with computers and laser printers.* Reading, MA: Addison-Wesley.

Glynn, S. M., Britton, B. K., and Tillman, M. H. (1985). Typographical cues in text: Management of the reader's attention. In D. H. Jonassen (Ed.), *The technology of text (volume two): Principles for structuring, designing, and displaying text* (pp. 192–209). Englewood Cliffs, NJ: Educational Technology Publications.

Hartley, J. (1987). Designing electronic text: The role of print-based research. *Educational Technology and Communication Journal, 35,* 3–17.

Hewson, D. (1988). *Introduction to desktop publishing.* San Francisco, CA: Chronicle Books.

Hooper, S., and Hannafin, M. J. (1986). Variables affecting the legibility of computer generated text. *Journal of Instructional Development, 9*(4), 22–28.

Kleper, M. L. (1987). *The illustrated handbook of desktop publishing and typesetting.* Blue Ridge Summit, PA: Tab Books.

Lang, K. (1987). *The writer's guide to desktop publishing.* London: Academic Press.

Lichty, T. (1989). *Design principles for desktop publishers.* Glenview, IL: Scott, Foresman and Co.

Miles, J. (1987). *Design for desktop publishing.* San Francisco: Chronicle Books.

Misanchuk, E. R. (1989). *Learner preferences for typeface (font) and leading in print materials.* Saskatoon, SK: Division of Extension and Community Relations, The University of Saskatchewan. (ERIC Document Reproduction Service No. ED 307 854)

Morrison, G. R. (1986). Communicability of the emotional connotation of type. *Educational Communications and Technology Journal, 34,* 235–244.

Paterson, D. G., and Tinker, M. A. (1932). Studies of typographical factors influencing speed of reading: X. Styles of type face. *Journal of Applied Psychology, 16,* 605–613.

Paterson, D. G., and Tinker, M. A. (1940). *How to make type readable.* New York: Harper and Row. Cited by Tinker, M. A. (1965). *Bases for effective reading.* Minneapolis: University of Minnesota Press.

Printing layout and design. (1968). Albany, NY: Delmar Publishers.

Publish! (1989a). *101 best desktop publishing tips, vol. 1.* San Francisco, CA: PCW Communications.

Shushan, R., and Wright, D. (1989). *Desktop publishing by design.* Redmond, WA: Microsoft Press.

Simonsen, R. (1985). The elements of design. *Popular Computing,* November, 59.

Spiegelman, M. (1987). Interior design for documents. *PC World,* March, 178–185.

Tinker, M. A. (1955). Prolonged reading tasks in visual research. *Journal of Applied Psychology, 39,* 444–446.

Tinker, M. A. (1963). *Legibility of print.* Ames, IA: Iowa State University Press.

Tinker, M. A. (1965). *Bases for effective reading.* Minneapolis: University of Minnesota Press.

Tinker, M. A., and Paterson, D. G. (1928). Influence of type form on speed of reading. *Journal of Applied Psychology, 12,* 359–368.

West, S. (1987). Design for desktop publishing. In The Waite Group
    (J. Stockford, Ed.), *Desktop publishing bible* (pp. 53–72). Indianapolis, IN:
    Howard W. Sams.

White, J. V. (1983). *Mastering graphics*. New York: Bowker.

Leading and Kerning

Leading (rhymes with wedding), as a verb, is the adjustment of the vertical space, usually measured in points, between adjacent lines of type. As a noun, it refers to the distance between adjacent lines of text. Its name derives from the practice, during the days of lead type, of inserting extra bars of that material as spacing between lines to improve legibility.

Type with no leading is said to be *set solid*.

Both practical experience and research have shown that optimal leading varies with the size of type and with the length of line, hence these factors also have to be considered when discussing leading.

Kerning, and its relative letterspacing, is the adjustment of the horizontal spacing between adjacent letters.

The term *leading* is sometimes used somewhat ambiguously. In some of the older literature (e.g., Tinker, 1963, 1965) it refers to the extra space between lines. For example, 2 points of leading might be used on 10-point text, yielding 10-point text on a 12-point line. In more recent usage, however, the tendency seems to be to use the sum of the type size and the extra space when referring to leading: 12-point leading would be the term used to designate a 12-point line. Fortunately, it is usually possible to determine from context which convention is being used.

A common method of describing type size and leading together is to represent them numerically, separated by a slash, thus: 10/13. This is read as "ten on thirteen," and indicates 10-point type on a 13-point line (which is how this book is set).

Since research has shown differences in line length and leading requirements between adults and children, they are addressed separately below.

Line Length and Leading (Adults)

There is general agreement among DTP experts, as well as research evidence to support the contention, that line length (or column width, in the case of multi-column pages) is related to the amount of leading needed. In general, the opinion is that as the length of the line is increased, the need for more leading and/or larger type size increases (Burns, Venit, and Hansen, 1988; Lang, 1987; *Printing layout and design*, 1968).

In Chapter 4 we noted that column width (which is the same as line length) was a matter on which diverse and conflicting advice was offered. Some say that a column of text should be only 35–40 characters long (West, 1987), while others would allow as many as 75 characters (*Publish!*, 1989b). Lang (1987) suggests that lines should optimally be 4.5" wide, and Lichty (1989) says that the line length should be 1.5 lower-case alphabets.

There is somewhat greater consensus with respect to leading, however: Kleper (1987) recommends line spacing of about 20% of the type size, while Lichty (1989) recommends 25%. Others state approximately the same things in different terms, by saying that two points of leading should be used for types sizes in the 9–12 point range (*Printing layout and design*, 1968).

Tinker (1965) summarizes the results of more than a dozen studies involving many thousands of subjects over a number of years. He concludes that leading (in moderation) improves legibility, and that the optimal amount of leading varies according to both type size and line length (or column width). The findings are represented in the table in Figure 7–1. In the table, the line length is represented in three different measurement systems: inches, centimeters, and picas (1 pica = $^1/_6$"). Since the original research was done in picas, the other measurements are converted approximations. For various combinations of line length and type size, those leadings found through research to be satisfactory are marked with a bullet. Tinker regarded these combinations as ones that printers should use.

To use the table, determine what column width (line length) and type size you wish to use, and enter the table with those values. Determine which leading values at that intersection contain a bullet; those are safe leading values to use. For example, if the line length is 9 cm (which is equal to 3 $^1/_2$" or 21 picas), and the type size you wish to use is 8 point, then either 2, 3, or 4 points of leading would be appropriate.

In order to make a generalization, some extrapolation from the research findings is necessary: In summary, what the table shows is that for type sizes between 9 and 12 points, and for line lengths between 2 $^1/_2$" and 5", 2-point leading is probably an adequate choice (although you might want to increase the leading by an additional point when the line length is near the high end of that range).

Within the limits established by Tinker's findings, however, there is still room for the designer to exercise choice. As in most things associated with design, moderation is probably a good idea: "Long lines of small type make it difficult for the reader to keep his or her place. Short lines of large type hinder the flow of the message by forcing frequent and disfiguring hyphenations" (Lichty, 1989, p. 53).

Type Size

Figure showing optimal leading for various type sizes and line lengths. Bullet (•) marks optimal combinations.

Line Length Inches	Cm.	Picas	6 Pt L1	6 Pt L2	6 Pt L3	6 Pt L4	8 Pt L1	8 Pt L2	8 Pt L3	8 Pt L4	9 Pt L1	9 Pt L2	9 Pt L3	9 Pt L4	10 Pt L1	10 Pt L2	10 Pt L3	10 Pt L4	11 Pt L0	11 Pt L1	11 Pt L2	11 Pt L3	11 Pt L4	12 Pt L0	12 Pt L1	12 Pt L2	12 Pt L3	12 Pt L4
2 3/8	6	14						•	•	•	•	•	•	•	•	•	•	•										
2 5/8	6.5	16																										
2 7/8	7	17																		•	•				•	•	•	•
3	7.5	18									•	•	•	•														
3 1/8	8	19																										
3 1/2	9	21	•	•	•	•	•	•	•	•					•	•	•	•										
4 1/8	10.5	25	•	•	•	•	•	•	•	•									•	•	•	•	•	•	•	•	•	•
4 5/8	12	28									•	•	•	•														
5	12.5	30																										
5 1/8	13	31														•												
5 1/2	14	33																		•	•				•	•	•	•
5 5/8	14.5	34					•	•	•	•																		
6	15	36																										

Figure 7–1. Optimal leading for various type sizes and line lengths (for adults) are marked with a bullet (•).

Line Length and Leading (Children)

Tinker also researched the same variables with children of different ages, to determine how generalizable his findings were. He concluded that children at about the fifth-grade level (age 10 or so) behaved very much like adults with respect to typographical variables (Tinker, 1965), and so could be treated the same as adults in that regard. He also concluded that line lengths between 2 $1/2$" and 5" are appropriate for younger children, although common practice was to use lengths between 2" and 3", except for first-graders, where shorter line lengths were common.

His recommendations for font size, line length, and leading for various grade levels are summarized in Figure 7–2.

Grade	Type size (points)	Line length (inches)	Leading (points)
1	14–18	$3\,^3/_8$	6–8
2	14–16	$3\,^3/_8 - 3\,^5/_8$	5–6
3–4	12–14	$3\,^3/_8 - 4$	3–4

Figure 7–2. Optimal leading for various type sizes and line lengths (for children).

Automatic vs. Fixed Leading

Normally, most Mac word processors will allow the mixing on a single line of fonts of different sizes. For example, they would typically allow for a single 30-point character in a line of 10-point text. They do this by automatically adjusting the leading to accommodate the largest character (see Figure 7–3).

If you perform particularly well, you

may be awarded a big ☆ in
recognition of your efforts. On the
other hand, if you perform poorly,
you should not expect to receive one.

Figure 7–3. Line set at 12 points. The text is 10-point; the star is
20-point. The large star causes an automatic increase in the leading.

MS Word, in particular, automatically provides this feature, whether
the line leading is set to **Auto** or to a user-specified size. In the main,
this is a useful feature that ensures that the large character does not get
clipped off at the top by the line above it or superimposed on it.

However, there are times when the extra leading thus inserted distracts
rather than enhances. For example, with some combinations of font
sizes, the extra leading may be unnecessary (i.e., the difference between
one size of font and the other is small enough to be accommodated
without extra leading), and the white space formed by the added leading
can become distracting (Figure 7–4).

If you perform particularly well,

you may be awarded a big ☆ in
recognition of your efforts. On
the other hand, if you perform
poorly, you should not expect to
receive one.

(a)

If you perform particularly well,
you may be awarded a big ☆ in
recognition of your efforts. On
the other hand, if you perform
poorly, you should not expect to
receive one.

(b)

Figure 7–4. The text in (a) is 10-point set on a 12-point line; that in
(b) is 10-point set on a –12-point line. The star is 20-point. The
unnecessary leading inserted automatically in (a) can be distracting.

In such cases, it may be desirable to fix the leading at a constant
amount. For example, if the text is 10/12, you could ensure that the
leading stays at 12 points by specifying a negative value for the **Line** size
(Figure 7–5).

```
╔═══════════════════════════════════════════╗
║ ≣≣≣≣≣≣≣≣≣≣≣ Paragraph ≣≣≣≣≣≣≣≣≣≣≣ ║
║ ┌Indents──────┐  ┌Spacing────────┐  ┌─────────┐ ║
║ │ Left:  │3.625in│  │ Line:  │ -12 pt │  │   OK  ↖ │ ║
║ │ Right: │-0.5in │  │ Before:│        │  └─────────┘ ║
║ │ First: │       │  │ After: │ 6 pt   │  ┌─Cancel─┐ ║
║ └─────────────┘  └───────────────┘  └─────────┘ ║
║                                      ┌─Apply──┐ ║
║  ☐ Page Break Before   ☐ Line Numbering    └────────┘ ║
║  ☐ Keep With Next ¶    ☐ Keep Lines Together         ║
║   ┌Tabs...┐   ┌Borders...┐   ┌Position...┐          ║
╚═══════════════════════════════════════════╝
```

Figure 7–5. Fixed leading. The minus sign before the numeral designating the leading causes the leading to be "frozen."

Note that fixing the leading by placing a minus sign before the numerals in the leading box (Figure 7–5) can have negative consequences, by cutting off or overlapping portions of very large characters or graphics (see Figure 7–6).

> If you perform particularly well, you
> may be awarded a big ☆ in
> recognition of your efforts. On the
> other hand, if you perform poorly, you
> should not expect to receive one.

Figure 7–6. Line set at –12 points. Text is 10-point; the star is 30-point.

If you insert a graphic into a paragraph that has fixed leading, only the bottom-most portion of the graphic (corresponding to the point size at which the leading is fixed) will show on the screen. When the page is printed, however, an even more rude surprise occurs. Instead of the usual situation wherein a graphic inserted into an MS Word document starts at the point of the cursor and fills downward, a graphic inserted into a fixed-leading line will fill upward from that line. That is, the graphic you insert will overlap any text immediately above the line upon which it is inserted.

Auto leading may give too much leading for display type, such as headings. Do not be afraid to adjust the leading of headings manually, but if you do so, make sure you are consistent across all headings.

Kerning

Kerning is the manual adjustment of horizontal spacing between adjacent letters. It is done, particularly with display type, to compensate for the fact that word processors and page layout programs sometimes do an inadequate job of providing a visually appropriate space. Most people would agree that the word on the right in Figure 7–7 looks better than the word on the left.

AWAKE   AWAKE

(a)   (b)

Figure 7–7. Words that are un-kerned, (a), and kerned, (b).

Some combinations of letters—A and V or W, or T and O, for example—are particularly troublesome, and need to be kerned. If letters are spaced mechanically, with exactly the same distance between their extremities, they tend to look awkward and disjointed (see Figure 7–8). Optically spaced letters, on the other hand, have approximately the same area between letters, and look better according to the "eyeball test."

(a)   (b)

Figure 7–8. Mechanically spaced letters, (a), have exactly the same distance between all letter combinations, but don't look as good as optically spaced letters, (b).

Hewson (1988) notes that it really isn't worthwhile kerning any type under 18 point, because the proximity of the small characters makes any aberrations all but unnoticeable. Even with larger (display) type, kerning is probably not worthwhile, in my opinion. Most DTP software now builds in some type of kerning procedure. Educators probably have better things to do with their lives than kerning every title and heading to make it absolutely perfect. If something comes off the printer simply screaming "Kern me!", then (and only then) may the job be worthwhile.

Letterspacing

Letterspacing is also an adjustment of the horizontal space between adjacent letters, but in a manner different from kerning. While kerning attempts to space differentially between certain pairs of letters, letterspacing adjusts the space between all letters by an equal amount. Letterspacing can be used to expand or contract the total length of a word or phrase (see Figure 7–9).

Avenueofthistypeisneeded

(a)

A venue of this type is needed

(b)

A   venue   of   this   type   is   needed

(c)

Figure 7–9. The letterspacing in these words has been adjusted: (a) is contracted, (b) is normal, and (c) is expanded.

In general, the recommendation is that letterspacing not be done at all (Kleper, 1987, p. 35). The reason for that recommendation is that uniformity of spacing leads to easier recognition of the letters, and hence their underlying meaning. If the learner has to struggle to connect (or disconnect) the letters making up a word or series of words, that is time taken away from the primary intention of instruction. Besides, letterspacing requires extra time and work, which might be better spent improving the substance of the instruction, rather than the letterspacing.

There is one study that shows no deleterious effects from letterspacing: Moriarty and Scheiner (1984) compared normal and close-set letter-spacing with both Times Roman and Helvetica fonts (11 point on a 25-pica line). Indeed, more text was read in a given period of time when the letters were close-set than when set normally, which Moriarty and Scheiner deemed to be an advantage. When one considers the content (the text of an advertising brochure on stereo speakers), the length of the passage read (not reported, but probably under 500 words, since the mean number of words read varied from 323–380 words), the extremely short reading time used (105 seconds), and the fact that no indexes of comprehension were used in this study, it would be unwise to generalize the results of this single study too much.

Ligatures

Kerning and letterspacing should not be confused with ligatures, which are separate entities. Ligatures are letters which have actually been formally combined to make a new character because the two original characters side by side appear more awkward than the ligature replacing them (Figure 7–10).

Character combinations	Ligatures
OE	Œ
AE	Æ
f i	fi
f l	fl

Figure 7–10. Samples of ligatures.

Ligatures are printed with special keystrokes (e.g., Œ is Shift-Option-Q on the Macintosh). Ligatures are part of the tradition of "professional"-looking type, but are not, in my estimation, worth the extra bother required to create them. If you do want to use ligatures, ignore them until you are completely finished with the document, then use the global search and replace to put them in.

References for Chapter 7

Burns, D., Venit, S., and Hansen, R. (1988). *The electronic publisher.* New York: Brady.

Hewson, D. (1988). *Introduction to desktop publishing.* San Francisco, CA: Chronicle Books.

Kleper, M. L. (1987). *The illustrated handbook of desktop publishing and typesetting.* Blue Ridge Summit, PA: Tab Books.

Lang, K. (1987). *The writer's guide to desktop publishing.* London: Academic Press.

Lichty, T. (1989). *Design principles for desktop publishers.* Glenview, IL: Scott, Foresman and Co.

Moriarty, S. E., and Scheiner, E. C. (1984). A study of close-set text type. *Journal of Applied Psychology, 69,* 700–702.

Printing layout and design. (1968). Albany, NY: Delmar Publishers.

Publish! (1989b). *101 best desktop publishing tips, vol. 2.* San Francisco, CA: PCW Communications.

Tinker, M. A. (1963). *Legibility of print.* Ames, IA: Iowa State University Press.

Tinker, M. A. (1965). *Bases for effective reading.* Minneapolis: University of Minnesota Press.

West, S. (1987). Design for desktop publishing. In The Waite Group (J. Stockford, Ed.), *Desktop publishing bible* (pp. 53–72). Indianapolis, IN: Howard W. Sams.

Principles of Page Layout

> Design advice abounds, and what makes a layout 'good' often
> seems to be a matter of opinion. The most universal examples
> of good layout, though, tend to be simple and maintain a
> delicate balance between unity and diversity. This balance is
> easily upset—too much diversity, when we use too many of the
> options provided by the microcomputer, or too much unity,
> when we use the microcomputer as a typewriter. (West, 1987,
> p. 53)

Page layout has to do with where on the blank page certain elements of
layout and composition, such as those listed below, fall (Burns, Venit,
and Hansen, 1988; West, 1987):

- titles or headings of various orders;
- body text;
- page numbers;
- running headers and/or footers;
- margins (including columns);
- tables;
- table headings;

- graphics (data graphics; illustrations):
    - line art;
    - photographs;
- figure captions;
- labels within figures;
- graphic elements (e.g., rules, boxes, bullets, icons, and dingbats);
- footnotes; and
- special sections, such as sidebars or summaries.

Equally as important as where on the page the above-listed elements fall is where they *don't* fall, i.e., what areas of the page are left blank. Such areas of white space, as it is called, can be a powerful feature when used with skill.

Page design is thus concerned with such things as the proportion of the paper used, the grid imposed upon it (which in turn involves consideration of the margins and column structure, if any), and the distribution of text and illustrations on the pages. Some of these concerns were first addressed in Chapter 4, Initial Design Considerations, as ones that should be thought about early in the process. However, some of the concerns are inter-related with others that were discussed in subsequent chapters (e.g., font size, leading, access structure), so we return to them now.

The reason for attention to page layout considerations is to facilitate instruction. West (1987) claims that layouts should attract a potential reader and then disappear (i.e., they should not interfere with the reading). While it is true that attracting the learner is important, the arguments developed in Chapter 1 regarding the differences between DTP and DTPI should be kept in mind. Congruent with the other lines of argument developed in this book, I suggest that the only valid criterion for judging page layout in DTPI is the efficacy of instruction. For this reason, some of the recommendations that follow fly in the face of the advice given by Felici and Nace (1987, p. 76) to "...avoid layout ad libbing—inventing ad hoc solutions can create a confused and unprofessional presentation. The best approach is to foresee your layout design needs and stick with a consistent plan."

While the virtues of a consistent overall plan are obvious (e.g., placement of headers, pagination, headings, etc.), layout of instructional material is precisely about the kind of page-by-page decision-making that Felici and Nace call "ad libbing." It is only through consideration for instructional effectiveness that instructionally reasonable decisions can be made about placement of blocks of text relative to other related blocks of text or relevant graphics. To follow Felici and Nace's advice would be to ad lib instructional decisions (as is indeed often done when graphic designers apply their rule of thumb to instructional materials, often with consequences that are detrimental to instruction); I would rather see the aesthetic dimension be ad libbed, if that's what it takes to make effective instruction.

Consider how a practitioner of DTP and a practitioner of DTPI would approach the same problem. Suppose in the course of laying out a document, a problem was encountered: A fairly large figure had to be placed into the document, and its intended location was such that most, but not all, of the figure would fit on the page, making some sort of re-arrangement necessary. The DTPer would ask himself or herself the question "How can I re-arrange the text and figure so that they would fit within the pre-set margins, and still look good?", probably without even making reference to the content of the text or the figure. The DTPIer, on the other hand, would ask "How can I arrange the text and figure so that they would be most effective instructionally?", and would pay a great deal of attention to what the content of the text was, especially as it related to the figure. In the course of laying out a single document, similar questions would typically have to be asked numerous times. Thus the DTPIer must, of necessity, "ad lib" through the document.

Principles of Design and Layout

Design and layout are primarily artistic activities, hence most of the advice available consists of generalizations derived from collective aesthetic experience.

Simplicity

The fact that desktop publishing is capable of producing complex designs and layouts of text should never be construed as an imperative—

or even as a licence—to exercise the capability. Rather, it should be the goal of the designer of instructional materials to make everything as simple as possible. Complexity usually interferes with communication, hence should be avoided. This is not to say that the design should be condescending, however; it should never "talk down" to the learner. Whether the decision is a choice between a single-column and a double-column layout, between mirror-image margins and alternatives, between using one font per page and using three, the decision boils down to one in which the principle of simplicity can be applied. Although I dislike the "put-down" inherent in a phrase that has become widely understood as the KISS principle (Keep It Simple, Stupid!), it does encapsulate the thought succinctly.

Burns, Venit, and Hansen (1988) note that creating documents which use the same grid on all pages is easier than producing documents which use grids that differ from page to page. Earlier it was noted that single-column layouts are easier to work with than multi-column ones, and that the number of different fonts used per document should be strictly limited. All these examples illustrate the principle of simplicity. The principle of simplicity is probably even more important in DTPI than in DTP, since instructional materials frequently undergo revision and re-publication.

Consistency

If variety is the spice of life, then surely consistency is the meat and potatoes. Zany layouts and attention-getting designs may indeed attract attention, but often the most attention-getting work does not communicate well. It is imperative in designing instructional materials that consistency prevail. Learners should not have to search about the page to find such elements as page numbers, headings, and the like. Footnotes should always appear in the same place on the page, in the same style and size of text. Major headings should all be alike, in size, in placement, and in amount of surrounding white space, so that they can be used as guides to the structure of the document. Captions should be located in the same position relative to their figures every time they are employed, so that no confusion is possible.

Consistency can be obtained handily through the use of template documents and word processor style sheets. If these are not used, and particularly if more than one person is involved in designing the instructional materials, write out and publicize precise specifications for fonts, styles, sizes, and white space surrounding each element of the layout (i.e., develop a style sheet).

As important as visual consistency is grammatical consistency. Settle on a style manual and dictionary beforehand and follow it religiously. Make sure all people working on the project know it (Burns, Venit, and Hansen, 1988).

Balance and Symmetry

Balance and symmetry are constructs often referred to by artists, and frequently mentioned by DTP experts as important to page layout decisions.

Balance and symmetry are closely related. Balance can be either formal or informal. Formal balance involves using matching elements of the same size and shape in a symmetrical arrangement (Figure 8–1), whereas informal balance involves using elements of differing sizes and/or shapes arranged about an axis so that the sum of the elements on one half appear equal to the sum of the elements on the other half.

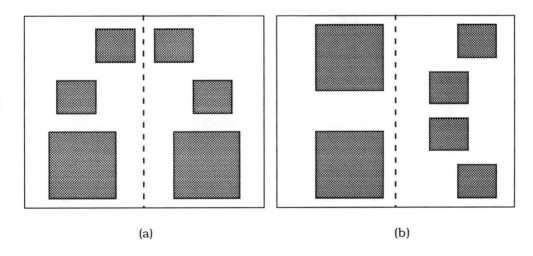

(a)   (b)

Figure 8–1. Balance can be either (a) formal or (b) informal. The dashed lines indicate the axes on which the shapes are balanced.

Consider a see-saw. If two people of equal size get onto a see-saw, they balance nicely if they are equidistant from the pivot point; if one of them gets closer to the pivot point, balance is lost. However, two small people on one side of the see-saw can arrange themselves at appropriate distances to balance one large person on the other side. So it is with elements on a page: Two (or more) smaller elements can offset a large element, creating informal balance.

Symmetry is related to balance insofar as a symmetrical arrangement has formal balance. The line of symmetry may be vertical, horizontal, or even diagonal (Figure 8–2). Asymmetrical arrangements lack formal balance, although they may have informal balance.

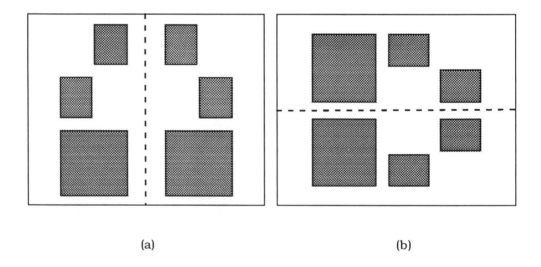

(a)   (b)

Figure 8–2. Layouts (a), (b), and (c) are symmetrical; (d) is asymmetrical. The dashed lines indicate the axes of symmetry. *(Figure continued on next page.)*

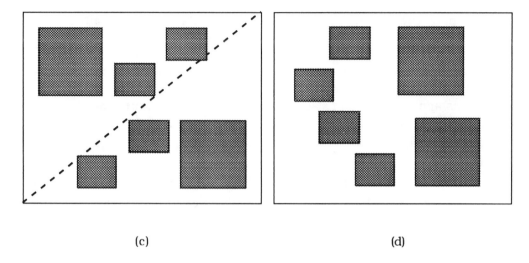

(c)   (d)

Figure 8–2. *(continued)*

Generally speaking, formally balanced, symmetrical layouts are considered static and prone to being boring. Most DTP experts suggest that interest is created by using informal balance and asymmetry.

Miles (1987) advises against mixing symmetry and asymmetry on the same page.

While principles of balance and symmetry should be kept in mind when laying out instructional materials, and guidelines given below applied whenever possible, it is important to remember that supremacy should be given to the logic of the content. If it makes logical and instructional sense that a certain illustration should be included next to text that refers to it, then that is where it should be placed, regardless of what happens to the symmetry or balance of the page. (Of course, you shouldn't be extreme or dogmatic about it.)

Unity, Harmony, and Rhythm

Unity, harmony, and rhythm are artistic constructs that are frequently referred to in the DTP literature when discussing page layout. They are applied in a variety of ways.

For example, the principle of unity is applied in the restriction of the number of fonts used, and in the use of the same fonts in figures and in body text; the principle of harmony is applied in the judicious selection of a second, contrasting font if one is used, or in the use for special purposes of various styles and sizes of the same font; the principle of rhythm is applied in the consistent placement of such features as headers and footers, page numbers, and figure captions.

Since the DTP literature usually approaches layout and design from the viewpoint of aesthetics, the arrangement of blocks of text and of illustrations on the page is often influenced by the principles of unity, harmony, and rhythm. In DTPI, however, these constructs play a secondary role. In those instances where they can be applied, *after* accommodating the instructional concerns, of course they should be.

Use of White Space

It is a natural action to attempt to put as much information or instruction on a page as possible in an attempt to communicate as much as possible for the least cost. If you do so, however, you should be aware that in fact what may happen is the opposite: You may end up communicating less than if you had left something out, because the document may be uninviting, intimidating, and overcrowded (Burns, Venit, and Hansen, 1988; Felici and Nace, 1987).

Well-designed documents contain plenty of white space—as margins, as separators between headings and body text and between adjacent paragraphs of text, as delineators of changes in expected activity or action, as demarcations of examples, figures, and tables. White space should not, however, be randomly placed on pages. It is a design element, not a left-over or residual. Its use must be planned (Lichty, 1989).

Content Should Determine Margins

A frequent problem with the way pages are laid out in textbooks or other instructional materials is that they are produced through the blind application of certain rules. For example, in most books, the bottom of each page (i.e., where the text ends) is kept constant, with very few exceptions. Designers of these books move illustrations (or tables, examples, etc.) to subsequent pages in order to accommodate uniform bottom margins. This frequently necessitates the moving forward of text that bears no relationship to the illustration, to fill in the extraneous white space created. The net effect is that the learner encounters text referring to the illustration, then is forced to make a decision: Turn the page to view the illustration, and keep flipping back and forth between the page containing the relevant text and the page containing the illustration; or forge ahead, reading first the text relevant to the illustration, then irrelevant text, then finally seeing the illustration. Making sense of it all is difficult either way, but especially so in the latter case. From an instructional point of view, it would be far better to keep the relevant text on the same page as the illustration, and not display the irrelevant text until after the illustration.

Most DTP experts insist that certain kinds of white space be held constant throughout a document, including margins. Many times, DTP advice is to adjust the leading of the text to ensure that margins are held constant from one page or spread to the next and that the space available on each page or spread is completely filled with text (a process called copy casting, or copy fitting), or to use devices such as pull quotes or fillers to lengthen the copy; indeed, sometimes designers are encouraged to edit the text to ensure that the margins are kept sacred.

While it seems important to maintain consistency in such matters as amount of white space allocated between headings and subsequent text, or between text and tables embedded in it, and even the location of top margins relative to the page, in my opinion there isn't much reason to maintain the sanctity of bottom margins with the same vigor.

Hartley (1978, 1982; Hartley and Burnhill, 1977a) argues convincingly that margins (and particularly bottom margins) should not be strictly adhered to. Rather, he suggests, the flow of the content should determine where page breaks occur. While it is currently common practice in the publishing industry to ensure that widows and orphans (single words or very short lines coming at the end of a page or column, or at the beginning of a subsequent page or column) are eliminated, Hartley is talking about much more: He is suggesting that column and/or page breaks be made when the logic of what is being said demands it, not necessarily when the bottom of the page is reached.

Indeed, there seems to be a good argument for *not* making the bottom margins uniform. Facilitating the order in which items are processed mentally by the learner is a legitimate aim of the deployment on the page of instructional text (Gropper, 1991), and adjacency of items aids association. Unfortunately, page breaks don't always fall at instructionally logical places. While it may not always be possible to have chunks of related content displayed adjacent to each other, often that goal can be assisted by judiciously forcing a page break before it would occur normally.

A ragged bottom margin can be seen on an increasing number of publications, and some DTP experts now recommend it (e.g., Burns, Venit, and Hansen, 1988, p. 301).

Hartley also carries his argument to the right margin. He states, for example, that right-justified text—which is common in the production of textbooks, novels, journals, magazines, and newspapers—should not be used at all. Not only does right-justified text slow the reader down, by virtue of the frequent hyphenation needed (a result confirmed by empirical studies, e.g., Trollip and Sales, 1986), but comprehension suffers as well. Line length should be variable, and based on sense. For example, consider the different arrangements of a single passage in Figure 8–3.

Even while retaining the archaic and confusing punctuation, the relationships and numbers seem clearer in the second arrangement.

Now the sons of Jacob were twelve. The sons of Leah;
Reuben, Jacob's firstborn, and Simeon, and Levi, and
Judah, and Issachar, and Zebulun. The sons of Rachel;
Joseph, and Benjamin: And the sons of Bilhah, Rachel's
handmaid; Dan, and Naphtali. And the sons of Zilpah,
Leah's handmaid; Gad, and Asher. These are the sons of
Jacob, which were born in Padan-aram.

Now the sons of Jacob were twelve.

> The sons of Leah;
> > Reuben, Jacob's firstborn, and
> > Simeon, and
> > Levi, and
> > Judah, and
> > Issachar, and
> > Zebulun.

> The sons of Rachel;
> > Joseph, and
> > Benjamin:

> And the sons of Bilhah, Rachel's handmaid;
> > Dan, and
> > Naphtali.

> And the sons of Zilpah, Leah's handmaid;
> > Gad, and
> > Asher.

These are the sons of Jacob, which were born in Padan-
aram.

Figure 8–3. Complicated, difficult-to-follow relationships can be
clarified by using space judiciously. (After Hartley, 1987)

It doesn't seem unreasonable to permit the occasional violation of the
left and right margins for the sake of expediency. If an educator has a
diagram that doesn't quite fit between the margins established for the
publication, but will still fit comfortably onto the page, my advice
would be to use the diagram as it is. Reserve the time—and money—saved
by not reducing the diagram to size, and apply it instead to improving
the quality of other aspects of the instruction being designed. (Case in
point: Figure 6–13 on p. 144.)

White Space as a Differentiating Feature

Another way of using white space is to ensure that graphics and tables in the text are easily distinguishable as entities. That is, there should be some white space allotted both before and after figures and tables to make them stand out from the surrounding text. This not only makes them stand out as separate elements, but also prevents confusion.

White Space and Headings as Indicators of Content Structure

As an educator and researcher, Hartley (1978, 1982; Hartley and Burnhill, 1977a; Hartley and Jonassen, 1985) recommends using white space differentially around different orders of headings, so that white space can contribute to an understanding of the structure of the content. Similar advice is generally given by DTP experts. As noted in the section on headings (Chapter 5), the higher the order of heading, the more space should be allocated before and after it.

Hartley and Burnhill (1977a) also recommend that space, rather than indention, be used to differentiate paragraphs.

Segmentation

Some evidence is emerging in the literature that some quite drastic departures from the norm in text arrangement have salutary effects. For example, Frase and Schwartz (1979) experimentally manipulated segmentation and indention of text. Segmentation was done on the basis of meaningfulness of the text, rather than on the basis of normal margins. That is, carriage returns were placed at locations where it made most sense to place them, in terms of the content of the text, rather than (as is usually the case) at the "end of the line" (i.e., where the margin occurs). For example, they might have arranged a passage thus:

> In a sense, well-executed instructional design
> should disappear into the background.
> That is, instructional materials that are well designed
> should produce learning in the learner
> without the learner being aware of the fact
> that there are materials mediating the process.

instead of in the more conventional form:

> In a sense, well-executed instructional design should
> disappear into the background. That is, instructional materials
> that are well designed should produce learning in the learner
> without the learner being aware of the fact that there are
> materials mediating the process.

Frase and Schwartz concluded that segmentation and indention can be used to facilitate comprehension, and that meaningfully segmented and indented text resulted in 14%–18% faster response times in verifying technical material.

Non-Breaking Spaces and Soft Carriage Returns

Recall the description of non-breaking spaces and soft carriage returns in Chapter 3. Non-breaking spaces (made with ⌘-Space Bar in MS Word) keep the two words or sets of characters on either side of them bound together. Soft carriage returns (Shift-Return in MS Word) cause carriage returns without adding extra spaces that might normally be added after a carriage return. These two techniques are useful for improving the readability of text in some circumstances.

Designers should keep an eye out for patterns of text that are dysfunctional, or difficult to follow, and which might be improved with the simple insertion of a carriage return or a non-breaking space. For example, consider this sentence:

> The accompanying text should have a rule with the left margin at 1
> $^1/_2$".

Without intervention, the word processor wrapped the line at a most inconvenient place, between the integer and the fraction, making the sentence difficult to follow and making the likelihood of a mistake quite high. By using a non-breaking space between the 1 and the $^1/_2$, however, the two are bound together, and both wrap to the following line, thus:

> The accompanying text should have a rule with the left margin at
> 1 $^1/_2$".

Sometimes the non-breaking space cannot solve the problem. In that case, a soft carriage return should be used to force text to the next line.

Placement of Tables, Figures, and Examples

Graphics (drawings, photographs, charts, figures, graphs), tables, and examples should be placed as close as possible to their referents in the text (Hartley and Burnhill, 1977a; Wright, 1982), rather than arranged on the page for aesthetic effect. Gropper (1991) notes that adjacency aids concurrent association and promotes a controlled order of processing. Because graphics usually cannot be "broken" across consecutive pages, and tables and examples generally should not be unless there is no other way to accommodate them, some rearrangement of either the graphics or the text may be necessary. I suggest that the recommended practice, from the point of view of instructional design, is to insert the appropriate graphic immediately after the paragraph of text which refers to it, regardless of how that affects bottom margins. The typical journal or book publication practice of placing those graphics at the top of the following page and filling in the space created with subsequent text, is not recommended.

As the layout of this book demonstrates, following that advice creates a publication which differs—sometime markedly—in appearance from most others. Of course, the more often the advice is applied, the less different it will begin to look. Ultimately, learners will accept as normal the sometimes large white spaces at the bottoms of pages. Indeed, they may come to recognize these "short pages" as non-normative cues (Gropper, 1991) that something that forms a cohesive "chunk" of instruction is just ahead.

Of course, this design rule of thumb should not be stretched to its limit. If, for example, a full-page graphic follows a page which, under the rule of thumb, would contain only three lines of text, it would probably make more sense to defer the graphic and fill the remainder of the page with text. It would be important in that circumstance to ensure that the reader is given directions as to the location of the graphic.

Another way of dealing with the same problem is sometimes possible—ruthless editing of the preceding text may make it possible to eliminate the offending three lines without adversely affecting comprehension.

Runarounds

Runaround is the description given to placing text around an irregularly-shaped graphic in such a way as to maintain a more-or-less consistent distance between the outermost portion of the graphic and the adjacent text (see Figure 8–4). That is, runarounds permit a constant-sized white "border" around an irregularly-shaped graphic. Some DTP advisors suggest that runarounds be used "...to avoid unnecessary and ugly white space around graphics" (Lang, 1987, p. 86). Recently popularized by software advertising its ability to do them automatically, runarounds are touted as a selling feature. Runarounds can also be done manually by judiciously altering the margins of each individual line of text—a very laborious and time-consuming process.

Figure 8–4. An example of a runaround.

Runarounds are probably rarely actually needed; indeed, I would argue that they almost never represent an improvement—let alone a necessity—for instructional materials. Sometimes runarounds are laid out so that the reader's eyes must skip over the graphic to continue reading the line (Figure 8–5a); other times they are laid out so that the text is more-or-less columnar (Figure 8–5b). Both set-ups have disadvantages, although the layout in (a) is considerably worse than the one in (b). Requiring a reader's eyes to jump over a graphic interruption—without losing track of which line is being read, let alone the thoughts it communicates—in order to continue reading text seems likely to be a major impediment to smooth reading. The layout in Figure 8–5b is better, at least insofar as the left column is concerned, but the varying location of the left margin of the right column is likely to slow reading; reading proceeds more smoothly when the location of the left margin is constant, since the eye has a fixed point to which to sweep.

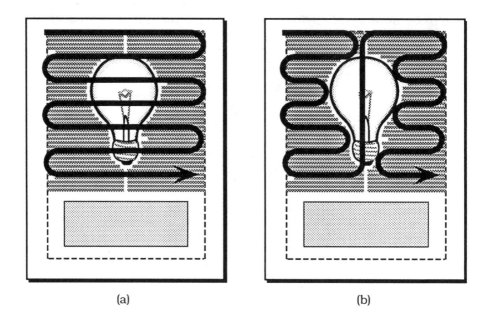

(a)   (b)

Figure 8–5. Runarounds may be set up in two ways: (a) text runs across graphic; (b) text stays on one side of graphic in each column.

In my judgment, if a graphic is sufficiently salient to be worth including, it is worth giving sufficient space for it to be placed normally in the text, without crowding text right up to its very edge. Only when non-salient graphics are used as embellishments (which ought not to be done in instructional materials under any circumstances; I violate the rule in the figures merely for purposes of demonstration) in limited space allocations, might runarounds be of any use. Side-by-side text and a small graphic—which is not a true runaround in any case—may be useful if you need to crowd text onto a page (e.g., if a chapter is running a little too long, or if placing the graphic without the runaround will push important and salient text onto another page), but by and large, you can just ignore them. Not using them usually just yields extra white space, which is probably more beneficial than harmful, in the sense that it makes the page lighter (Lang's comments about "ugly white space" notwithstanding).

Lichty makes the point well when he says that runarounds

> ...are more like technological posturing than design features...[which] provoke irregular word spacing, dissolve the conceptual border between text and graphics, and are often poorly produced. Unfortunately...runarounds have become a measure of software performance....Runarounds are rarely warranted. Don't let Madison Avenue convince you otherwise. (Lichty, 1989, p. 129)

Another disadvantage of runarounds is that they virtually demand right justified margins (otherwise text to the left of the graphic will not have a uniform white border around the graphic), and the variable inter-word spacing (and, often, hyphenation) induced by right justification interferes with efficient reading.

Widows and Orphans

Widows and orphans are most often described as single words or short lines (which are variously defined as two words, three words, or a few words; or less than one-third or one-half the width of the column) that end a paragraph (Bove and Rhodes, 1989; Burns, Venit, and Hansen, 1988; Davis, Barry, and Wiesenberg, 1986; Miles, 1987; Shushan and Wright, 1989), although Lichty (1989) defines as a widow the *first* line of a paragraph at the bottom of a column or page.

Widows and orphans are generally deemed unsightly and undesirable, particularly if they fall at the bottom of a column or page, or if they form the first line of a column or page. Whether they are called widows or orphans depends upon whether they form the last line or the first line on a column or a page, but trying to figure out which is which is a real challenge: Burns, Venit, and Hansen (1988, p. 210) and Davis, Barry, and Wiesenberg (1986, p. 49) define a widow as a short last line of a paragraph, regardless of whether it falls at the end of a column or page, or within a column or page. Shushan and Wright (1989, p. 39), Bove and Rhodes (1989, p. 134), and Miles (1987, p. 26) call the short last line of a paragraph a widow if it appears at the top of a column or page, and Lichty (1989, p. 58) calls the *first* line of a paragraph a widow if it appears at the bottom of a column or page.

Davis, Barry, and Wiesenberg (1986, p. 49) call the short last line of a paragraph an orphan if it occurs at the top of a column or page, and Lichty (1989, p. 58) defines an orphan as the last line of a paragraph at the top of a page or column. Bove and Rhodes (1989, p. 134) and Shushan and Wright (1989, p. 39) use the name orphan for a short last line of a paragraph at the bottom of a column or page.

Exactly *why* widows and orphans are considered bad form is unclear, although Shushan and Wright (1989) suggest that they "...make the type appear uneven on the page and in some situations interrupt the reader's eye movement" (p. 39). Although they admit that ragged right margins make widows less of a problem than does justified text, particularly when white space is used between paragraphs, most other DTP experts appear not to be so forgiving. Some of the remedies suggested for widows and orphans include rewriting the text to lengthen or shorten it, hand-kerning letters (!), changing margins, or adjusting the word spacing, letterspacing, or column length. All the remedies seem to be rather extreme and labor-intensive, especially since they address what may well be a non-problem: No research was located on whether widows and orphans constitute instructional problems.

In DTPI, widows and orphans should be viewed in a manner different than in regular DTP, in my opinion. The question to ask is not whether the line at the bottom or the top of the page is complete, but rather whether the thought is. That is, widows and orphans shouldn't be judged on the basis of what they look like, but on the basis of how much sense they make. If the interruption of changing columns or pages can be accommodated without losing the thought, the widow or orphan should be allowed to stand. If not, then the offending word or phrase should be forced forward or back, or rewritten. On the other hand, although I am not persuaded that widows and orphans are detrimental per se, I see no harm in avoiding them, particularly if avoidance can be done automatically. MS Word, like some other word processing and page layout programs, offers an optional control over the existence of widows. That is, by turning on an appropriate "switch" (**Widow Control** under the **Document** command in the **Format** menu, in MS Word), the word processor can be made to eliminate widows automatically by forcing an additional line of text to a subsequent page when not doing so would create a widow.

My usual procedure is to leave this switch turned on, but to over-ride it if it becomes necessary to create a widow or an orphan in order to circumvent a subsequent problem of keeping related text together. That is, if in formatting a document I encounter an area where there is a problem of keeping related text adjacent, I have no qualms about deliberately producing a widow or an orphan in earlier text if doing so will help me with the problem of keeping subsequent related text together. Of course, turning off the widow control means that particular attention will have to be paid to all page bottoms in the entire document.

In a related matter, it makes sense, in my view, to follow a widespread rule of thumb in DTP that a title or heading should not appear at the bottom of a page if there is not room for a significant amount of text following it. Once again, exactly how much text should follow the heading is open to opinion, as there seems to be no research on the topic. In my view, at least two or three lines of text should follow a heading, but, once again, I have no qualms about breaking this rule of thumb if I find it necessary to place only one line of text after a heading in order to produce a more sensible layout on a subsequent page.

Similarly, headings followed immediately by sub-headings, without intervening text, should always be kept together rather than being allowed to appear on separate pages.

Practical Considerations in Layout

When the time finally comes for you to begin viewing your nearly-finished document on the screen, in page preview mode, you will likely find all sorts of places where you have been unable to accommodate all the rules and suggestions in this book and still come up with a halfway decent looking document. Page breaks will occur at the most inopportune times; figures will be just a smidgen too large to be accommodated on the same pages as their captions; descriptions that you really want to be on the same page or spread as the figures they refer to simply won't cooperate.

Don't despair.

First try to apply some of the simpler solutions, like editing or re-arranging some of the content. Although you may have been careful to present your material in the most considered order, you may find it possible in some circumstances to interchange one section with another, without doing violence to the overall work. Sometimes just moving one paragraph before another can make all the difference in the world to your layout. In doing the final layout and pagination of this book, I had to do that a few times, and I would bet you would be hard pressed to identify where I made those changes. Of course, you shouldn't make the changes in order of content if they do impair the comprehensibility of the document.

A second line of defense is to cheat a little bit. Although I tried to impress upon you the importance of uniformity and consistency, I was stating an ideal. If you had decided, for example, to allow a certain amount of space before major headings, and you find a truculent page or two that would lay out better if you just had two points less space above the major heading, remove the space. A few times in this book, I had to shave two points off the space before a caption, just to get it to fit on the same page as the figure it referred to. Now that you know about it, you may be able to spot where I did it, but I doubt you would have noticed if I hadn't raised the issue.

Despite the ideal stated earlier of not hyphenating words, sometimes it is possible to make text fit the constraints of a page better with a few judiciously-placed hyphens.

Finally, if all else fails, take the rules with a grain of salt, violating them where absolutely necessary. Accept that there is just no way to get the verbal references to a figure onto the same page as the figure itself, and place things where they fall (e.g., see Figures 3–5 through 3–9, and surrounding text, beginning on p. 40). Break a figure across two pages, even though you know it would be better to have both parts on a single page or spread. After all, you have to be practical. The rules and guidelines set out in this book represent an ideal. If you have to deviate from them, *c'est la vie*. Be careful, however, not to be too cavalier about violating them, or the look and effectiveness of your product may suffer.

References for Chapter 8

Bove, T., and Rhodes, C. (1989). *Desktop publishing with PageMaker for the Macintosh.* Toronto: John Wiley and Sons.

Burns, D., Venit, S., and Hansen, R. (1988). *The electronic publisher.* New York: Brady.

Davis, F. E., Barry, J., and Wiesenberg, M. (1986). *Desktop publishing.* Homewood, IL: Dow Jones-Irwin.

Felici, J., and Nace, T. (1987). *Desktop publishing skills: A primer for typesetting with computers and laser printers.* Reading, MA: Addison-Wesley.

Frase, L. T., and Schwartz, B. J. (1979). Typographical cues that facilitate comprehension. *Journal of Educational Psychology, 71*, 197–206.

Gropper, G. L. (1991). *Text displays: Analysis and systematic design.* Englewood Cliffs, NJ: Educational Technology Publications.

Hartley, J. (1978). *Designing instructional text.* London: Kogan Page.

Hartley, J. (1982). Designing instructional text. In D. H. Jonassen (Ed.), *The technology of text: Principles for structuring, designing, and displaying text* (pp. 193–214). Englewood Cliffs, NJ: Educational Technology Publications.

Hartley, J. (1987). Designing electronic text: The role of print-based research. *Educational Technology and Communication Journal, 35*, 3–17.

Hartley, J., and Burnhill, P. (1977a). Fifty guidelines for improving instructional text. *Programmed Learning and Educational Technology, 14*, 65–73.

Hartley, J., and Jonassen, D. H. (1985). The role of headings in printed and electronic text. In D. H. Jonassen (Ed.), *The technology of text (volume two): Principles for structuring, designing, and displaying text* (pp. 237–263). Englewood Cliffs, NJ: Educational Technology Publications.

Lang, K. (1987). *The writer's guide to desktop publishing.* London: Academic Press.

Lichty, T. (1989). *Design principles for desktop publishers*. Glenview, IL: Scott, Foresman and Co.

Miles, J. (1987). *Design for desktop publishing*. San Francisco: Chronicle Books.

Shushan, R., and Wright, D. (1989). *Desktop publishing by design*. Redmond, WA: Microsoft Press.

Trollip, S. R., and Sales, G. (1986, January). *Readability of computer-generated fill-justified text*. Paper presented at the Annual Convention of the Association for Educational Communications and Technology, Las Vegas, NV.

West, S. (1987). Design for desktop publishing. In The Waite Group (J. Stockford, Ed.), *Desktop publishing bible* (pp. 53–72). Indianapolis, IN: Howard W. Sams.

Wright, P. (1982). A user-oriented approach to the design of tables and flowcharts. In D. H. Jonassen (Ed.), *The technology of text: Principles for structuring, designing, and displaying text* (pp. 317–340). Englewood Cliffs, NJ: Educational Technology Publications.

Tables

There are three primary ways of representing numerical information in print: in text, in tables, and in data graphics (graphs and data charts). There is considerable agreement that the first way is a poor one for reporting numerical information (Feliciano, Powers, and Kearl, 1963; Macdonald-Ross, 1977b; Tufte, 1983). This chapter deals with the second way, and the next chapter with the third.

When to Use a Table

Tables are often used to present a maximum amount of numerical information in a minimum amount of space; indeed, Macdonald-Ross (1977a, 1977b) identifies compactness as the main benefit of tables. However, tables have some disadvantages, too (elaborated below). The choice to put data into a table (as opposed to text or data graphics) can hinge on a number of things. One—compactness—has already been mentioned. Efficacy, intended use, and amount of data to be represented are others.

> The conventional sentence is a poor way to show more than two
> numbers because it prevents comparisons within the data....
> Tables are clearly the best way to show exact numerical value....
> Tables are preferable to graphics for many small data sets
> (Tufte, 1983, p. 178).

Care should be taken to consider fully the reasons that the use of a table is being contemplated, as well as how and by whom it is intended to be used.

Feliciano, Powers, and Kearl (1963) are unequivocal about the use of tables: "Under no circumstances should text be used by itself to convey important statistical data if more than a very few facts are to be presented" (p. 38). Based on their research, they aver that tables "...gain in effectiveness when they reinforce or are reinforced by text repeating the same information" (p. 38). The American Psychological Association (*The Association*, 1983), on the other hand, suggests that tables should supplement, rather than duplicate, information presented in the accompanying text. The text should be used to highlight and to point out particular features of the table, but should not refer to every entry. It should be noted that the audience for whom the Association is recommending that approach is one which can be expected to be familiar with reading tables. Clearly the nature of the intended audience must figure into the decision whether or not to use tables.

Research shows that, in general, people find tables daunting and confusing, and difficult to use correctly and quickly (Wright, 1968; Wright and Fox, 1970, 1972). Although it is a common response for a subject-matter specialist to consider using a table, that decision ought not to be reached without due consideration. The relatively small amount of space saved by the use of a table, or of a particular type of table, may be bought at a high cost in understanding and facility on the part of the learner.

Macdonald-Ross (1977b) contends that tables are preferred for professional audiences, and when exactitude is needed in the data retrieved, while graphs—the subject of the next chapter—are the preferred means of communicating "...trends and comparisons for education or general information for the lay reader" (p. 369) and where exact numbers are less important.

Initial Considerations
in Table Design

Having decided to use a table, the designer must give consideration to some overarching concerns before setting out to construct the table: which way the table should be oriented, and how much redundancy it should contain.

To facilitate discussion about table design and construction, the item located to enter the table will be called the *target entry*, and the item in the table that matches or corresponds to the target entry will be called the *answer*. That is, using a table involves locating a target entry, then reading the corresponding answer from the table.

Orientation of Tables

Tables can be either horizontally oriented or vertically oriented (Hartley and Burnhill, 1977a; Miles, 1987; Wright, 1968; Wright and Fox, 1970). That is, they can be designed so that the user scans for a target entry predominantly by moving his or her eyes either vertically (Table 9–1) or horizontally (Table 9–2).

Table 9–1.   Average Daily High
              Temperatures in
              Selected Saskatchewan
              Communities (°C)

	Jan–Mar	−9
North	Apr–Jun	16
Battleford	Jul–Sep	22
	Oct–Dec	0
	Jan–Mar	−1
Maple	Apr–Jun	18
Creek	Jul–Sep	24
	Oct–Dec	6
	Jan–Mar	−9
Hudson	Apr–Jun	15
Bay	Jul–Sep	21
	Oct–Dec	−1
	Jan–Mar	−7
Weyburn	Apr–Jun	17
	Jul–Sep	24
	Oct–Dec	2

Table 9–2.   Average Daily High Temperatures in Selected Saskatchewan
              Communities (°C)

North Battleford				Maple Creek				Hudson Bay				Weyburn			
Jan–Mar	Apr–Jun	Jul–Sep	Oct–Dec	Jan–Mar	Apr–Jun	Jul–Sep	Oct–Dec	Jan–Mar	Apr–Jun	Jul–Sep	Oct–Dec	Jan–Mar	Apr–Jun	Jul–Sep	Oct–Dec
–9	16	22	0	–1	18	24	6	–9	15	21	–1	–7	17	24	2

Research results indicate that, wherever possible, the vertical format
(e.g., Table 9–1) should be used (Wright, 1968; Wright and Fox, 1970,
1972). When a two-dimensional table is necessary, the table should be
arranged so that the most likely method of entering the table is vertical.

There is some evidence (described below) that tables designed for use by
the general populace should be designed differently than tables for use
by professionals or by people specifically trained in their use.

Redundancy in Tables

The compactness of tables is usually accomplished through the
elimination of redundancy. However, Wright (1982) reminds us that the
elimination of redundancy can be a false economy, since it usually
means that learners will have more problems, and will make more
errors, in retrieving information from the table. She suggests that it is
easier for readers to use tables if the structure of the list of items
(i.e., the target entries) making up the table is made obvious. Many
times, this means that redundancy is called for.

For example, Table 9–3 is generally more difficult for learners to read
and use than Table 9–2, although it represents the more common
design. Table 9–2 does contain some redundancy in headings, hence
takes somewhat more space.

Table 9–3.   Average Daily High Temperatures in
Selected Saskatchewan Communities (°C)

	North Battleford	Maple Creek	Hudson Bay	Weyburn
Jan–Mar	−9	−1	−9	−7
Apr–Jun	16	18	15	17
Jul–Sep	22	24	21	24
Oct–Dec	0	6	−1	2

In particular, Wright (1982) offers evidence that people frequently have problems interpreting and dealing with matrix tables (e.g., Table 9–4), and advocates a "binary-decision" approach to table design instead, claiming it is more "user-friendly" (see Table 9–5).

Table 9–4.   Distances Between Selected Saskatchewan
Cities (Km.)

	Lloydminster	Regina	Saskatoon	Yorkton
Lloydminster	—	535	276	607
Regina	535	—	259	189
Saskatoon	276	259	—	331
Yorkton	607	189	331	—

Table 9–5.   Distances Between
               Selected Saskatchewan
               Cities (Km.)

	Regina	535
Lloydminster to	Saskatoon	276
	Yorkton	607
	Lloydminster	535
Regina to	Saskatoon	259
	Yorkton	189
	Lloydminster	276
Saskatoon to	Regina	259
	Yorkton	331

Wright's recommendations are based on a series of more than a dozen studies she and Fox undertook (Wright, 1968; Wright and Fox, 1970, 1972) which used as their foci a real-life problem in table use: Britain underwent a change in coinage system in 1971, and the entire citizenry had to be provided with a means of facilitating the conversion. Size of the table (insofar as it affected portability) was a consideration. So was the educational background and intellectual capacity of the intended users (Wright reminds us that by definition half the population is below average in ability).

Wright found it convenient to distinguish between explicit tables and implicit tables. The former are either linear (lists of pairs of entries, such that locating only the target entry is necessary to determine the answer) or two dimensional (i.e., matrices, where two target entries must be located and their intersection specifies the answer). The key feature of explicit tables is that each target entry can be read directly from the table. Tables 9–1, 9–2, and 9–3 are explicit tables.

Implicit tables, on the other hand, give only part of the information, and require interpolation or some other activity by the reader to come up with some of the answers (e.g., combining the answers associated with two or more target entries). Statistical tables (e.g., *F* distribution) and tables of logarithms are examples of implicit tables; usually, two target entries have to be looked up and added together to yield the answer.

The studies repeatedly indicated the superiority of explicit, linear tables, although some of the superiority was obviated with practice. Even when people are shown how to use matrices, some still have difficulty using them, and this generalization holds whether the contents of the table are numbers or text.

The context of these studies should be kept in mind when applying the results. When a task aid is required (such as a table for currency conversion), an explicit linear table is demonstrably superior. However, there may be many cases in which it is the specific focus of instruction to have learners become facile with matrices. In such cases, deliberate instruction, with several examples and considerable practice, should be provided to ensure facility.

Table Construction

General Design Principles

Ehrenberg (1977) puts forth some principles that should guide the design of a table which is to be used to indicate trends to non-professional audiences:

- Numbers should be rounded off to no more than two significant figures to facilitate learners' making comparisons.

- Averages of rows and columns (as appropriate) should be given to facilitate learners' making comparisons of individual cell entries to them.

- Put the most important comparisons into columns (rather than rows), as columns make for the easiest comparisons.

- Numbers in rows or columns should be arranged in some meaningful order whenever possible (e.g., increasing or decreasing).

Note that the first rule should not be applied when necessary detail will be lost, or when professionals are expected to read the table for detailed information.

Based on her series of studies, Wright (1968; Wright and Fox, 1970, 1972) offers the following guidelines for the construction of tables to be used by the general populace (Wright and Fox, 1970, p. 241):

- All the information the learner will need should be presented in the table. That is, the learner should not be required to interpolate, combine entries, draw inferences, or otherwise manipulate the contents of the table in order to determine the correct answer. Rather, the learner should only be required to scan the list to find the correct target entry.

- Type size used in the table should be between 8 and 12 point.

- Items should be arranged vertically in the table rather than horizontally (i.e., the list of target entries should be vertical).

- Items within columns should be grouped and separated from other groups by either white space or rules (lines) in order to facilitate reading without accidentally moving to another row. Groups should contain no more than five items.

- Redundant abbreviations of units should not be included within the table entries [although they should be included in the column or row headings].

- 'Landmarks' or sub-headings—certain target entries in the table highlighted by using bold type or a larger font (e.g., every tenth entry, starting with 10, 20, 30, etc.) as an intended aid to locating entries—should not be used, since they appear to be ineffective and possibly confusing.

- It is useful to have adjacent columns printed in different fonts or styles to distinguish between them. That is, there is less chance of erroneous reading of the table if the column of target entries is in normal text (for example) and the column of associated answers is in boldface text.

- Related pairs of items in adjacent columns should be spaced closely together (i.e., the eyes should not have to traverse a great distance between the target entry and the associated answer).

- Whenever possible, columns should be arranged so that the target entries are to the left of the answers.

One common-sense rule needs to be added to the list of design guidelines:

- All the text in a table should be set horizontally (i.e., normally); in other words, avoid setting text vertically or at an angle. Although there seems to be no research on this topic specifically in connection with tables, there is evidence (discussed in Chapter 11) from research on diagrams that horizontal text is a better choice than vertical or slanted text.

Spacing of Columns and Rows

Spacing of columns need not (indeed, perhaps should not) be equal. Equal white space between columns may satisfy an aesthetic criterion, but contribute little to an instructional one. It is more reasonable, Wright (1982) argues, to have functional groupings, in which items which relate to one another logically are grouped closer together than items which are not so logically related. It is undesirable to spread the columns across the page, just because the space is available (Hartley, 1978); proximity of the columns to one another is more desirable.

Spacing of rows is another matter. To facilitate eye movement without losing track of which row is being traversed, there should be extra white space between every fourth or fifth row (Tinker, 1965).

Horizontal and Vertical Rules in Tables

Rules, in the language of typography, are straight lines, either horizontal or vertical. Whether or not they need to be used in tables seems to be more a matter of opinion than of empirical evidence. For example, Hartley (1978) recommends that rules never be used; white space should be used instead. Miles (1987), on the other hand, suggests that the dominant direction of the table can be emphasized by the use of rules. To add my opinion, here are guidelines for the use of rules in tables:

- Use white space instead of rules wherever possible to delineate rows and columns.

- Use horizontal rules when necessary to span columns and define the range over which column headings apply.

- Avoid vertical rules unless they are necessary to reduce confusion caused by columns being crowded together.

Tables should not be boxed in (Hartley, 1978; Miles, 1987). Not only is boxing in tables time-consuming and costly, but it is also unnecessary. If isolation of the table from the surrounding text is what is sought, white space may be as effective or more so.

> When you are preparing tables or charts that contain a lot of text, be sure to give them enough space to be easily legible. Too often, tables are crammed into a tight space, which makes sorting one item out from another too difficult. Readers become confused when they try to read across a crowded table that doesn't leave enough room between individual elements. A general rule is to add 25 percent to the size you think a table will require—then you can put some space between the elements to segregate them into logical groups. (Davis, Barry, and Wiesenberg, 1986, p. 44)

Some writers suggest that rules may be used as a design device to separate a table from its title. Tufte (1983) advises that rules that separate a table from the accompanying text should be avoided.

Font Choices for Tables

Some designers favor using a different font for tables than for body text; others favor using the same one. The argument for using a different font is that tables done this way stand out more from the surrounding text. The counter-argument is that using too many fonts and styles on the same page makes for a cluttered look. In light of Wright's (1968; Wright and Fox, 1970, 1972) research-based recommendation that adjacent columns be printed in a different font or a different style to minimize learners' looking at the wrong column, the notion of having too many fonts on a single page is significant. (It would be a mistake to interpret Wright's recommendation that every column in a table be done in a different font or style; merely alternating between normal text and boldface may be adequate, for example.) Furthermore, isolation of the table from the surrounding text can be accomplished with either white space or rules.

With respect to size of font used in tables, try to use no smaller than 8-point and no larger than 12-point text (Hartley and Burnhill, 1977a; Tinker, 1963, 1965; Wright and Fox, 1970). Many people will have difficulty reading 6- and 7-point text. Even if they don't, having to use such small text probably means that you are trying to put too much information into a single table.

Whatever size and font you finally choose for table entries, try to be consistent. Make your largest table first, and use that to determine what font size to use for the rest of the tables. (Of course, if you have only a single very large table requiring very small type, and a number of smaller ones, you might be better off standardizing the text in all but the very large one.)

Placement of Tables

Although each table should be self-contained and capable of standing on its own, tables should generally not be presented in isolation; there should be text accompanying them and referring to them. Research has shown that tables accompanied by text referring to them are more effective than text alone (Feliciano, Powers, and Kearl, 1963). It has become customary to place tables after the first reference to them in the text. References to tables made in the text should be followed as soon as possible by the table itself (Hartley and Burnhill, 1977a; Tufte, 1983). In my opinion, it is preferable to leave white space at the bottom of a page rather than fill the space with subsequent text, if the remaining space on the page is insufficient to accommodate the table. However, if doing so causes the page layout to appear very discontinuous, the space may be filled in with subsequent text.

The table itself should be separated visually from the text before and after it by at least one extra carriage return. If, as is customary, source information is included with the table, it should be placed immediately beneath the table, in a smaller font size, with the extra white space following it.

Tables should not be artificially expanded horizontally to fill the width of the column in which they are placed. That is, if a table—constructed with reasonable, proximate spacing of columns, and with related columns closer together than unrelated ones—is not wide enough to span the text column, extra space between the columns should not be added (Hartley, 1978). Increasing the distance between columns to satisfy aesthetic concerns such as matching the width of the text column is likely to increase the possibility of errors in reading the table.

If a table is narrower than the text column, it can either be centered in the column or set flush left.

> It is our impression...that left-ranging tables would present no more difficulty to readers than conventional [centered] ones. We have not actually tested this impression, but in another experiment, using more complicated tabular structures than those reported here, we were unable to find differences between the speed of retrieval from different tabular structures. (Hartley, Young, and Burnhill, 1975, p. 42)

Hartley, Young, and Burnhill's (1975) study did show that the typing of tables that were centered took longer and resulted in more errors than did the typing of tables that were arranged flush left. It is unclear from the description of the experimental method what it was that was centered: both the contents of the table and the table as a whole with respect to the margins, or just the former. Either way, to the extent that word processors now make both centering text within columns and centering tables between the margins almost trivial (i.e., tables can be typed flush left, then centered as a unit), perhaps Hartley, Young, and Burnhill's findings are no longer relevant, particularly in light of their own admission that centered tables do tend to stand out from the surrounding text.

Dealing with Large Tables

Since research has shown that short tables are more effective than long tables for learners who have little or no formal training and/or experience with them (Feliciano, Powers, and Kearl, 1963), large tables should be used for those learners only when there is no other choice. (Both large and small tables were found to be equally effective for groups well-versed in table use, however.)

Hartley and Burnhill (1977a) recommend placing row headings on both the right and left sides of tables that are wide and contain many columns. They also suggest numbering or lettering columns and rows if there are many. Footnotes, they suggest, should be avoided if possible. If footnotes must be used, Miles (1987) suggests they should be:

- set in a font one or two sizes smaller than the text used in the table (as is usual);

- set in line lengths that are relatively short (i.e., in columns that are half or one-third the width of the table); and

- identified by symbols that are not likely to be confused with data in the table. If there are only few footnotes, symbols such as §, †, or * can be used. If numerals must be used, ensure that the font and size used are clearly different from the numerals forming the body of the table.

One method of dealing with a large table is to rotate it 90° on the page. Do this only if absolutely necessary, as learners may become irritated at having to rotate pages frequently to read tables (Miles, 1987). If it must be done, ensure that all tables are rotated in the same direction—counter-clockwise—and avoid placing text (other than the title and source) on the same page, whether or not the table completely fills the page.

If rotating the table is inadequate, the table may have to be broken over two or more pages. This is a drastic and messy tactic, and usually indicates that you have not sufficiently thought through what must be included in the table and what can be excluded. It should be avoided wherever possible: Break the table down into several smaller ones. If it simply cannot be avoided, ensure that column headings are replicated on every page, and that all but the last page carry a message indicating that the table is continued on another page.

If the instructional materials are printed on two sides of the page (e.g., in a bound book), consider placing the large table across two facing pages (even if this means leaving a blank page before the table; simply print on the blank page "This page left blank intentionally," so that learners will not incorrectly infer that some information is missing). Ensure that the binding method used will adequately maintain the alignment of rows in the table and that the binding is located at a logical (inter-columnar) place in the table (Miles, 1987).

If the materials are printed in loose-leaf (ring binder) format, consider having learners remove one page and place it alongside another to yield the complete table. Provide explicit instructions (perhaps with a thumbnail diagram to show relative position) on how this is to be done; do *not* assume that how to do it is obvious!

Text Tables

Some tables contain only text in their cells. While some writers (e.g., Winn and Holliday, 1982) use the term *charts* to refer to such tables, the more common meaning of *charts* is bar charts, pie charts, flow charts, and the like. Thus, here such tables are referred to as text tables.

Text tables can be used to provide summaries of topics that are related in a way that can be represented by a matrix. There are a few points to remember when designing text tables:

- Keep them as simple and as brief as possible. If they are meant as summaries, that is what they should be. Elaborations can accompany them in the body text, if necessary.

- Ensure that the font used for the text in each cell is sufficiently large to be legible.

- Set the text in each cell flush left (unjustified), not centered.

In addition, the guidelines set forth earlier for numerical tables should apply to text tables.

Instruction on Using Tables

Tables are not necessarily easy to use or familiar to most learners. It is probably necessary to include instruction on how to read and use tables, unless there is compelling evidence that such instruction is unnecessary. It is inadequate to assume that learners know how to read a table, no matter what level of learner you are dealing with (including college).

In particular, if it is important that a learner, as a practitioner of a discipline, know how to make use of complex tables, and especially matrix tables, then instruction should be included. Several examples of using the table are likely to be necessary.

Software for Creating Tables

Today's word processors—with their left- and right-aligned tabs, centered tabs, and decimal tabs; their adjustable rulers; and their ability to employ a variety of fonts and sizes within the same table— make table construction far easier than with typewriters. However, if you make a lot of tables (or even just a few, but complicated ones) you might want to look into specialized software for table construction (e.g., TableTools™). Table construction software is sometimes built right into a high-end word processor (e.g., the **Insert Table...** command under the **Document** menu of MS Word). These programs typically allow you to pre-specify the number of rows and columns in the table (allowing you to change those numbers later, of course, if necessary), making the software do much of the bull work of deciding how to set tabs to get the proper number of columns into the space allotted. Since they effectively allow you to set different rulers for each cell in the table, it is easy to have combinations of centered, left- and right-aligned, and decimal tabs within the same column. Too, word wrapping occurs automatically within each cell, which is a real boon if tables are created in one font size, then later changed to a smaller or larger size (particularly in text tables). Table-creation software typically allows considerable flexibility in setting vertical and horizontal rules as well, permitting individual cells or groups of cells to be outlined in a variety of ways, including varying weights and numbers of lines.

Object-oriented graphics programs can also be used to create tables, although the extra effort involved makes that avenue worthwhile only in special cases. Lack of effective use of tabs in object-oriented graphics programs is a major limitation in their use for table construction (particularly for aligning decimal numbers), since each cell must be created as a separate entity, then aligned with other cells. However, setting rules is generally much more under the designer's control than it is in table-creation software. Furthermore, object-oriented programs will permit the rotation of text, something not all table-creation software does. (Although the rotation of text in tables is generally not a good idea, as it interferes with comprehension, sometimes it is necessary.)

References for Chapter 9

American Psychological Association. (1983). *Publication manual of the American Psychological Association* (3rd ed.). Washington, DC: The Association.

Davis, F. E., Barry, J., and Wiesenberg, M. (1986). *Desktop publishing.* Homewood, IL: Dow Jones-Irwin.

Ehrenberg, A. S. C. (1977). Rudiments of numeracy. *Journal of the Royal Statistical Society A, 140,* 277–297. Cited by Wright, P. (1982). A user-oriented approach to the design of tables and flowcharts. In D. H. Jonassen (Ed.), *The technology of text: Principles for structuring, designing, and displaying text* (pp. 317–340). Englewood Cliffs, NJ: Educational Technology Publications.

Feliciano, G. D., Powers, R. D., and Kearl, B. E. (1963). The presentation of statistical information. *AV Communication Review, 11*(3), 32–39.

Hartley, J. (1978). *Designing instructional text.* London: Kogan Page.

Hartley, J., and Burnhill, P. (1977a). Fifty guidelines for improving instructional text. *Programmed Learning and Educational Technology, 14,* 65–73.

Hartley, J., Young, M., and Burnhill, P. (1975). On the typing of tables. *Applied Ergonomics, 6*(1), 39–42.

Macdonald-Ross, M. (1977a). Graphics in text. In L. S. Shulman (Ed.), *Review of research in education, vol. 5.* Itasca, IL: F. E. Peacock.

Macdonald-Ross, M. (1977b). How numbers are shown: A review of research on the presentation of quantitative data in texts. *AV Communication Review, 25,* 359–409.

Miles, J. (1987). *Design for desktop publishing.* San Francisco: Chronicle Books.

Tinker, M. A. (1963). *Legibility of print.* Ames, IA: Iowa State University Press.

Tinker, M. A. (1965). *Bases for effective reading.* Minneapolis: University of Minnesota Press.

Tufte, E. R. (1983). *The visual display of quantitative information.* Cheshire, CT: Graphics Press.

Winn, W., and Holliday, W. (1982). Design principles for diagrams and charts. In D. H. Jonassen (Ed.), *The technology of text: Principles for structuring, designing, and displaying text* (pp. 277–299). Englewood Cliffs, NJ: Educational Technology Publications.

Wright, P. (1968). Using tabulated information. *Ergonomics, 11*(4), 331–343.

Wright, P. (1982). A user-oriented approach to the design of tables and flowcharts. In D. H. Jonassen (Ed.), *The technology of text: Principles for structuring, designing, and displaying text* (pp. 317–340). Englewood Cliffs, NJ: Educational Technology Publications.

Wright, P., and Fox, K. (1970). Presenting information in tables. *Applied Ergonomics, 1*(4), 234–242.

Wright, P., and Fox, K. (1972). Explicit and implicit tabulation formats. *Ergonomics, 15*(2), 175–187.

Data Graphics

This chapter deals with those types of graphics that are used to represent numerical information in graphic form. A few words about terminology are in order, since there is considerable variability in the literature regarding the use of such terms as *graph*, *chart*, and *diagram*.

Macdonald-Ross' (1977b) definition of a graph as "...a line drawn on a coordinate grid to show the relationship between two [or three, I would add] variables" (p. 366) will apply here. According to this definition, devices such as bar charts and circle or pie charts, which are often called bar graphs and circle graphs, are not graphs at all.

(Incidentally, the line representing the relationship between or among variables on a graph is called a curve—even if it happens to be straight).

Charts form a rather catch-all category, including the aforementioned bar and circle (pie) charts, Neurath's Isotype pictorial charts, organizational charts, and flowcharts. If the charts are based on data (e.g., bar charts, pie charts, Isotype charts) they are collectively referred to here as data charts; otherwise (e.g., flow charts, organizational charts) they are simply referred to as charts. This category of charts does not include one type of "chart" described by Winn and Holliday (1982). Their "...single words or short phrases placed in the rows and columns of a rectangular matrix, accompanied by category headings" (p. 277) seems better described by the term *text table*, dealt with in Chapter 9.

It is an acknowledged terminological anomaly that graphs and data charts share certain common characteristics (e.g., axes in graphs and some types of data charts), while charts and diagrams share others (e.g., position of elements reflecting actual spatial or temporal relationships). These shared characteristics influenced the decision to discuss data charts in this chapter and the remaining types of charts in the next chapter, along with illustrations and graphics of other kinds.

Macdonald-Ross (1977b) noted the relative lack of experiments in education involving graphs and data charts, a situation that appears to have improved only slightly in the intervening years. Given the facility with which educators can construct graphs and data charts on computers, and the consequent likely increase in their use, this lack of research ought to be addressed.

When to Use Data Graphics

The use of graphs for communication, which lay largely dormant for four decades, began to flourish in the late 1960's as the result of novel graphical ideas exploited by the noted statistician and data analyst, John Tukey (Tufte, 1983). Furthermore, although graphs have been used by scientists and mathematicians for a couple of centuries, it is only recently that there has been a concerted effort to develop a theoretical base for the way in which people perceive and interpret graphs (Cox, 1978; Dunn, 1988; Tufte, 1983).

The use of graphs to portray numbers has often been associated in the public mind with distortion of the truth. According to popular opinion, graphs are only used when one wants to lie with statistics. While there is no doubt that graphs have been, and will probably continue to be, used for nefarious purposes, there is nothing inherently unscrupulous about presenting data in graphical form. Quite the contrary; in science, for example, graphs are valued for their lucidity and conciseness. In the last decade, a number of newspapers and newsmagazines have taken to presenting a great deal more information via graphs and data charts than ever before. Not all of these data graphics are good ones (Tufte, 1983); still, they increase the amount of information seen in this form by the average person.

When should graphs or data charts be used? The power of the visual to support and augment the verbal should not be overlooked. However, gratuitous use of graphs and data charts is undesirable.

> Charts, graphs, and tables can complement text in communicating information clearly. When you have information, such as numeric values, that is especially suited for presentation in charts and graphs, don't overlook the opportunity to use it as a graphic element in your document. Avoid using charts, graphs, or tables as mere adornments, however. They can confuse your readers, who may attach extra importance to them and wonder why they are there if the need for them is not apparent. (Davis, Barry, and Wiesenberg, 1986, p. 43)

On the one hand, research done as early as 1927 concluded that numerical data should never be presented in text form if there are more than one or two items to be presented (Macdonald-Ross, 1977b). Tufte (1983), whose work on graphs is one of the most comprehensive and thoughtful available, says "The conventional sentence is a poor way to show more than two numbers because it prevents comparisons within the data" (p. 178). On the other hand, Tufte also states "Tables usually outperform graphics in reporting on small data sets of 20 numbers or less" (p. 56). Wainer (1984) contends that the less information carried in a graph, the worse it is. Wainer refers to Tufte's (1983) data density index (DDI), defined as the number of numbers plotted per square inch, and says that the higher that index is, the better the graph is. He particularly deplores graphical presentations of only a few data points (low DDI), such as are often found in today's newspapers and newsmagazines. These displays, because they lack an adequate amount of real data to create an interesting graph, are often beefed up with what Tufte calls "chartjunk"— elaborate illustrations and embellishments (often with multiple colors) that do more to obfuscate than to clarify.

> The interior decoration of graphics generates a lot of ink that does not tell the viewer anything new. The purpose of decoration varies—to make the graphic appear more scientific and precise, to enliven the display, to give the designer an opportunity to exercise artistic skills. Regardless of its cause, it is all

non-data-ink or redundant data-ink, and it is often chartjunk.
(Tufte, 1983, p. 107)

Choosing to use a graph or data chart (as opposed to simply reporting the data in text form) therefore appears to be a judgment call: use them, but not when there aren't really enough data to warrant their use.

In other words, maximize the DDI.

This is not the same as crowding great quantities of data onto a graph, however. Placing too many curves on one graph is liable to be confusing to the learner. If possible, break complex multi-curve graphs into several simpler ones, unless direct comparisons are required. Macdonald-Ross (1977b) cites research that indicates that for the purpose of reading individual points, putting several curves on one graph and making several individual graphs—each with one curve—are equally good approaches. However, for making comparisons, putting several curves on one graph is superior.

Tufte (1983) believes there are bad reasons for using graphs, and implies that all too often, those are the ones used to make the choice. He lays the blame squarely at the feet of those who are more interested in the aesthetics of presentation than the accuracy, and rejects the notion that statistical presentations must be "jazzed up" in order to make them palatable to the average reader:

> Many believe that graphical displays should divert and entertain those in the audience who find the words in the text too difficult.... What E. B. White said of writing is also true of statistical graphics: "No one can write decently who is distrustful of the reader's intelligence, or whose attitude is patronizing." Contempt for graphics and their audience, along with the lack of quantitative skills among illustrators, has deadly consequences for graphical work: over-decorated and simplistic designs, tiny data sets, and big lies. (Tufte, 1983, p. 81)

> Inept graphics...flourish because many graphic artists believe that statistics are boring and tedious. It then follows that decorated graphics must pep up, animate, and all too often exaggerate what evidence there is in the data.

> If the statistics are boring, then you've got the wrong numbers. (Tufte, 1983, p. 79–80)

> Graphical competence demands three quite different skills: the substantive, statistical, and artistic. Yet now most graphical

> work, particularly at news publications, is under the direction
> of but a single expertise—artistic. Allowing artist-illustrators to
> control the design and content of statistical graphs is almost
> like allowing typographers to control the content, style, and
> editing of prose. (Tufte, 1983, p. 87)

Although graphs may be daunting initially, learners can usually be taught to read them with facility. Bryant and Somerville (1986) found, for example, that even very young children (aged 6 and 9) were able to extrapolate *x* and *y* values from a line graph, when given appropriate instruction. (The key consideration here is contained in the last four words of the previous sentence; learners cannot and should not be expected to make use of graphs until they are explicitly taught how.)

Macdonald-Ross (1977b) distinguishes between educational purposes ("visual arguments") and operational purposes of graphs (sources of precise data for action). He contends that graphs and data charts are the preferred means of communicating "...trends and comparisons for education or general information for the lay reader" (p. 369) and where exact numbers are less important, while tables are preferred for the professional audience, and when exactitude is needed in the data retrieved. This chapter concentrates on the former purpose and audience, on the assumption that most professional audiences are dealt with by using tables. It omits consideration of some of the specialized graphs (like various nomograms and cartograms, topics well covered by Macdonald-Ross, 1977a) and specialized maps (like choropleths and isopleths, also covered by Macdonald-Ross and by Dunn, 1988), and deals only with the more common types.

Selecting and Organizing Information

Graphs and data charts have two kinds of information in them: the data themselves and the supporting information such as titles, labels, and coding devices designed to help the reader interpret the data. For maximum impact and efficiency, both kinds of information must be carefully chosen and organized. An important question for the designer to ask is "What needs to be included?" Equally important is the question "What can be left out?"

Design decisions regarding graphs and data charts necessarily include consideration of how the data are to be organized for presentation. The designer must decide beforehand what message needs to be communicated or bolstered by the graph or data chart, and arrange the data accordingly.

> ...the design and the accuracy of the data are only two elements that affect the clarity of the information [depicted in a graph]. A major consideration is the right view of the information being presented. Just as a grammatically correct paragraph of text can confuse the reader with obscure terminology or incomplete description, an illustration can be both visually pleasing and technically accurate without conveying the underlying message clearly. (Burns, Venit, and Hansen, 1988, p. 225)

Wainer (1984) warns against presenting graphical information out of context, by selectively re-arranging intervals or by dropping data that would reflect badly on the argument being made, or by presenting only part of, or adjusting the scale of, relevant axes. He also points out that sometimes ordering graph elements alphabetically can be misleading, in that comparisons can be easily overlooked under that arrangement, so the decision to lay out data that way should be carefully considered.

The amount of supporting information included must also be balanced against the possibility that its inclusion will interfere with the clear communication of the graph. Cox (1978) identifies various methods of showing supplementary information on a graph:

- attaching names to points;
- using different shapes to identify points;
- using color; and
- using lines of different lengths emanating in different directions from points.

However, Vinberg (1980) cautions against over-use of supporting information by postulating the following common-sense rules for graph construction:

- Do not over-annotate graphs. Let the visual component prevail. If exact detail and precision are important, a table is a more suitable medium.

- Do not include all the information. Graphs should provide impressions. Once again, detail is best left to tables.

Cleveland (1984) warns against cluttering graphs and data charts with textual material in the area of the plotted data, possibly obscuring patterns in the data, particularly in scientific publications. Tordella (1988) suggests that, since the idea behind using a graph is to save space, a designer ought not to provide too much supporting detail (e.g., lengthy titles, too many labels on axes).

Making the difficult decisions whether or not to use a graph or data chart—and, if so, what data and supporting information to include and exclude, and how to arrange it—is not easy or clear-cut. The amount of knowledge (indeed, even opinion) available to guide you is small. Hopefully, however, just being cognizant of the points identified above will cause you to make conscious decisions, rather than glossing over them unthinkingly.

General Design Principles

As already noted, Tufte's (1983) thoughtful and reasoned discourse on the design and construction of graphs provides some of the best advice available to the would-be graph designer. Particularly useful are his generalized principles of graph design. His overall goal is encapsulated in the statement "Graphical excellence is that which gives the viewer the greatest number of ideas in the shortest time with the least ink in the smallest space" (Tufte, 1983, p. 51). To achieve that goal, he says, graphs should:

- show the data

- induce the viewer to think about the substance rather than about methodology, graphic design, the technology of graphic production, or something else

- avoid distorting what the data have to say

- present many numbers in a small space

- make large data sets coherent

- encourage the eye to compare different pieces of data

- reveal the data at several levels of detail, from a broad overview to the fine structure

- serve a reasonably clear purpose: description, exploration, tabulation, or decoration

- be closely integrated with the statistical and verbal description of a data set. (Tufte, 1983, p. 13)

Tufte takes strong issue with those who use graphs to deceive, either intentionally or unintentionally. To increase the integrity of graphs, he postulates the following principles:

- the representation of numbers, as physically measured on the surface of the graphic itself, should be directly proportional to the numerical quantities represented (p. 56)

- clear, detailed, and thorough labelling should be used to defeat graphical distortion and ambiguity. Write out explanations of the data on the graphic itself. Label important events in the data (p. 56)

- show data variation, not design variation (p. 61)

- in time-series displays of money, deflated and standard-ized units of monetary measurement are nearly always better than nominal units (p. 68)

- the number of information-carrying (variable) dimensions depicted should not exceed the number of dimensions in the data (p. 71)

- graphics must not quote data out of context. (p. 74)

Presentation Considerations

Completely operationalizing and explicating Tufte's fairly general design principles would require more space than is available here; besides, Tufte has already done so. Still, a few more specific guidelines for the presentation of graphs can be identified. They are collected below under the categories of attention-getting; friendliness; accuracy; proportions; axes and grids; labels, legends, and keys; and the data-ink ratio and defaults.

Attention-Getting

Getting attention is one of the legitimate goals of graphs. However, don't be too clever. Straightforward presentations may not be as attention-getting as clever designs, but they usually communicate better (Vinberg, 1980). Novelty is a less important criterion than clarity, and just because a graph has been done a particular way in the past is not a valid reason for doing it a different way this time (Wainer, 1984).

Friendliness

Tufte speaks of the "friendliness" of graphs and data charts. Specific guidelines for achieving friendliness and avoiding unfriendliness are presented in the form of a table (taken verbatim from Tufte, 1983, p. 183):

Friendly	*Unfriendly*
words are spelled out, mysterious and elaborate encoding avoided	abbreviations abound, requiring the viewer to sort through text to decode abbreviations
words run from left to right, the usual direction for reading occidental languages	words run vertically, particularly along the Y-axis; words run in several different directions
little messages help explain data	graphic is cryptic, requires repeated references to scattered text
elaborately encoded shadings, cross-hatching, and colors are avoided; instead, labels are placed on the graphic itself; no legend is required	obscure codings require going back and forth between legend and graphic
graphic attracts viewer, provokes curiosity	graphic is repellent, filled with chartjunk

Friendly	***Unfriendly***
colors, if used, are chosen so that the color-deficient and color-blind (5 to 10 percent of viewers) can make sense of the graphic (blue can be distinguished from other colors by most color-deficient people)	design insensitive to color-deficient viewers; red and green used for essential contrasts
type is clear, precise, modest; lettering may be done by hand	type is clotted, overbearing
type is upper-and-lower case, with serifs	type is all capitals, sans serif

Accuracy

That accuracy in plotting data is a requirement for good graphs goes without saying. However, there are also things that can be done to ensure that accuracy in *interpretation* of graphs is maximized.

Quantitative information should be made to stand out from the supporting information by ensuring that the different items on a graph can be easily visually distinguished (Cleveland, 1984).

The presentation should not stand in the way of interpretation. For example, fine lines should generally be used for curves so as not to obscure data points underlying them (Cox, 1978; Tufte, 1983). Data should be presented to an appropriate degree of accuracy (i.e., number of decimal places) (Wainer, 1984). The scale chosen should not be too large (requiring the reader to "look at the data from far away," as Wainer puts it), causing variation in the data to appear minimal.

Be aware of the perceptual distortion that can be brought to bear by changing the scale on one of the axes. In Figure 10–1, the same data are represented in both (a) and (b), but the effect appears stronger in (b) because the curve is steeper by virtue of a changed scale on the *x*-axis.

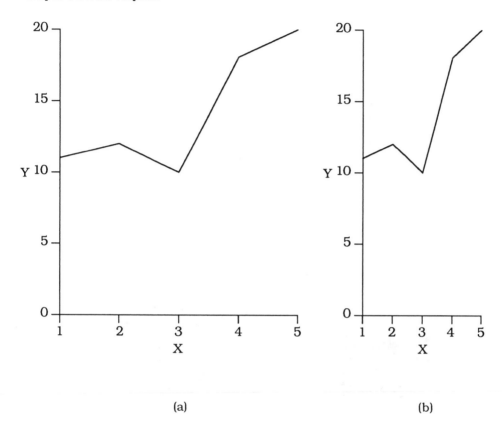

(a)   (b)

Figure 10–1. Changing the scale of one axis can distort the interpretation of the data. Although the data are the same in both graphs, the effect appears greater in (b) due to the increased steepness of the curve caused by a change in the scale of the x-axis.

Keep the visual metaphor underlying the graph constant (Wainer, 1984). For example, if two graphs comparing exports are presented side-by-side, and the area representing exports in one graph is shaded with the same color as the area representing imports in the other, accuracy will surely suffer.

Also, keep the number of dimensions in the underlying metaphor the same as reality (e.g., if what is being graphed is based on length, but area is portrayed, distortion will occur) (Wainer, 1984). If what is essentially a bar graph is given a second dimension (e.g., represented as a dollar bill), the learner tends to interpret the area represented by the two-dimensional dollar bill, rather than the length of it. Hence a doubling of the length will result in a four-fold increase in the area, and likely a concomitant misinterpretation (Figure 10–2).

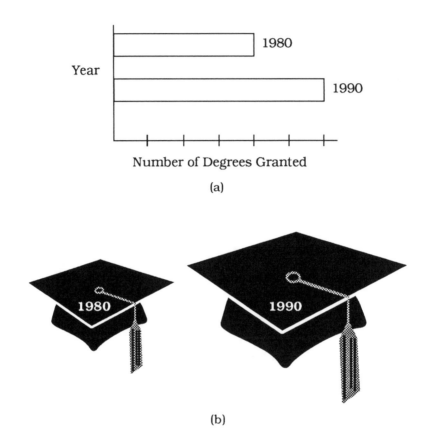

(a)

(b)

Figure 10–2. Using a two-dimensional representation of single-dimension data will likely cause misinterpretation. Although the widths of the mortarboards in (b) are in the same proportions as the lengths of the bars in (a), the 1990 mortarboard appears to be much more than one and one-half times the size of the 1980 one. (Data are fictitious.)

Data should be presented with an appropriate number of dimensions (i.e., don't make a three-dimensional graph out of two-dimensional data) (Wainer, 1984). Adding a third dimension to bar charts to make volume charts is unnecessary and may be potentially confusing (Hartley and Burnhill, 1977a; Hartley, 1978, Tufte, 1983).

Proportions

The nature of the data should be allowed to determine the overall proportions of the graph, if possible. Otherwise, try to keep graphs mostly horizontal, about one and one-half times as wide as tall (Tufte, 1983). If comparisons are to be made between and among graphs, keep their proportions identical.

Distorting graphs (perhaps by drawing them as viewed at an angle) can distort their interpretation (Lichty, 1989). Avoid three-dimensional views of one- or two-dimensional data, special effects, shadows, and other "frills" on graphs (Tordella, 1988).

Axes and Grids

With the exception of circle or pie charts, all graphs and data charts will have two or three axes. Cox (1978) suggests that a good graph will have the following characteristics with respect to axes:

- the axes should be clearly labelled with the names of the variables and the units of measurement

- scale breaks should be used for false origins

- comparison of related diagrams should be made easy, for example by using identical scales of measurement and placing diagrams side by side

- scales should be arranged so that systematic and approximately linear relations are plotted at roughly 45° to the *x*-axis. (p. 6)

When presenting more than one graph, try to avoid using different scales if possible, especially if learners are expected to make comparisons between the graphs.

Grids superimposed on the graph area to extend the axis scales can be useful for making accurate readings and interpolating on a graph (Tufte, 1983). With many graphing software programs, adding a grid to a graph can be done with the click of a mouse. But should it be?

Wainer (1984) suggests that grids should not be used on graphs, particularly in combination with dimly-plotted points, because the data become hidden (i.e., there is more ink used—to plot the grid—in relation to the amount of data plotted, making the graph harder to read). Vinberg (1980) recommends that grids be used sparingly and only when necessary, as they can clutter the visual field of a graph. Tufte agrees, noting that a grid increases the data-ink ratio, and suggests that if one is used, it should be muted relative to the data. He proposes using a gray grid (rather than a black one) with a delicate line. For bar graphs, he promotes the use of a negative (or reverse) grid, in which the grid lines appear as fine white lines where they intersect the shaded bars, and of course disappear entirely into the white background of the majority of the graph area. Unfortunately, most contemporary graphing software does not offer the option of such a reverse grid. Creating such a grid would require exporting the graph to an object-oriented graphics program to make the necessary modifications.

Labels, Legends, and Keys

As is the case for tables and other types of graphics, there should be a thoughtfully chosen caption or title for every graph and data chart. As was the case for tables, good labels and legends should make graphs and data charts capable of standing on their own (Cox, 1978), even though they should not be required to do so; there should also be reference in the body text to the graph and its contents.

> It is nearly always helpful to write little messages on the plotting field to explain the data, to label outliers and interesting data points, to write equations and sometimes tables on the graphic itself, and to integrate the caption and legend into the design so that the eye is not required to dart back and forth between textual material and the graphic. (Tufte, 1983, p. 180)

> Graphs must be clearly described. The combined information of the figure legend and the text of the body of the paper should provide a clear and complete description of *everything* that is on the graph. Detailed figure legends can often be of great help to the reader. First describe completely what is graphed in the display, then draw the reader's attention to salient features of the display, and then briefly state the importance of these features. (Cleveland, 1984, p. 268)

In addition to titles or captions, graphs and data graphics typically contain labels (e.g., on axes and/or data points) and legends or keys (cross-referring the shapes of data points and/or type of fill or shading to their meaning). Both labels and legends should be printed in a font size that is adequately large (eight-point minimum) and legible. If possible, labels should be placed directly on bars or lines, and the text in labels and titles should be horizontal rather than vertical. Font and size of type should be consistent with that used in the text; smaller type sizes may be needed to include all relevant information, but sizes under eight points should generally not be used (Lichty, 1989). Note that not all graph-producing software does this as a default. Some do not even permit it; avoid using them. Wainer (1984) urges that labels be legible, complete, correct, and unambiguous.

With respect to the use of legends or keys, there seems to be some disparity in advice. A number of research studies have highlighted the importance of a good legend or key for each graph and chart (Dunn, 1988). However, based on research done by Culbertson in 1959, Macdonald-Ross (1977b) recommends that keys should not be used with bar charts or with graphs. Rather, the labels should be placed directly on the graph or charts, next to the referent elements. Cleveland (1984) suggests that when keys are used, that as much of the text as possible be placed outside the area of the plot, unless there is absolutely no possibility of the key interfering with the perusal of the data.

The Data-Ink Ratio and Defaults

Tufte (1983) devised a statistic called the data-ink ratio (DIR), which is the amount of ink used to represent data compared to the total amount of ink used to print the graph. He says the data-ink ratio should be maximized, the amount of ink devoted to non-data should be minimized (within reason), and redundant data ink should be deleted (also within reason).

Graphs should be carefully edited and revised to accomplish these goals—a point especially noteworthy to users of highly automated graph-production software that will substitute default values for a number of decisions that should probably have more careful consideration. After a graph is produced by software, it will often need to be "touched up" to meet the requirements of a healthy DIR.

Tordella (1988) reminds us to go beyond the default values of graphing software. For example, he identifies the maximum and minimum values on the axes as items to which the designer should give special attention. While a graphing/charting program will undoubtedly assign maximum and minimum values to any data set being plotted, they may not be reasonable ones in terms of interpreting the message of the graph in a forthright manner. The same is also true for the symbols used to indicate points on a graph, or the type of fill or "shading" assigned to elements in a data chart.

Placement of Graphs
and Data Charts

Like tables, graphs and data graphics should be placed into the body text at the point at which first reference is made to them.

> Tables and graphics should be run into the text whenever possible, avoiding the clumsy and diverting segregation of "See Fig. 2".... If a display is discussed in various parts of the text, it might well be printed afresh near each reference to it, perhaps in reduced size in later showing. The principle of text/graphic/ table integration also suggests that the same typeface be used for text and graphic and, further, that ruled lines separating different types of information be avoided. (Tufte, 1983, p. 181)

Of course, in those situations where placement simply cannot be made according to Tufte's suggestion, cross-references to the figure should be made in the body text.

Pros and Cons of Some Types
of Graphs and Data Charts

Many types of graphs are readily (and quite automatically) available to the designer through spreadsheet programs like (on the Mac) Microsoft® Excel, WingZ™, and Microsoft® Works; statistical analysis programs like StatView™ SE + Graphics, StatWorks™, and Data Desk®; and graphing programs such as DeltaGraph™. As well, graphs could be constructed with graphics packages like MacDraw® II, Canvas™, SuperPaint, or FullPaint™. There are some guidelines available from research to assist in making appropriate choices of graph type.

Some kinds of graphs are clearly superior to others in certain situations or for certain kinds of data. It is clear, however, that there is no one type of graph that is best for all purposes. Macdonald-Ross (1977b) recaps the extended debate among researchers seeking to determine the superiority of either pie charts or bar charts by meticulously examining their research methods and their criteria for superiority. He concludes that when the "good" research is sifted out from the "bad" (my terms, not his), bar charts appear to have an edge, although graded keyed circle charts and pie charts may also be viable. (Graded keyed circle charts are ones that have a key which depicts the range of the circles used, in stepped sizes.) He also concludes:

> ...continuous sized and unkeyed circles, segmented bars, and three-dimensional figures should not be used. The chief "competitors" to the bar and circle formats are (for professional readers) the data in tabular form and (for lay readers) pictorial charts of the Isotype format. (p. 375)

Of course, there are many more types of graphs and charts than just the two studied in the research reviewed by Macdonald-Ross. In addition, there are opinions about graphs and charts, even about the ones that have been researched. Many of these opinions and research studies are examined below. Please note that in the graphs presented below to illustrate certain principles of good graph construction, other principles may have been ignored for simplicity.

Pie Charts

Pie charts (and circle charts) are considered useful for showing propor- tions of the whole. One of the benefits claimed for pie charts is that they do not take up as much space as bar graphs do. However, since most people can't make fine distinctions in angular size, they cannot make comparisons as readily on pie charts as on bar charts.

At the risk of a glaring over-generalization, pie charts seem to be recommended by writers who have not delved very deeply into the pros and cons of their use. The usual claim is that pie charts are easy to understand. Those opinions are not held by individuals who have given the genre serious thought, however:

> A table is nearly always better than a dumb pie chart; the only worse design than a pie chart is several of them.... Given their low data-density and failure to order numbers along a visual dimension, pie charts should never be used. (Tufte, 1983, p. 178)

Tordella (1988) suggests that pie charts be avoided on the grounds that they make it difficult to estimate how much each segment represents without reference to numbers. He recommends bar graphs instead.

Lichty (1989) recommends that pie charts should not be used where there are more than seven components. He also recommends that the line delineating the largest portion of the pie be placed at the twelve o'clock position.

If pie charts are used, they should under no circumstances be given an artificial perspective to make them three-dimensional (Figure 10–3), as this distortion makes angular comparisons even more difficult than usual. Note how areas B and C are equal in Figure 10–3a; yet C appears larger than B in Figure 10–3b. Similarly, in the (b) view, C seems relatively larger compared to D, than in the (a) view.

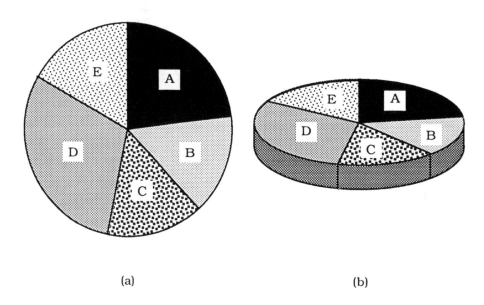

(a)   (b)

Figure 10–3. Adding perspective to a pie chart makes angular comparisons extremely difficult. In the three-dimensional view, (b), note the apparent differences in sizes of equal-sized segments.

Bar Charts

Bar charts, favored for showing general trends and relationships where at least one variable is categorical, are generally better for that purpose than either circle (pie) charts or line graphs (Macdonald-Ross, 1977a).

Bar charts can be either horizontal or vertical (the latter sometimes being referred to as column charts) (Figure 10–4). In addition to the normal bar charts, there are multiple bar charts (where several bars are grouped together in clusters to facilitate comparisons) and stacked bar charts (where the top of one bar forms the base for the succeeding bar) (Figures 10–5 and 10–7, respectively). Macdonald-Ross (1977b) favors horizontal bar charts over vertical bar charts, since there is generally more room available for placement of the labels. Research done by Feliciano, Powers, and Kearl (1963) determined that horizontal bar graphs with supporting text were superior to either long or short tables and to text alone.

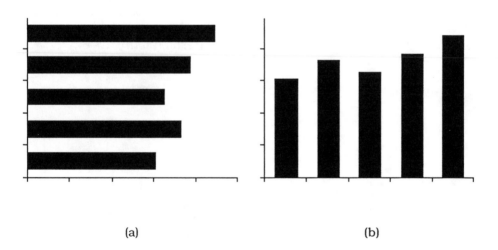

(a)   (b)

Figure 10–4. Bar charts can be horizontal (a) or vertical (b). Vertical bar charts are sometimes called column charts.

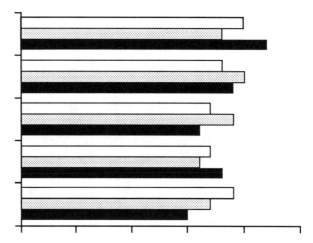

Figure 10–5. Multiple bar chart.

The bars in a bar chart should be equidistant from one another, with the bars wider than the spaces between them (Lichty, 1989). For maximum visual appeal, the shading or patterns chosen to fill the bars should be restrained, with a dark-to-light (black-gray-white) progression preferable to an arbitrary mixture of patterns (Figure 10–6).

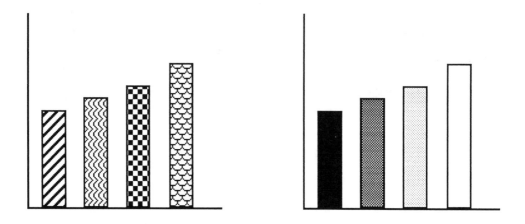

Figure 10–6. Bar charts will look more pleasing if shades of gray in an ordered progression are used rather than a wild mixture of patterns. (After Lichty, 1989)

In a stacked bar chart, keep the dark tones at the bottom, and lighten them as you work upward (Figure 10-7).

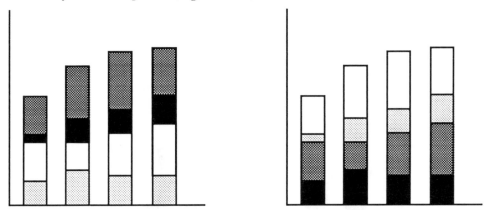

Figure 10–7. In stacked bar charts, arrange the fill or shading of the bars so that the lighter colors are on top, progressing to darker colors on the bottom, rather than placing them in an arbitrary order. (After Lichty, 1989)

Vinberg (1980) recommends organizing the bars on a bar chart for visual emphasis (e.g., highest to lowest, or vice versa), rather than putting them in some other order (e.g., alphabetically). This advice should be taken cautiously: If there is a rational, logical order to the elements composing the chart, then it should prevail.

Vinberg (1980) suggests that numerical labels not be used on bar charts. His speculation is that the visual impact of using them may be that the brain will unconsciously add the length of the digits to the bars, creating distortion. However, Feliciano, Powers, and Kearl (1963) cite research indicating that labeling bars or other graph elements is better than presenting the same information in a legend. Tufte feels that putting numbers on bar charts is redundant data-ink, and should be avoided, unless redundancy has a "distinctly worthy cause" (Tufte, 1983, p. 100).

In keeping with his principle of minimizing the data-ink ratio, Tufte (1983, p. 126–128) recommends that bar charts (or any charts or graphs, for that matter) can be improved by taking the following steps:

- Remove (or do not draw) a box around the chart.

- Erase the vertical axis, except for the ticks.

- Do not use a grid, unless you use a white grid, which then obviates the tick marks (and which should then be removed, leaving the numerical labels associated with the white grid lines).

- Use a thin baseline or eliminate the baseline entirely.

These features are incorporated into the chart in Figure 10–8.

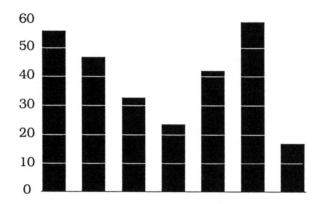

Figure 10–8. A bar chart incorporating Tufte's recommendations.

Line Graphs

A line graph is usually used when time is one of the variables; time is typically plotted along the *x*-axis. Sometimes several curves are plotted on the same axis, creating a multiple-line graph (Figure 10–9). Multiple-line graphs permit ready comparison between two or more curves.

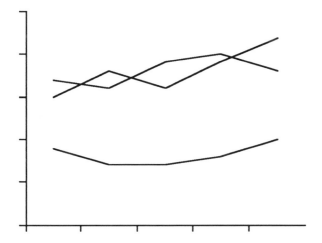

Figure 10–9. A multiple line graph permits comparisons between curves.

The decision to plot multiple curves on a single set of axes should be made on the basis of the audience's familiarity with graphs. Lichty (1989) recommends that no more than five lines be plotted on the same axes, and that the graph be broken into several simpler graphs if the multiple lines cross each other repeatedly. However, as noted earlier, if comparisons must be made, a multiple-line graph is better than several single-line graphs (Macdonald-Ross, 1977b).

Scatter Graphs

Scatter graphs, also known as scatterplots, correlation graphs, or *x-y* graphs, have continuous variables on both axes.

Scatterplots, suggests Tufte (1983), can be improved by replacing the axes with a *range-frame*, which is composed of axis-like lines that stretch only from the lowest to the highest plotted values in the graph (Figure 10–10). The range-frame makes visual the maxima and minima, hence actually increases the amount of information available in the graph, while minimizing the data-ink ratio. Tick marks, of course, can be placed directly on the range-frame. Off-setting an appropriate portion of the line forming the range-frame can illustrate the interquartile range, as well, and breaking that offset line at the median illustrates its value. Thus, simply by erasing and modifying lines normally printed on a scatterplot, Tufte suggests, ten new bits of information can be included in the display: the minimum, the maximum, two quartiles, and the median, for each of the two variables.

Some software packages (e.g., Data Desk) use the range-frame by default, but with most other graphing packages, one would have to modify the graph with a graphics program to obtain a range-frame. Even Data Desk does not contain all the elements Tufte suggests, however.

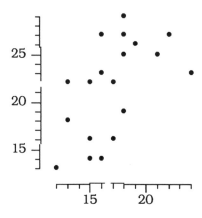

Figure 10–10. A scatterplot with improvements suggested by Tufte (1983). Note the offset portions of the range frame, indicating the interquartile range, and the gaps signifying the medians.

Area and Volume Charts

Area and volume charts use shapes or symbols of two or three dimensions, respectively, to depict comparisons (Figure 10–11). Despite the fact that some DTP writers (e.g., Lichty, 1989) sanction their use, they are generally thought by researchers to be very poor devices, as they are difficult to interpret accurately. Macdonald-Ross (1977b) notes that people cannot compare sizes readily or exactly, and that various attempts at overcoming the psychophysical problem in perception have effectively met with failure.

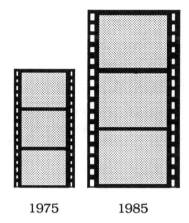

1975   1985

Number of Motion Pictures Produced

(a)

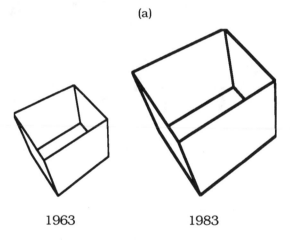

1963   1983

The Proliferation of Paper Boxes

(b)

Figure 10–11. Area charts, (a), and volume charts, (b), are poor choices. (NOTE: Data are fictitious.)

Isotype System

In the 1930's and '40's, Otto Neurath developed a pictorial charting system called the Isotype System. It involved using icons to represent quantities (Figure 10–12). Practical use of the system for some fifty years has led to some guidelines for designing charts of this type (Macdonald-Ross, 1977b):

- Let each icon represent the same quantity.

- Make clear the quantity each icon represents.

- Keep all icons the same size. Represent greater quantities with a larger number of icons, not with icons of increased height, area, or volume.

- Use icons to make explicit comparisons. Leave out anything not critical to the explicit comparison.

Figure 10–12. A typical Isotype System chart. Each icon represents a given quantity.

Stacked Area Graphs

Stacked area graphs (also known as segmented graphs) stack several curves on top of one another, in a manner similar to multiple-line graphs. However, in multiple-line graphs the axis forms the baseline for all curves, whereas in stacked area graphs, the baseline for each curve is considered to be the curve immediately below it. That is, it is the area between successive curves that represents the quantity being depicted. The area above or below one line is usually shaded to highlight the sum or difference.

Vinberg (1980) clearly demonstrates the potential for misinterpretation with stacked area graphs (see Figure 10–13). It would appear in the graph in Figure 10–13a that the profit (light gray) appears (to most people) to be maximal in the eighth quarter; in fact, the profit in the tenth quarter is 20% larger than in the eighth, a fact shown clearly if profit is plotted below net cost (Figure 10–13b).

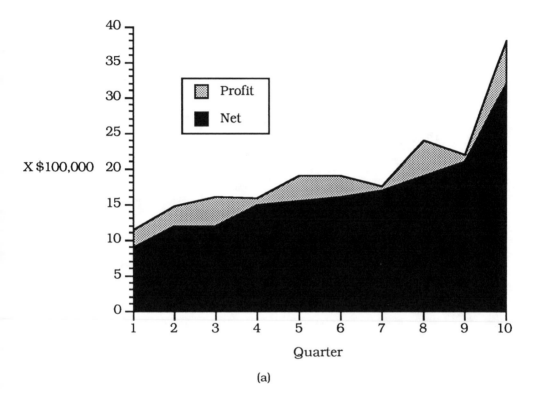

(a)

Figure 10–13. Stacked area graphs offer much potential for misinterpretation. Notice how Profit seems to be maximized in the eighth quarter in (a). When the graph is re-drawn, (b), it is clear that maximum profits actually occur in the tenth quarter. (After Vinberg, 1980) *(Figure continued on next page.)*

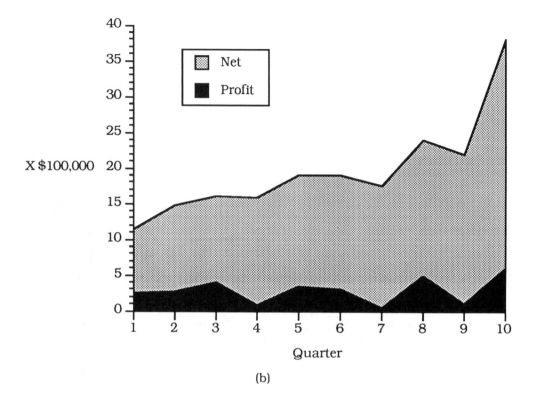

(b)

Figure 10–13. *(continued)*

"Making comparisons is always aided when the quantities being compared start from a common base" (Wainer, 1984, p. 143). "Jiggling" the baseline, says Wainer, diminishes the effectiveness of a graph. Stacked area graphs are particularly prone to this difficulty, and for that reason, should be avoided. (This point is also made forcefully by Vinberg [1980]; Macdonald-Ross [1977b] agrees). Stacked area graphs purport to show cumulative totals vividly. I suppose they do that, but they also beg to be misinterpreted. It seems far better to use line graphs, with a separate line for the total, if showing the total is important (Figure 10–14).

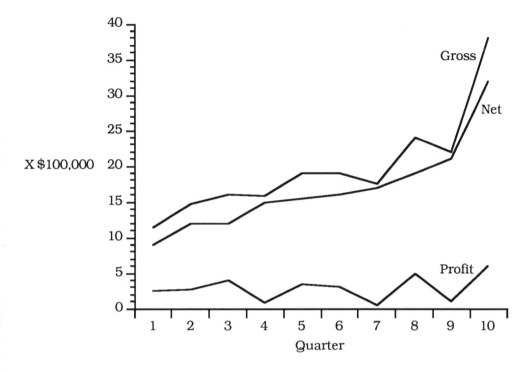

Figure 10–14. This view, showing gross, net, and profit as separate lines based on a common axis, is probably better than either of the views in Figure 10–13. (After Vinberg, 1980)

References for Chapter 10

Bryant, P. E., and Somerville, S. C. (1986). The spatial demands of graphs. *The British Journal of Psychology*, 77, 187–197.

Burns, D., Venit, S., and Hansen, R. (1988). *The electronic publisher.* New York: Brady.

Cleveland, W. S. (1984). Graphs in scientific publications. *The American Statistician*, 38, 261–269.

Cox, D. R. (1978). Some remarks on the role in statistics of graphical methods. *Applied Statistics*, 27, 4–9.

Davis, F. E., Barry, J., and Wiesenberg, M. (1986). *Desktop publishing.* Homewood, IL: Dow Jones-Irwin.

Dunn, R. (1988). Framed rectangle charts or statistical maps with shading: An experiment in graphical perception. *The American Statistician, 42,* 123–129.

Feliciano, G. D., Powers, R. D., and Kearl, B. E. (1963). The presentation of statistical information. *AV Communication Review, 11*(3), 32–39.

Hartley, J. (1978). *Designing instructional text.* London: Kogan Page.

Hartley, J., and Burnhill, P. (1977a). Fifty guidelines for improving instructional text. *Programmed Learning and Educational Technology, 14,* 65–73.

Lichty, T. (1989). *Design principles for desktop publishers.* Glenview, IL: Scott, Foresman and Co.

Macdonald-Ross, M. (1977a). Graphics in text. In L. S. Shulman (Ed.), *Review of research in education, vol. 5.* Itasca, IL: F. E. Peacock.

Macdonald-Ross, M. (1977b). How numbers are shown: A review of research on the presentation of quantitative data in texts. *AV Communication Review, 25,* 359–409.

Tordella, S. J. (1988). How to create good graphics. *American Demographics, 10*(10), 40–41.

Tufte, E. R. (1983). *The visual display of quantitative information.* Cheshire, CT: Graphics Press.

Vinberg, A. (1980). *Designing a good graph.* (ERIC Document Reproduction Service No. ED 222 192)

Wainer, H. (1984). How to display data badly. *The American Statistician, 38,* 137–147.

Winn, W., and Holliday, W. (1982). Design principles for diagrams and charts. In D. H. Jonassen (Ed.), *The technology of text: Principles for structuring, designing, and displaying text* (pp. 277–299). Englewood Cliffs, NJ: Educational Technology Publications.

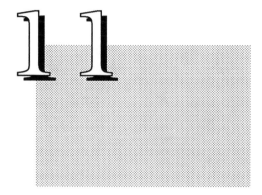

Illustrations and Other Graphics

The terms *graphics* and *art work* are often used in DTP to apply to anything that isn't text. The terms, therefore, cover a multitude of things—illustrations or pictures (such as photographs or drawings), graphs, charts, ruled lines, boxes, shaded or tinted areas, and patterns. Due to the breadth of the topic of graphics and to the commonalities in graphs and data graphics, the latter two topics were treated in separate chapters devoted to each. This chapter deals with illustrations (the more iconic form of graphics, such as drawings, paintings, pictures, photographs, and diagrams), functional and decorative graphic elements (borders, boxes, and rules), and some specialized kinds of graphics (graphic organizers and cartoons).

Prior to venturing into the realm of graphics, a couple of terms—line art and halftone art—need to be distinguished, since they will be found in several subsequent discussions.

In the publishing industry, a distinction is made between two kinds of artwork or graphics: line art and halftone art. The distinction is necessitated by the methods used to reproduce each kind. In keeping with the assumptions laid out in Chapter 1, the discussion here will be restricted to black-and-white printing, not color.

Line art is black-and-white; it contains no grays. A synonym for line art is high-contrast artwork. Pen-and-ink drawings, woodcuts, and photographs made with high-contrast film produce line art. On the other hand, halftone artwork contains shades of gray, or continuous tones. Photographs made with regular panchromatic film produce halftone artwork.

Line art is easily reproduced via xerography and other typical printing processes. Halftone art, however, requires special processing before it can be printed. Since single-color printing processes can only either print a color or not print it, continuous tones must be represented by dots of differing sizes. That is, photographs must be changed (via a process called *screening*) into a collection of dots before they can be printed. (If screening is unfamiliar to you, examine closely a photograph in a newspaper; you will note it is made up of a collection of dots of varying size.) The screening process, being an additional step, generally makes the use of halftone artwork more expensive than the use of line art.

Line art can be easily generated and handled by computer programs; its creation and placement are fairly straightforward. Until fairly recently, however, continuous tone illustrations had to be handled manually, and set into place after the master copy of the text came off the laser printer. Recently, however, the improvement of scanners and of photo-editing software has changed that situation, and even more improvements can be expected in the near future.

Choosing and Using Illustrations

Is a picture really worth a thousand words? The literature of DTP pays a good deal of attention to the use of graphics of all kinds, including illustrations. By and large, graphics are viewed as devices to break up the "monotony of the printed page." After reading most books on DTP, one would conclude that Felici and Nace (1987) are atypical of the DTP perspective when they state that the functions of illustrations accompanying text are twofold: to expand and elaborate upon the subject addressed in the text, and to make the page more visually appealing. Of course, from the point of view of the educator, their first-mentioned reason is the primary one; indeed, I am tempted to argue, it should be the only one. It is their second function, however, that typifies the DTP perspective. West (1987) seems to regard illustrations (she uses the words *pictures* and *diagrams*) as left-overs, to be dealt with last. Graphics appear to be regarded as optional—niceties that can be added or not added to the text, according to whether space and aesthetic considerations permit, but basically unimportant for consideration as functional components of communication. This posture, observe Duchastel and Waller (1979), is common in the publishing industry—but inappropriate, particularly in an educational context.

Since graphics of any kind (either line art or halftone) are relatively more expensive to produce than text, their use should be considered carefully. Furthermore, careless or inappropriate use of graphics may actually do more harm than good, by acting as a distraction. Most importantly, graphics should be used in a way that clearly facilitates instruction. If instructional facilitation is not highly probable, then concern for both the economics and the potential for distraction dictates that graphics should not be used in instructional materials.

Other than going on gut feeling, how does an educator go about making the decision of whether or not to include an illustration, and if so, which one? As before, we can turn to research to help provide an answer. The use of visuals in instruction has been researched extensively, over a span of many years. The results are anything but straightforward to interpret, however. Illustrations can have any of a variety of effects on the effectiveness of instruction, or they can have no effect at all (Levie and Lentz, 1982). The reason that the research results are so mixed is probably that many variables are involved, among which are "the type of illustration, its relationship to the text, its physical characteristics, its placement in the text, and the purpose of its existence in the learning situation..." (Hurt, 1987, p. 85). There is a great deal of interdependence between and among the characteristics of the learners, learning task, pictorial materials used, and assessment procedures which Rieber (1991) likened to a jumble of pick-up sticks: The moment one variable is tinkered with, others are inevitably affected. Still, some generalizations have emerged from the large number of studies, meta-analyses, and reviews done within the past two decades.

In general, Merrill and Bunderson (1981) found that the old adage that a picture is worth a thousand words, although appealing to instructional designers, had simply not been upheld by the empirical research. Their response to that finding was to focus on the question "What types of graphics should be used under various conditions?", a question whose answer is of particular value to educators.

Illustrations for Different Types of Learning

In reviewing a substantial body of research, Merrill and Bunderson took the view that illustrations might be differentially effective with respect to different categories of learning. Their conclusions are presented so succinctly that they are reproduced virtually verbatim below, organized by instructional category (Merrill and Bunderson, 1981, p. 7).

Concepts

- pictorial graphics should be used as examples of concepts that have concrete referents

- in the initial stages of learning, simplified pictorial graphics should be used to isolate and highlight critical attributes

- in later stages of learning, more realistic pictorial graphics should be used to facilitate transfer

- pictorial graphics are not necessary and may be distracting if they are used as signs for concepts, objects, or events with which the learner has had considerable experience

- pictorial graphics are helpful and vital when learners are exposed to new concepts, objects, or events for which they have no labels and/or corresponding visual images.

Discriminations

- discriminations can be learned through considerable drill and practice (with corrective feedback) using graphics of actual objects or symbols

- color may enhance learning when used to emphasize relevant cues and when actual color discrimination is required.

Rules

- learning complex procedures can be facilitated with the use of flowcharts.

Problem solving

- training in problem solving should involve instruction in the use and interpretation of tables and figures.

Verbal information

- diagrams can provide organization and meaning which facilitate storage and retrieval of verbal information

- pictures inserted in text often have a neutral effect on performance since they only illustrate concepts that could have been visualized easily for the text descriptions provided. However, they are generally attractive and interesting to learners and are therefore preferred by them, which may reduce attrition.

Motor skills

- slow motion pictorial graphics can demonstrate the continuity of movement while slowing it down to a speed at which the critical aspects of the movement can be perceived.

Attitudes

- human modelling seems to be the most effective approach to attitude learning. The human model may appear either in graphic form (either still or motion) or in text form.

Thus Merrill and Bunderson's analysis led to a decision-making tool for the educator deciding whether or not to use graphics, based on the kind of learning expected. Theirs is but one of several possible approaches. Another way of approaching the problem is to focus on characteristics of the pictures themselves.

Representational Pictures vs. Analogical Pictures

According to some researchers, there are two distinct categories of pictures or illustrations, the first encompassing those pictorial materials called representational pictures—"...those that share a physical resemblance with the thing or concept that the picture stands for" (Alesandrini, 1984, p. 63)—and the second encompassing analogical pictures—those that "...[convey] a concept or topic by showing something else and implying a similarity" (Alesandrini, 1984, p. 68).

Representational Pictures

One use of representational pictures is to supplement verbal presentations, as opposed to pictures being the primary vehicle of instruction. In this role, Alesandrini (1984) concludes, pictures do help learners learn new concepts. Apparently basing this generalization on the many studies done by Dwyer and his associates (Dwyer, 1978), she states that

> ...Dwyer concluded that when visuals are used to supplement verbal information that the learner is already familiar with, no facilitation will occur. On the other hand, if the material to be learned is too complex, presenting a realistic visual may not facilitate learning either. (Alesandrini, 1984, p. 64)

While learners prefer to learn from illustrated materials (Levie, 1987), and while it appears that learners prefer to look at visuals that contain much detail (e.g., concrete pictures), Dwyer (1978) also concluded that "...simple line drawings are most helpful to learners while overly concrete or detailed visuals, such as photographs, do not aid learning" (Alesandrini, 1984, p. 66).

"One general finding of Dwyer's research is that pictures are most helpful in achieving objectives that entail visual discriminations (such as identifying the parts of the heart)" (Levie, 1987, p. 16). In terms of teaching concepts, however, studies on the use of pictures, while more limited in number, yield more mixed results: There is some evidence that the use of pictures may inhibit the learning of abstract concepts, but there is also evidence that, for concrete concepts at least, pictures may be beneficial, especially where they are used to illustrate the critical attributes of the concept (Levie, 1987). The amount of research available on the usefulness of pictures in teaching problem solving, critical thinking, and other higher-order processes, as well as affective responses to pictures, seems to be limited (Levie, 1987).

Levie and Lentz (1982) summarize their meta-analysis of research on representational pictures thus:

- illustrations facilitate learning the information in the written text that is depicted in the illustrations

- illustrations have no effect on learning text information that is not illustrated

- when the test of learning includes both illustrated and nonillustrated text information, a modest improvement may often result from the addition of pictures. (p. 213)

Analogical Pictures

Theoretically, analogical pictures should help a learner make relationships between what is being learned and what the learner already knows. Hurt (1987) showed that analogical illustrations did better at clarifying abstract or non-phenomenal information—information that has "...no tangible existence or is too large, too small, too distant or too transient to be recorded" (p. 86)—than did literal illustrations, and vice versa. In the process, he confirmed that gender differences, at least for college-aged learners, was not an issue.

Levie and Lentz (1982) concluded that non-representational pictures may be less reliable in their effects than representational pictures, perhaps as a consequence of learners' not being practiced at using them.

In summary, Levie and Lentz (1982) provide what they call guides for further research—tentative guidelines based on previous research— which might well be used by designers as guidelines for design until the additional research is completed:

- in normal instructional situations, the addition of pictorial embellishments will not enhance the learning of information in the text....[where embellishments are defined as] illustrations that present information that does not overlap the text content

- when illustrations provide text-redundant information, learning information in the text that is also shown in pictures will be facilitated

- the presence of text-redundant illustrations will neither help nor hinder the learning of information in the text that is not illustrated

- illustrations can help learners understand what they read, can help learners remember what they read, and can perform a variety of other instructional functions

- illustrations can sometimes be used as effective/efficient substitutes for words or as providers of extralinguistic information

- learners may fail to make effective use of complex illustrations unless they are prompted to do so

- illustrations usually enhance learner enjoyment, and they can be used to evoke affective reactions

- illustrations may be somewhat more helpful to poor readers than to good readers

- learner-generated imaginal adjuncts are generally less helpful than provided illustrations. (p. 225–226)

Although some researchers reached the conclusion that empirical evidence did not support the espoused value of illustrations in instruction, there has been in the last decade and a half a plethora of research and meta-analysis of previous studies that has come to exactly the opposite conclusion. Levin and Lesgold (1978, p. 233) say "...there is solid evidence that pictures facilitate prose learning," at least with children, provided that the prose passages are fictional narratives presented orally, the prose passages and the pictures overlap in content, and that factual recall is the criterion of learning. Schallert's (1980) review removed some of the qualifications that Levin and Lesgold attached to their conclusion, and concluded that "...illustrations benefitted reading as well as listening comprehension, adults as well as children, expository as well as narrative prose, and non-redundant as well as redundant text" (p. 519). Several research studies (e.g., Anglin, 1985, 1986a, 1986b, 1987; Hurt, 1986; Levin and Berry, 1980; Peng and Levin, 1979) supported Schallert's conclusion. Anglin and Kwak's (1991) recent review of new literature confirmed that the generalization is standing up over time.

Some specific generalizations based on recent research into the instructional value of illustrations include:

- Waddill, McDaniel, and Einstein (1988) concluded that pictures serve the function of supplementing the text, helping learners represent and remember information in the pictures that is consistent with the text. However, they believe that the text must provide specific instruction to the learner with respect to what in the picture must be processed and how, and that without those special processing instructions, pictures "...do not help learners encode information that is not ordinarily encoded in the first place" (p. 463).

- Ogunyemi (1983) found that "...the addition of black-and-white pictures as supplements to verbal instruction will improve a subject's test score [by]...13 percentile points" (p. 8).

- Hannafin (1984) found that both immediate and delayed post-test scores were better for children taught with both pictures and text than for children given text-only teaching. The results held true for both concrete and abstract content.

- Research by van Dam, Brinkerink-Carlier, and Kok (1986) found that "embellishments" (drawings depicting the gist of each verbal passage) facilitated recall of the embellished material. However, verbal embellishments (verbal details) did the same, and the enhanced recall was attained at the expense of a decrement in recall of un-embellished text.

- Hurt (1987) highlights the importance of considering the function of the illustration vis-à-vis the text. In his research, illustrations containing both phenomenal information and non-phenomenal information (e.g., analogies) aided in the overall comprehension of a text passage, but they "...served different functions to achieve that assistance, by addressing different types of information" (p. 93). Furthermore,

  > The group that read the passage with an illustration which served the function of identifying properties of phenomenal information did significantly better on comprehension of that type of information than did the group reading the passage with an illustration serving another function. Conversely, the group reading the passage with an illustration which served the function of clarifying nonphenomenal information did significantly better on comprehension of that information than did the other group. (p. 92)

Probably the primary reasons that earlier reviewers of the literature mistakenly came to the conclusion that there was insufficient empirical evidence to support the contention that pictures aid learning were the interdependence of variables identified in Rieber's pick-up sticks analogy, and the fact that much of the early research was insufficiently attentive to the functions that illustrations were being expected to play.

Functions of Illustrations

According to most books on DTP, the function of illustrations is to break up the monotony of the gray page, and to provide interest. These rather vague rationalizations are unsatisfactory to educators, who have undertaken more rigorous examinations of the reasons for including illustrations in text.

Duchastel (1978) suggested three roles for illustrations in text:

- attentional—attempting to motivate the learner;

- explicative—explaining some aspect of the verbal content or showing something which would be difficult or impossible to communicate solely with words; and

- retentional—aiding recollection by virtue of having the information encoded both verbally and iconically.

The explicative role, the most important one for instructional materials, is further sub-divided into seven functions (Duchastel and Waller, 1979):

- descriptive—showing what an object looks like (e.g., a photograph of a starfish);

- expressive—having an impact on the learner by evoking an affective response in the learner (e.g., a photograph depicting the horrors of war);

- constructional—demonstrating how component parts relate to one another (e.g., an exploded view of an internal combustion engine);

- functional—simplified visual representation of organizational relationships (e.g., an organizational chart);

- logico-mathematical—line graphs;

- algorithmic—flow charts; and

- data-display—bar charts, pie charts, histograms, stem-and-leaf constructions, density maps, and the like.

Duchastel's typology is useful to designers of instructional materials in addressing the question of whether or not a particular illustration should be included: If one or more of the roles are fulfilled by an illustration, then it might be a candidate for inclusion; if none are, then the illustration should not be included. When using Duchastel's typology, be wary of ascribing the attentional role too readily. Altogether too many illustrations get placed into instructional materials on the vague premise that they will somehow increase motivation.

Levin (1981) also devised a typology for functions of pictures in texts, which may be of even greater use than Duchastels in helping a designer decide whether or not to include an illustration in instructional materials. He identified eight functions:

1. decoration—to increase the attractiveness of the text;

2. remuneration—to help increase sales;

3. motivation—to increase readers' interest in the text;

4. reiteration—to bolster the message in the text;

5. representation—to make more concrete the information in the text;

6. organization—to help integrate the information in the text;

7. interpretation—to make more comprehensible the information in the text; and

8. transformation—to make the information in the text more memorable.

Levin dismissed the first two functions as being irrelevant to an anticipated contribution to improved learning (I share his viewpoint), and expected little or no contribution to that end from the third and fourth. The fifth function, however, he expected to provide a moderate contribution. The sixth and seventh functions were expected to provide a moderate to substantial contribution, and the eighth, a substantial one. Clearly, Levin's typology is hierarchical with respect to anticipated contribution to learning. In applying his typology to decision-making, then, a designer need only determine how far down the list a particular illustration's function falls. The lower it is, the more powerful the reason to include it, and vice versa. Certainly, illustrations fulfilling only the first or second function should not be considered for inclusion.

Relevance of Illustrations to Text

Too often, graphics are used without any reference whatsoever to the text in which they are embedded. Indeed, sometimes that appears to be the thrust of advice given in DTP books—art for art's sake. For example: "Even abstract geometric shapes can intrigue and invite and add movement to the page" (Shushan and Wright, 1989, p. 11).

Maybe so, but they can also distract learners from the intended communication (which presumably isn't couched in the abstract geometric shapes).

The tendency to add just one more cute little graphic to a page, just to attract the learners' attention, is probably more of a rationalization of the opportunism of electronic clip-art than it is good design practice. Fortunately, some DTP writers give more reasoned advice:

> Remember, communication is our business (not art), and anything placed between the reader and the message that interferes with communication should be questioned, no matter how elegant (or amusing, or clever) it may be. (Lichty, 1989, p. 135)

> As desktop publishers (and not designers), we must always exercise skepticism and restraint, especially with regard to nontypographical elements. Our tools are so convenient and flexible that the temptation to overdesign is almost irresistible.

> Resist that temptation. (Lichty, 1989, p. 146)

Recent research has indisputably established the effectiveness of pictures, but under certain conditions. Of particular importance is the relevance of the pictures to the accompanying text. Anglin (1985, 1986a, 1986b, 1987) found that learners who read prose with accompanying relevant pictures did from 10%–18% better on both immediate and delayed post-tests (administered up to as much as 55 days later) than did learners who read only the prose.

Levin, Anglin, and Carney (1987) suggest that what is known about the effects of pictures on learning from prose can be summarized in three statements:

- in cases where text-embedded illustrations are relevant to (i.e., largely over-lapping or redundant with) the to-be-remembered content, moderate to substantial prose-learning gains can be expected

- in cases where text-embedded illustrations are not relevant to the to-be-remembered prose content (i.e., they depict unrelated—or worse, conflicting—text information), no prose-learning facilitation is to be expected

- in cases where "pictures" consist of self-generated visual images that are relevant to the to-be-remembered content, some positive effects can be expected, but these are much more modest and more variable than those associated with actual illustration. (p. 52)

Levin, Anglin, and Carney also assert that "...at least as far as text-relevant illustrations are concerned[,] ...*pictures in text consistently produce prose-learning benefits*" [italics theirs] (p. 53). Levie and Lentz (1982) agree, stating it thus: "In experimental comparisons in which the test measured the learning of information presented in both print and pictures, the illustrated text version was consistently better than the text-alone version" (p. 225).

The problem of irrelevance of illustrations in instructional materials is all too common. Levin's (1981) decoration and remuneration functions do unfortunately tend to prevail in many graphic designers' and publishers' decision-making.

> However gratifying it would be to think that pictures are
> selected on the basis of their instructional value, supported by
> empirical evidence, pictures are probably most often selected
> for more mundane reasons such as their attractiveness, cost,
> and availability. (Brody, 1982, p. 301)

Instructional designers, many of whom have an affinity for things audiovisual, are susceptible to including gratuitous illustrations on the premise that pictures are inherently good. This tendency has to be counteracted with stringent reference to the function—selected from one of the typologies of functions described earlier—the illustration can reasonably be expected to play (NOTE: expected, not merely hoped).

Intertwined with this notion of relevance of the picture to the text is the idea that learners may have to be shown or told the relationship between the two. Levie and Lentz (1982) note that while students may look at pictures that accompany text, they likely don't actually use them to learn from unless told to do so. Peeck (1978) agrees that at minimum, the text must call attention to the picture before any benefits can be expected from the picture. However, she believes that merely calling attention may be insufficient, and cites several studies which indicate that requiring the learner to be actively involved with the picture (through such mechanisms as labelling parts of the picture) has beneficial results.

Brody (1982, p. 303) puts it quite forcefully: "...for a picture to be used most effectively, it is necessary to control both what the learner is looking at and when it is to be examined." Part of the control has to do with placement of the picture, both in relation to the page and to the text referring to it. Brody notes that there has not been a great deal of research done on this question, and that picture placement decisions appear to be done primarily on the basis of aesthetic considerations. The single empirical study I found on this topic was done by Fleming (1984), who experimentally manipulated the placement of pictorial material with respect to accompanying text (picture first, then words; vs. words first, then picture), and found no significant difference. Of course, he was dealing with very sophisticated learners (graduate students), which may have had an effect on his observations.

Another part of the control Brody mentions has to do with ensuring that for every illustration, there is some statement in the body text indicating when the learner should attend to it, how it relates to the body text, and what he or she should attend to and extract from it. Captions for the illustrations should also be provided, but the burden of the control mentioned should not be carried by captions alone. Many times illustrations are plunked into text without such cross-references, and often with such succinct or generally-worded captions as to make their purpose unclear. The likelihood of real learning occurring from those illustrations is minimal.

Creating Your Own Illustrations

"But I can't even draw a straight line!"

That's what many educators would say if prompted to provide illustrations for their instructional materials. Disregarding for the moment whether or not a straight line is an appropriate criterion, microcomputers have made it possible for almost anyone to either create or modify existing artwork quickly and easily.

There are several avenues that can be taken to creating your own illustrations. Graphics for DTPI can be:

- drawn right on the computer;

- scanned or traced into the computer from existing line drawings or photographs; or

- purchased in the form of electronic clip-art, and used "as-is" or modified.

Although considered by some to be old fashioned, another method is surprisingly often the most reasonable and most economical. Graphics can also be:

- pasted into camera-ready copy manually.

Computer Graphics

For all intents and purposes, computer-drawn graphics can be classified as one of two types: bit-mapped or object-oriented, also known as paint-type and draw-type, respectively. These two types of graphics are conceptually similar to the two types of fonts—bit-mapped and outline—described in Chapter 6.

Bit-mapped graphics are those in which each pixel is represented internally in the computer as a 1 or 0, on or off. Consider the square depicted in Figure 11–1.

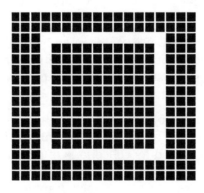

Figure 11–1. A square created with a computer graphics program.

In a paint-type (bit-mapped) program, the square would be described as a series of 1's and 0's, corresponding to whether or not each successive pixel was illuminated. Hence the description would be something like that in Figure 11–2.

```
0 0 0 0 0 0 0 0 0 0 0 0 0 0 0 0 0 0 0 0
0 0 0 0 0 0 0 0 0 0 0 0 0 0 0 0 0 0 0 0
0 0 0 1 1 1 1 1 1 1 1 1 1 1 1 1 0 0 0 0
0 0 0 1 0 0 0 0 0 0 0 0 0 0 1 0 0 0
0 0 0 1 0 0 0 0 0 0 0 0 0 0 1 0 0 0
0 0 0 1 0 0 0 0 0 0 0 0 0 0 1 0 0 0
0 0 0 1 0 0 0 0 0 0 0 0 0 0 1 0 0 0
0 0 0 1 0 0 0 0 0 0 0 0 0 0 1 0 0 0
0 0 0 1 0 0 0 0 0 0 0 0 0 0 1 0 0 0
0 0 0 1 0 0 0 0 0 0 0 0 0 0 1 0 0 0
0 0 0 1 0 0 0 0 0 0 0 0 0 0 1 0 0 0
0 0 0 1 0 0 0 0 0 0 0 0 0 0 1 0 0 0
0 0 0 1 0 0 0 0 0 0 0 0 0 0 1 0 0 0
0 0 0 1 1 1 1 1 1 1 1 1 1 1 1 1 0 0 0 0
0 0 0 0 0 0 0 0 0 0 0 0 0 0 0 0 0 0 0 0
0 0 0 0 0 0 0 0 0 0 0 0 0 0 0 0 0 0 0 0
```

Figure 11–2. The square in Figure 11–1 as represented internally in a paint-type program.

In a draw-type (object-oriented) program, on the other hand, only the graph coordinates (x and y) of the figure are used to represent the square; the program "knows" that the points specified should be connected with lines. Hence the square can be represented with only this information:

(3,4) (3,15) (14,15) (14,3)

which says, in effect, draw a line from coordinate (3,4) to (3,15), then to (14,15), then to (14,3), and finally back to (3,4).

As in the case of fonts, curves are represented by mathematical equations. Although these equations can sometimes be quite complex, object-oriented graphics are still usually more compact than bit-mapped graphics when the graphic is large.

Object-oriented graphics enjoy another advantage over bit-mapped graphics: They can be moved and re-sized as units. Bit-mapped graphics have to be moved and re-sized as collections of pixels. Moreover, because object-oriented graphics are based on equations, they do not exhibit increased jaggedness as bit-mapped graphics do when they are increased in size. On the other hand, they generally cannot be edited or have portions erased, as bit-mapped graphics can.

In terms of use, the difference between bit-mapped and object-oriented graphics programs is that with the latter, you construct your diagram from a number of basic objects (e.g., horizontal, vertical, or diagonal lines; squares or rectangles, with either square or rounded corners; circles or ovals; regular and irregular polygons; arcs; free-form lines) each of which can be drawn with "pens" of different widths and/or using different "ink" (shading, cross-hatching, etc.). Objects can be made larger or smaller without changing the line width or shading employed, and objects can be moved around the screen by simply dragging them to the new position. Parts of an object cannot be erased. For example, the right side of a square could not be removed to create a squared-off C shape. (However, a rectangle drawn with a white pen and filled with white could be laid over the right side of the square to yield the same effect.)

With bit-mapped graphics, similar basic shapes can be created in much the same manner as with object-oriented graphics. Once the object is drawn, it cannot be re-sized unless portions of it are erased and re-drawn. This may mean, for example that if you don't get the size or shape of a circle just right the first time, you must erase it and begin again. Bit-mapped graphics have a number of additional tools available (e.g., spray paint, eraser, paint brush) for additional flexibility. Editing (adding or removing "ink") can be done on a pixel-by-pixel basis. Objects cannot be re-sized conveniently or accurately; while crude forms of re-sizing can be done, unless the entity being re-sized is composed entirely of horizontal and/or vertical lines, the character of the picture changes.

Of course, text can also be combined with either type of graphic.

Historically, programs specifically designed to create graphics were either paint-type (e.g., MacPaint) or draw-type (e.g., MacDraw). Recently, however, a number of programs have come onto the market that handle both types of graphics seemingly simultaneously (e.g., SuperPaint, Canvas). (Strictly speaking, they don't handle both types of graphics simultaneously. Rather, each type is handled in a separate layer, managed by a sub-program of the appropriate type. The net effect to the user, however, is that the output from the graphics program appears to combine both types, whether the output is viewed on the screen or printed on paper.) Since there is now a blending of capabilities, graphics programs are sometimes now classified as "mostly drawing" (e.g., Adobe Illustrator 88™, Aldus Freehand™, Claris™ CAD 2.0), or "mostly painting" (e.g., Claris™ MacPaint 2.0, Digital Darkroom™).

Most people involved in DTPI want access to both bit-mapped and object-oriented graphics creation and editing capabilities. Since the programs named above (and others) vary widely in their power and capabilities (and therefore in their learning curve requirements), those contemplating purchase of graphics programs would do well to investigate the field more thoroughly than can be done here.

Scanners

Scanners are devices that convert existing artwork (either color or black and white) to digital form so that it can be manipulated and stored in a computer.

There are several types of scanners. Sheet-fed scanners require that the artwork being scanned travel through the machine, along a curved path. This makes it impossible for graphics in books to be copied unless they are photocopied first. Bed scanners have a flat surface on which the artwork is placed, much like most photocopy machines. Hand-held scanners are just that—held in the hand and drawn over the artwork to make the copy. Although bed scanners are probably the best choice, they are also the most expensive, and some users report good results with the less expensive models.

Scanners are a godsend for people who cannot draw. Even if the exact graphic required cannot be found, often one that is almost right can be. Since most scanner software also includes some editing capabilities, the user can modify the original artwork as necessary.

One important point should be remembered by scanner users: Images created by someone else, whether in their original medium or scanned, whether in their original form or modified, still enjoy the protection of copyright. Many people who would never break the copyright laws by using text illegally seem to feel that graphics are a whole different ball game; that if they only make a few modifications to the graphic, they are somehow not in violation of the copyright laws. I wouldn't presume to give legal advice here, but if you check into it, I think you'll find that so long as a graphic is still recognizably based on a copyright-protected original, copyright laws apply.

The consensus amongst DTP experts at this time seems to be that scanners are not yet capable of producing the high resolution (600 dpi minimum) needed for reproduction of halftone illustrations. Educators may be able to afford slightly more lenient standards, and choose to use lower-quality reproductions for instruction than the publishing industry would sanction, especially if it comes down to a choice between the lower resolution versus not being able to use a picture at all. However, that choice should be made only if the detail and clarity of the illustration are such that interpretation and comprehension are certain not to suffer. Be wary of deciding that the contents of a picture are clear enough, only because you already know what the picture represents! Test a questionable picture with naive viewers.

Scanners should not be used to reproduce photographs if there is any possibility that the work will eventually end up on a printer with higher resolution than 300 dpi. While scanned photographs will look okay when printed on the 300-dpi printer, they will look terrible on a higher resolution device (Hewson, 1988). If the scanning software offers a choice, match the scan resolution to the resolution of the printer that will be finally used.

Electronic Clip Art

A sizable number of firms offer electronic clip art for sale. These generic images are intended as building blocks for graphics. Users can take part or all of a clip art image and modify and adapt it to their needs. Usually, these clip art collections (which cover a variety of topics) are sold for the express purpose of allowing the user to modify them, hence copyright is not a concern. However, it would be wise to read carefully any copyright notices that come with a clip art collection to be sure that there are no provisos limiting the use of the images.

Clip art, of course, comes in both bit-mapped and object-oriented forms, although it is unusual to see the same images offered in both forms— usually, they are one or the other. Clip art collections can also be either line art or halftone art. Sometimes non-standard graphics file formats are used in clip art collections, and you may find out that the clip art you purchased cannot be edited or even used with your existing software, so investigate clip art carefully before buying it. (This problem is especially troublesome in the DOS world, but also exists in the Mac world.)

Manual Paste-Ups

Sometimes DTP enthusiasts get so wrapped up in their work, so inflated with the power of their systems, that they forget that getting the job done is their ultimate aim. Their new aim becomes to do the job elegantly (if not necessarily wisely). I have seen users spend half a day trying to get a graphic scanned, edited, and correctly placed in an electronic document when a pair of scissors, a bottle of white-out, some transparent tape, and ten minutes could have accomplished the same job.

To be sure, there are times when it is worthwhile spending the extra time and energy involved to convert illustrations to electronic form. For example, if you are producing a document that will likely undergo a number of modifications in between various print runs, doing the conversion will eliminate having to do manual paste-ups before each printing. On the other hand, if the document is likely going to be printed only once, the quick and simple way of dealing with many—if not all—of the illustrations is probably manual paste-up.

Principles for Designing Illustrations

While the topic of designing illustrations is too broad to address here in much more than a cursory way, following are a number of guiding principles and tips that have emerged from either the collective experience of graphic artists or research studies on the use of illustrations in instruction:

Simplification

- Combine pictures and words; they will complement each other, encourage dual encoding, and help retention (Parrish, 1990).

- Keep the amount of information (both verbal and visual) in the illustration to a minimum; don't overwhelm with information. Eliminate extraneous elements, and reduce the complexity of the illustration as much as possible while still meeting the instructional objective (Burns, Venit, and Hansen, 1988; Parrish, 1990).

- Rather than use a complex illustration, break it into several simpler ones (Parrish, 1990).

- Avoid placing too much emphasis on diagrams with low-ability learners, who have difficulty using them (Winn and Holliday, 1982).

Organization

- Organize the information in such a way that the most important information is most prominent (Burns, Venit, and Hansen, 1988).

- Create visual focal points in order to highlight importance and to maintain interest (Burns, Venit, and Hansen, 1988).

- Organize the elements of the illustration to reflect their conceptual or real-world organization (Parrish, 1990; Winn and Holliday, 1982).

- Arrange sequences to be read from left to right and top to bottom (NOTE: this is likely to be culturally-bound) (Parrish, 1990; Winn and Holliday, 1982).

Interaction

- Encourage learner interaction with the illustration by building in questions, or requiring the learner to label parts. Ensure that questions cover all the material to be learned, not just part, but be careful that they do not over-prompt learners (Parrish, 1990; Winn and Holliday, 1982).

Proportions

- The Golden Section (also sometimes known as the Golden Rectangle) is a proportional relationship that can be found frequently not only in objects considered beautiful over the entire span of human existence, but also in nature and in mathematics (Doczi, 1981). Without going into the mathematics underlying the Golden Section, suffice it to say that it represents approximately the ratio 5 : 8 (or 1 : 1.618). A rectangle 5 units by 8 units is claimed to be more universally pleasing to the human eye than a rectangle of any other proportion. This rule of thumb, known since the time of the ancient Greeks and evident in their architecture, is often touted as the one that should be kept in mind when designing graphics.

- Tufte (1983) acknowledges that the Golden Section has survived the test of time, but calls it a "dubious rule of aesthetic proportion," noting that several other proportions yield rectangles "...for which aesthetic claims might be made" (Tufte, 1983, p. 189), as well:

    - $1 : \sqrt{2}$ (or 1 : 1.414)

    - $1 : \sqrt{3}$ (or 1 : 1.732) and

    - 1 : 2.

    Figure 11–3 shows rectangles of these various proportions, including the Golden Section. Tufte summarizes the results of some 130 years of research on the matter by noting that while psychologists have found a mild preference for the Golden Section, the range of preferred ratios of height and length has been quite wide, and highly context-dependent.

| 1 : 1.414 | 1 : 1.618 | 1 : 1.732 | 1 : 2 |

Figure 11–3. Rectangles whose proportions are thought to have particularly aesthetic qualities.

Layout

- Make the overall composition of the diagram tight but not crowded (Burns, Venit, and Hansen, 1988).

- Highlight critical elements of the illustration, and eliminate or down-play non-critical elements (Parrish, 1990).

- Ensure that the critical elements of the illustration stand out well from the background (Parrish, 1990).

- Use arrows to indicate direction and sequence (Winn and Holliday, 1982).

- Avoid placing text vertically in diagrams (Parrish, 1990).

- Use contrast within diagrams (in line weight and in shading) to heighten interest and alleviate boredom; avoid too much symmetry (Burns, Venit, and Hansen, 1988).

- Enforce consistency across all diagrams with respect to things such as ruled line lengths and weights, fill patterns, and alignment of text (Burns, Venit, and Hansen, 1988, p. 229).

Labels and Captions

- Groups things (e.g., labels) that are logically related (Burns, Venit, and Hansen, 1988; Parrish, 1990). Try to keep the number of elements in a group to seven or fewer.

- Ensure that the distances between the labels in the diagram reflect the semantic distance between the elements labelled. If there is a sequential relationship between any elements, ensure that the layout of elements reflects it (Winn and Holliday, 1982).

- Lines connecting labels to referents should be at the same angle whenever possible. Also, the distance between illustrations and labels should be constant across illustrations (Burns, Venit, and Hansen, 1988).

- Keep titles and captions simple and short; make points in the body text, with clear reference to the illustrations to tie them together (Burns, Venit, and Hansen, 1988).

Technical Considerations

- Consider final paper quality when selecting or creating an illustration; do not include fine detail when the quality of paper to be used is low, since the details will not reproduce adequately (Burns, Venit, and Hansen, 1988).

- Plan ahead for any necessary reduction of diagrams. Ensure that line width is adequate (e.g., a two-pixel line reduced 50% will yield a one-pixel line). Also ensure that text, when reduced, is of the appropriate size (e.g., if labels in diagrams are 9-point, and you must reduce a particular diagram by 50%, use 18-point labels).

- Use graphic software commands to align elements, rather than trusting your eyes (unless magnification is possible and rulers can be made very accurate).

- Match your use of screens (gray areas) to the printer to be used for the final copy. A LaserWriter printer will yield different gray densities than will a Linotronic™. Generally, grays of less than 50% printed on a high-resolution printer will appear lighter than the same gray printed on a LaserWriter. Grays of more than 50% printed on a high-resolution printer will appear darker than the same gray printed on a LaserWriter (Burns, Venit, and Hansen, 1988; (*Publish!*, 1989a).

Placement of Illustrations

Page layout programs (e.g., PageMaker, Quark Xpress™, etc.) permit extremely accurate placement and sizing of a variety of graphic elements, including illustrations, virtually anywhere on the page. Even high-end word processors may have powerful graphics placement facilities (e.g., the **Position** command in MS Word). On the Mac, most graphics can simply be dragged into an appropriate position, since the view on the screen is pretty much WYSIWYG. However, for really accurate placement, it is better to use software commands rather than trust your eyes (unless considerable magnification power is available).

Programs such as PageMaker 4.0 can place an element accurately to within 0.0003".

As has been the case in a number of instances, DTP experts offer differing advice with respect to where on the page illustrations should be placed. On the one hand, Lang (1987) believes that figures and tables should be kept as close as possible to the text that refers to them. On the other hand, West (1987) says:

> If you show a number of visuals, try clustering them, rather than spotting them evenly around the spread. You might even assign them a particular area—across the bottom or clustered in the center, so that the visuals have their own area. (p. 69)

Visual appeal once again appears to be the criterion used by DTP experts, rather than the criterion preferred by educators—instructional significance. "Don't break the grid—that is, place an element arbitrarily on the page. The whole purpose of the grid, after all, is to ensure visual organization. Find other ways of creating interest on the page" (West, 1987, p. 68).

This may be good advice for some kinds of documents, but it is probably not good advice for instructional materials. As noted earlier in this chapter, very little research has been done on this topic, but I would argue that guidelines for the placement of illustrations should be similar to those for tables (see Chapter 9):

- They should be placed as close as possible to the text that refers to them (and there should always be text that refers to them).

- If possible, they should be placed after the first reference to them, even if that means leaving white space at the bottom of a page.

- If the referent text is extensive, make every effort to keep it all together, as well as keep it with the graphic (i.e., don't split the text across pages so that learners have to constantly flip back and forth between the illustration and the referent text).

- Have a caption for each illustration, and always keep it in the same place relative to the illustration (e.g., below, to one side, etc.).

- Separate the illustration and its caption from the surrounding text with a consistent amount of white space.

- Illustrations should not span two pages unless they have been designed to be displayed that way; it is often an indication that the illustration is too complex or too filled with information if it cannot be put onto a single page.

For some types of publications, this appears to be a good common-sense guideline:

> If a similar image (such as a computer screen) appears regularly, especially if on sequential pages, find a consistent place for it. This way, your reader can find that particular kind of information easily. For instance, if your technical manual has several sequential pages with a screen image on each, make each screen the same size and put it in the same place. (West, 1987, p. 69)

Captions and Labels

A *caption* is a name or description of an entire graphic, and usually either immediately precedes or follows the graphic. *Label* is the term used here for a word or words within a graphic that describe or name pictorial elements of the graphic. Labels are often connected to their referents by *leader lines*.

If possible, keep leader lines parallel to one another to avoid visual clutter (Figure 11–4).

Arrow-heads on leader lines are probably unnecessary, since they usually only serve to increase visual clutter.

Labels within a figure can be flush left, flush right, or centered with respect to either their referents or the leader lines tying them to their referents. There seems no reason to prefer one alignment over another, but the use should be consistent across all diagrams.

Aligning in-figure labels vertically wherever possible helps reduce visual clutter and allows for grouping of related elements. Vertical grouping of labels would also seem to be advantageous since:

> Objects and events encountered in proximity with each other, i.e., close together in time or space or in the same context, will tend to be perceived as somehow related, e.g., ideationally,

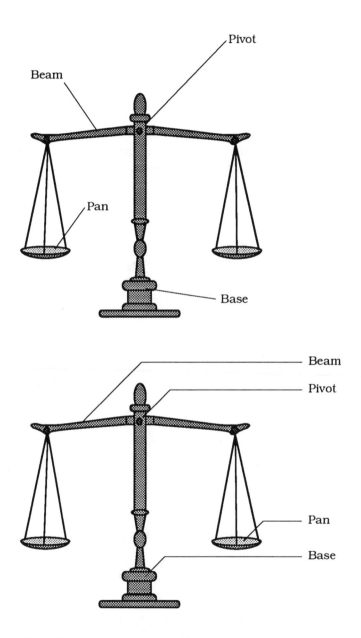

Figure 11–4. Keep leader lines parallel to each other whenever possible, and consider grouping labels attached to related elements, and aligning labels vertically to aid legibility.

> functionally, etc. Comparisons will be facilitated, both similar-
> ities and differences becoming apparent. (Fleming and Levie,
> 1978, p. 71)

> Learning to associate or relate two or more objects or events
> (stimuli and/or responses) is facilitated where they occur or are
> encountered in contiguity, i.e., close together in time and/or
> space. (Fleming and Levie, 1978, p. 100)

When importing a diagram containing labels from a graphics program
(and especially when changing its size in the process), you may inadvertently change the size of the labels (i.e., the font size). Take pains to
avoid this, or plan ahead for it. If you know that you must reduce a
figure 50% after creating it, use a font twice as large as you want the
labels to be in the finished product.

The necessity of captions for illustrations has already been mentioned
in the discussion on relevance of illustrations to text. Brody (1982)
notes that most publishers appear not to use instructional criteria for
developing their captions; it is clear that captions can be powerful
influences with regard to what learners perceive in illustrations, and
their content should be carefully considered. Each illustration should
have a meaningful caption. If you find it difficult to conceive of a
meaningful caption, you should question whether the illustration will
really make a contribution to learning, as opposed to being merely
decorative.

Captions should be as consistent as any other element in a well-
designed document. They should always be found in the same location
relative to the illustration, and they should always have the same form
and appearance. It is often useful to number illustrations so that
reference to them in the text is easy; if that is done, the illustration or
figure number should appear as part of the caption.

Generally speaking, DTP advisors suggest making captions look
different from body text:

> Because they are physically separate from the main body text,
> captions should be treated in a contrasting typographic style,
> either by using a variant (bold, italic or condensed, perhaps), a
> different point size, a different measure, or a different, but
> complementary typeface—or perhaps by a combination.
> (Collier and Cotton, p. 36)

> Captions should supplement an illustration, rather than
> compete with it for attention. If you are using a serif typeface

> such as Times Roman for the body of your text, consider using a
> sans serif typeface such as Helvetica for the captions, or
> perhaps a smaller size of the Times Roman. If a smaller size is
> difficult to read, consider using italics. (Davis, Barry, and
> Wiesenberg, 1986, p. 53)

Should captions be created in the graphics program, or the word
processing or layout program? There are pros and cons to each method.

An advantage of creating the caption in the graphics program is that the
caption becomes permanently tied to the figure; it therefore cannot be
lost or inadvertently swapped for another one. However, the disadvantage is that much more care must be taken to achieve the proper
alignment of the caption with respect to the ultimate placement of the
figure in the text. Furthermore, text size may have to be adjusted to
compensate for any enlargement or reduction of the figure prior to
insertion in the text. Also, last-minute changes in the caption become
awkward, as it is necessary to go right back to the graphics program to
make them.

If a word processor is being used for layout, captions can simply be
created along with the text, perhaps using a different style sheet. Figures
can be inserted later, at positions marked by place-holders such as
##INSERT FIGURE "figure name" HERE.

If a layout program is being used, the captions can be included right
with the text. This has the advantage of increasing the likelihood that
the figures will ultimately appear in the correct position with respect to
the text. However, it necessitates a great deal of cutting and pasting
within the layout program, as the captions will probably have to be
isolated from the surrounding text in order to achieve proper placement
and sizing. All that cutting and pasting increases the possibility that a
caption will inadvertently get misplaced or lost, with the net result that
a caption-less figure will be left over at the end.

A second approach is to type in the captions "on the fly," as figures are
placed in the final copy. This bypasses the normal proofreading, and
risks the incorrect matching of captions with figures unless a very tight
method of cross-referencing is in place.

A third solution is to place all the captions in a separate text file, and
bring them into the layout program one at a time. This method can
work well, but care must be taken to ensure that this additional file gets

proofread, and that a rigid cross-referencing system is in place to ensure that the right captions end up with the right figures.

Charts and Diagrams

A diagram contains pictorial elements displayed in a consistently-depicted relationship to one another, often with accompanying text. A diagram may be quite iconic (e.g., a line drawing of a flower, rich with detail) or quite abstract (e.g., a schematic for an electronic circuit). Maps are a special kind of diagram that depicts geographical or astronomical features.

Winn and Holliday (1982) identify a number of points of concern to someone designing charts or diagrams:

- Contrary to popular opinion, diagrams are not easy devices for learners to use; certain mental skills are required for the successful use of diagrams. They are a good way for high-ability students to learn, but not necessarily for all students. This does not mean they should not be used, however—only that in some situations, instructions on how to interpret and use diagrams may be necessary.

- Actual conceptual and real-word relationships should be reflected in the spatial arrangement of the elements in the diagram or chart. Parts of a chart or diagram should be arranged so that superordinate concepts are presented before subordinate concepts (in a left-to-right, top-to-bottom sequence), particularly when teaching classification. When sequences of concepts are involved, arrange them left-to-right, top-to-bottom on the page.

- If possible, make the distances between elements in the chart or diagram correspond to the semantic distances between the concepts they represent (i.e., concepts that are closely related conceptually should be placed near one another on the chart, and vice versa). Ensure that sequential relationships are accurately depicted by using arrows and lines to indicate direction and sequence. Boxes and similar graphic devices can be used to create separation among concepts.

- Include small drawings or pictures within a chart to facilitate learners' identification of the concepts being depicted, particularly for low-ability learners.

- Supplementing diagrams with text should be done cautiously. Learners tend to exert the least possible amount of effort required to attain their objectives, hence often choose the most familiar medium to use. Thus learners may attend primarily to the text (since that is most familiar to them), and miss information included in the diagram. This may necessitate specific instructions (in the text) to refer to the diagram.

- Study questions can form an important adjunct to diagrams by focusing learners' attention on the important information contained in the diagram. However, unless the questions are very carefully constructed, they can be dysfunctional; learners may focus only on those items addressed by the questions. Therefore it is necessary to ensure that all important questions relevant to and addressed by the diagram are asked (i.e., that all aspects of the diagram that are important have a question). It is also important to ensure the questions don't over-prompt the learner. If the answers to the questions are so obvious that the learner does not need to think about what is in the diagram, then the diagram probably will not be used.

Borders, Boxes, and Rules

Borders, boxes, and rules are some of the designer's tools that can be used to direct and limit the movement of the reader's eyes across and about the page. Not long ago, educators were limited to rows of either the underscore character (_), the hyphen (-), the period, or the asterisk. Now, borders, boxes, and rules have become elements of design and layout that are relatively easy to incorporate into documents using page layout programs, the output of graphics programs pasted into word processors, or, in fact, word processors themselves.

Borders and Boxes

The distinction between borders and boxes apparently varies from one author to the next. Borders and boxes do the same job—separate some elements on the page from other elements. To my way of thinking, borders enclose large areas (complete pages, or large portions thereof), while boxes contain relatively smaller areas.

Lichty (1989) claims that borders can be used to:

- separate a part of the text from the remainder, for emphasis

- provide some typographical color to an otherwise gray page

- break text into smaller, more appealing groupings

- provide an appropriate border for line art or photographs. (p. 127)

There seems to be no research on the effects, if any, that borders and boxes have on instruction, but prudence seems to suggest that if borders are used, simple designs should be chosen, and they should be used with restraint, so as not to overwhelm or distract the learner. Boxes can be used to separate text within them from other text on the page, and can be effective for highlighting important points or setting off distinctly different material. Miles (1987) believes that boxed material should probably have subject titles or headings of their own, but it seems to me that titles would be necessary only if the boxes contained ancillary material. My view is that boxes, like other graphic devices, should be used with restraint and consistency, if at all.

Rules

Rules, in the language of text design and layout, are what lay persons call lines. They can be delicate or heavy, solid, dotted, or dashed, vertical or horizontal. Rules can be used to organize and separate elements on the page, to define areas on the page, and to provide emphasis (Lichty, 1989). It is my view that most rules can be replaced with white space, with a better overall effect. However, there are times that nothing else will do. For example, when headings must span two or more columns, a rule may be necessary to separate the material above the heading from the heading itself, to provide a kind of fence to tell the reader's eyes where to look next.

There is a rule of thumb in the publishing industry that using a contrast rule (a heavy rule next to a light rule) sets up a progression from thick to thin, to lead the eye to the focal point of the message. That is, to lead the eye into a graphic or some other focus of attention, one could place contrast rules above and below the graphic as depicted in Figure 11–5a and b. The effect may be magnified with fancy rules (e.g., 1–5c and d) (*Printing layout and design.* 1968, p. 47). Of course, placing the rules the opposite way around would have the opposite effect, and lead the eye away from the center of attention.

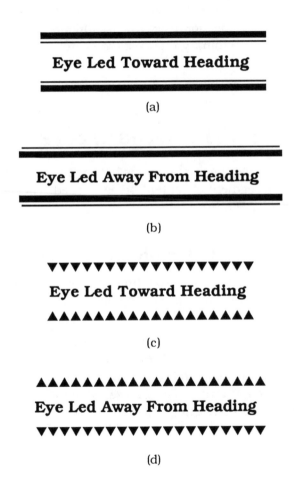

Figure 11–5. Rules can lead the eye toward or away from the headline.

Different weights of rules can take on different meanings, too: More important categories of information can be designated with heavier rules, while less important ones can be signified by lighter ones (Davis, Barry, and Wiesenberg, 1986). If you use rules to signal these differences, make sure that:

- the meanings are clearly explained before the rules are used; and

- not too many different types of rules are assigned meaning, as the learner is likely to become confused.

There does not seem to be much research on the effect of using rules to guide the eye about the page. Johnsey, Wheat, and Morrison (1990) have done some, but their preliminary report is too sketchy to cite any conclusions.

Graphic Organizers

Graphic organizers show the relationships between and among the key ideas and terms in a segment of content being learned. They appear as tree-like diagrams (e.g., Figure 11–6).

Research on Graphic Organizers

A meta-analysis of 23 studies investigating graphic organizers (Moore and Readence, 1984) led to the following guidelines.

Originally used as a type of advance organizer for teacher-directed learning, graphic organizers yielded mixed performance. However, newer studies focusing on the use of graphic organizers by learners rather than by teachers yielded more positive findings. The discussion that follows is couched in terms of effect size, which is "...the difference between the means of a treatment group and a control group divided by the standard deviation of the control group" (Moore and Readence, 1984, p. 12).

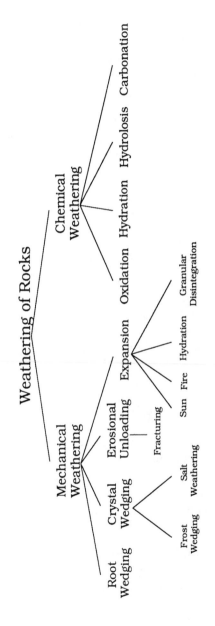

Figure 11-6. An example of a graphic organizer. (Based on Barnes, 1988)

In general (i.e., over all studies), the effects of graphic organizers were small but positive: Learners using graphic organizers outperformed control learners by about one-fifth of a standard deviation. However, when the results of the studies were examined from the point of view of selected variables, more powerful effects were observed, leading to the following rules of thumb:

- Graphic organizers are more effective when learners construct them after the learning task, rather than prior to the learning, or in conjunction with questions, study guides, or small group discussions.

- Graphic organizers are more effective when used to learn vocabulary than when used for general comprehension.

- Graphic organizers are more effective with university students than with either elementary or secondary students.

- Qualitative meta-research suggests that care must be taken to explain to learners the value of constructing graphic organizers, or else they may view the activity as isolated and irrelevant, and not grasp the utility of using them. In other words, learners will probably have to be convinced of the utility of using graphic organizers, as well as being taught how to construct them.

Pictorial Elements in Graphic Organizers

Hawk, McLeod, and Jonassen (1985) recommend going beyond the use of simple tree-diagrams, and using pictorial elements in graphic organizers in an attempt to capitalize on the hypothesis that pictorial material is processed and encoded differently than textual material. They also posit the use of participatory organizers, in which learners are required to add to the organizational structure provided.

Research by Tajika, Taniguchi, Yamamoto, and Mayer (1988) showed that fifth-grade learners given an integrated advance organizer (i.e., a concrete drawing that gave a meaningful context for the text passage it accompanied) recalled more both immediately and one week later than did learners given a fragmented pictorial advance organizer (one in which the visual components did not relate to one another in a meaningful way), the text passage only, or nothing.

Cartoons

Cartoons are often incorporated into instructional materials on the rationale that they "add interest," and, based on their review of the research, Sewell and Moore (1980) conclude that there may be some validity to that claim. However, their research showed that cartoons contributed nothing toward comprehension. Cartoon embellishments (i.e., cartoons which do not depict exactly or support directly what is being taught by the text) may even be harmful, in that they may distract the learner. Bryant, Brown, Silberberg, and Elliott (1981) determined that humorous illustrations had no effect on the acquisition of information and on motivation, had positive effects on enjoyment and likelihood of purchasing the book, and had negative effects on the credibility of the book.

Obviously, cartoons must be used with care if they are used at all!

References for Chapter 11

Alesandrini, K. L. (1984). Pictures and adult learning. *Instructional Science, 13,* 63–77.

Anglin, G. J., (1985, January). *Prose-relevant pictures and older learners' recall of written prose.* Paper presented at the Annual Convention of the Association for Educational Communications and Technology, Anaheim, CA. (ERIC Document Reproduction Service No. ED 256 305)

Anglin, G. J., (1986a, January). *Effect of pictures on recall of written prose: How durable are picture effects?* Paper presented at the Annual Convention of the Association for Educational Communications and Technology, Las Vegas, NV. (ERIC Document Reproduction Service No. ED 267 755)

Anglin, G. J. (1986b). Prose-relevant pictures and older learners' recall of written prose. *Educational Communications and Technology Journal, 34,* 131–136.

Anglin, G. J. (1987). Effect of pictures on recall of written prose: How durable are picture effects? *Educational Communications and Technology Journal, 35,* 25–30.

Anglin, G. J., and Kwak, E. (1991, February). *Research on pictures: Knowledge acquisition, visual thinking, and cognitive skill acquisition: A guide to the literature, 1986–1990.* Paper presented at the Annual Convention of the Association for Educational Communications and Technology, Orlando, FL.

Brody, J. P. (1982). Affecting instructional textbooks through pictures. In
D. H. Jonassen (Ed.), *The technology of text: Principles for structuring,
designing, and displaying text* (pp. 301–316). Englewood Cliffs, NJ:
Educational Technology Publications.

Bryant, J., Brown, D., Silberberg, A. R., and Elliot, S. C. (1981). Effects of
humorous illustrations in college textbooks. *Human Communication
Research, 8,* 43–57.

Burns, D., Venit, S., and Hansen, R. (1988). *The electronic publisher.* New York:
Brady.

Davis, F. E., Barry, J., and Wiesenberg, M. (1986). *Desktop publishing.*
Homewood, IL: Dow Jones-Irwin.

Doczi, G. (1981). *The power of limits.* Boulder, CO: Shambhala Publications.

Duchastel, P. C. (1978). Illustrating instructional texts. *Educational Technology,
18*(11), 36–39.

Duchastel, P., and Waller, R. (1979). Pictorial illustration in instructional texts.
Educational Technology, 19(11), 20–25.

Dwyer, F. M. (1978). *Strategies for improving visual learning.* State College, PA:
Learning Services.

Felici, J., and Nace, T. (1987). *Desktop publishing skills: A primer for typesetting
with computers and laser printers.* Reading, MA: Addison-Wesley.

Fleming, M. (1984, January). *Visual attention to picture and word materials as
influenced by characteristics of the learners and design of the materials.*
Paper presented at the Annual Convention of the Association for Educational
Communications and Technology, Dallas, TX. (ERIC Document Reproduction
Service No. ED 243 420)

Fleming, M., and Levie, W. H. (1978). *Instructional message design.* Englewood
Cliffs, NJ: Educational Technology Publications.

Hannafin, M. J. (1984, January). The relative effectiveness of pictures versus
words in conveying abstract and concrete prose. Paper presented at the
Annual Meeting of the Association for Educational Communications and
Technology, Dallas, TX. (ERIC Document Reproduction Service No.
ED 243 422)

Hawk, P., McLeod, N. P., and Jonassen, D. H. (1985.) Graphic organizers in tests,
courseware, and supplemental materials. In D. H. Jonassen (Ed.), *The
technology of text (volume two): Principles for structuring, designing, and
displaying text* (pp. 158–186). Englewood Cliffs, NJ: Educational Technology
Publications.

Hewson, D. (1988). *Introduction to desktop publishing.* San Francisco, CA:
Chronicle Books.

Hurt, J. A. (1987). Assessing functional effectiveness of pictorial representations used in text. *Educational Communications and Technology Journal, 35,* 85–94.

Johnsey, A. L., Wheat, N. H., and Morrison, G. R. (1990, January-February). *Layout design making: The placement of illustrations.* Paper presented at the Annual Convention of the Association for Educational Communications and Technology, Anaheim, CA.

Lang, K. (1987). *The writer's guide to desktop publishing.* London: Academic Press.

Levie, W. H., (1987). Research on pictures: A guide to the literature. In D. M. Willows and H. A. Houghton (Eds.), *The psychology of illustration, volume 1* (pp. 1–50). New York: Springer-Verlag.

Levie, W. H., and Lentz, R. (1982). Effects of text illustrations: A review of research. *Educational Communications and Technology Journal, 30,* 195–232.

Levin, J. R. (1981). On functions of pictures in prose. In F. J. Pirozzolo and M. C. Wittrock (Eds.), *Neuropsychological and cognitive processes in reading* (pp. 203–228). New York: Academic Press.

Levin, J. R., and Berry, J. K. (1980). Children's learning of all the news that's fit to picture. *Educational Communications and Technology Journal, 28,* 177–185.

Levin, J. R., and Lesgold, A. M. (1978). On pictures in prose. *Educational Communications and Technology Journal, 26,* 233–243.

Levin, J. R., Anglin, G. J., and Carney, R. N. (1987). On empirically validating functions of pictures in prose. In D. M. Willows and H. A. Houghton (Eds.), *The psychology of illustration, volume 1* (pp. 51–86). New York: Springer-Verlag.

Lichty, T. (1989). *Design principles for desktop publishers.* Glenview, IL: Scott, Foresman and Co.

Merrill, P. F., and Bunderson, C. V. (1981). Preliminary guidelines for employing graphics in instruction. *Journal of Instructional Development, 4*(4), 2–9.

Miles, J. (1987). *Design for desktop publishing.* San Francisco: Chronicle Books.

Moore, D. W., and Readence, J. E. (1984). A quantitative and qualitative review of graphic organizer research. *Journal of Educational Research, 78,* 11–17.

Ogunyemi, O. A. (1983). *An analytic study of the efficacy of black-and-white pictorial instruction on achievement.* (ERIC Document Reproduction Service No. ED 286 252)

Parrish, P. (1990). *Illustrations for instruction: A guide for instructors.* Westminster, CO: Front Range Community College.

Peeck, J. (1987). The role of illustrations in processing and remembering illustrated text. In D. M. Willows and H. A. Houghton (Eds.), *The psychology of illustration, volume 1* (pp. 115–151). New York: Springer-Verlag.

Peng, C. Y., and Levin, J. R. (1979). Pictures and children's story recall: Some questions of durability. *Educational Communications and Technology Journal, 27*, 39–44.

Printing layout and design. (1968). Albany, NY: Delmar Publishers.

Publish! (1989a). *101 best desktop publishing tips, vol. 1.* San Francisco, CA: PCW Communications.

Rieber, L. (1991, February). Chairman's concluding remarks at the session *The effects of pictures and illustrations in learning* at the Annual Convention of the Association for Educational Communications and Technology, Orlando, FL.

Schallert, D. L. (1980). The role of illustrations in reading comprehension. In R. J. Spiro, B. C. Bruce, and W. F. Brewer (Eds.), *Theoretical issues in reading comprehension: Perspectives from cognitive psychology, linguistics, artificial intelligence, and education* (pp. 503–524). Hillsdale, NJ: Lawrence Erlbaum Associates.

Sewell, E. H., and Moore, R. L. (1980). Cartoon embellishments in informative presentations. *Educational Communications and Technology Journal, 28*, 39–46.

Shushan, R., and Wright, D. (1989). *Desktop publishing by design.* Redmond, WA: Microsoft Press.

Tajika, H., Taniguchi, A., Yamamoto, K., and Mayer, R. E. (1988). Effects of pictorial advance organizers on passage retention. *Contemporary Educational Psychology, 13*, 133–139.

Tufte, E. R. (1983). *The visual display of quantitative information.* Cheshire, CT: Graphics Press.

van Dam, G., Brinkerink-Carlier, M., and Kok, I. (1986). Influence of visual and verbal embellishment on free recall of the paragraphs of a text. *American Journal of Psychology, 99*, 103–110.

Waddill, P. J., McDaniel, M. A., and Einstein, G. O. (1988). Illustrations as adjuncts to prose: A text-appropriate processing approach. *Journal of Educational Psychology, 80*, 457–464.

West, S. (1987). Design for desktop publishing. In The Waite Group (J. Stockford, Ed.), *Desktop publishing bible* (pp. 53–72). Indianapolis, IN: Howard W. Sams.

Winn, W., and Holliday, W. (1982). Design principles for diagrams and charts. In D. H. Jonassen (Ed.), *The technology of text: Principles for structuring, designing, and displaying text* (pp. 277–299). Englewood Cliffs, NJ: Educational Technology Publications.

References

Alesandrini, K. L. (1984). Pictures and adult learning. *Instructional Science, 13*, 63–77.

American Psychological Association. (1983). *Publication manual of the American Psychological Association* (3rd ed.). Washington, DC: The Association.

Anglin, G. J. (1985, January). *Prose-relevant pictures and older learners' recall of written prose.* Paper presented at the Annual Convention of the Association for Educational Communications and Technology, Anaheim, CA. (ERIC Document Reproduction Service No. ED 256 305)

Anglin, G. J. (1986a, January). *Effect of pictures on recall of written prose: How durable are picture effects?* Paper presented at the Annual Convention of the Association for Educational Communications and Technology, Las Vegas, NV. (ERIC Document Reproduction Service No. ED 267 755)

Anglin, G. J. (1986b). Prose-relevant pictures and older learners' recall of written prose. *Educational Communications and Technology Journal, 34,* 131–136.

Anglin, G. J. (1987). Effect of pictures on recall of written prose: How durable are picture effects? *Educational Communications and Technology Journal, 35,* 25–30.

Anglin, G. J., and Kwak, E. (1991, February). *Research on pictures: Knowledge acquisition, visual thinking, and cognitive skill acquisition: A guide to the literature, 1986–1990.* Paper presented at the Annual Convention of the Association for Educational Communications and Technology, Orlando, FL.

Barnes, C. W. (1988). *Earth, time, and life: An introduction to physical and historical geology* (2nd ed.). New York: John Wiley and Sons.

Bove, T., and Rhodes, C. (1989). *Desktop publishing with PageMaker for the Macintosh.* Toronto: John Wiley and Sons.

Briggs, L. J., Gustafson, K. L., and Tillman, M. H. (Eds.) (1991). *Instructional design: Principles and applications* (2nd ed.). Englewood Cliffs, NJ: Educational Technology Publications.

Brody, J. P. (1982). Affecting instructional textbooks through pictures. In D. H. Jonassen (Ed.), *The technology of text: Principles for structuring, designing, and displaying text* (pp. 301–316). Englewood Cliffs, NJ: Educational Technology Publications.

Brooks, L. W., Danserau, D. F., Spurlin, J. E., and Holley, C. D. (1983). Effects of headings on text processing. *Journal of Educational Psychology, 75,* 292–302.

Bryant, J., Brown, D., Silberberg, A. R., and Elliot, S. C. (1981). Effects of humorous illustrations in college textbooks. *Human Communication Research, 8,* 43–57.

Bryant, P. E., and Somerville, S. C. (1986). The spatial demands of graphs. *The British Journal of Psychology, 77,* 187–197.

Burnhill, P., Hartley, J., and Young, M. (1976). Tables in text. *Applied Ergonomics, 7*(1), 13–18.

Burns, D., Venit, S., and Hansen, R. (1988). *The electronic publisher.* New York: Brady.

Clark, R. E. (1984). Research on student thought processes during computer-based instruction. *Journal of Instructional Development, 7*(3), 2-5.

Cleveland, W. S. (1984). Graphs in scientific publications. *The American Statistician, 38,* 261–269.

Coles, P., and Foster, J. (1975). Typographic cueing as an aid to learning from typewritten text. *Programmed Learning and Educational Technology, 12,* 102–108.

Collier, D., and Cotton, B. (1989). *Basic desktop design and layout.* Cincinnati, OH: North Light Books.

Cowart, R., and Cummings, S. (1989). *The ABC's of Ventura.* San Francisco, CA: Sybex.

Cox, D. R. (1978). Some remarks on the role in statistics of graphical methods. *Applied Statistics, 27,* 4–9.

Crouse, J. H., and Idstein, P. (1972). Effects of encoding cues on prose learning. *Journal of Educational Psychology, 63,* 309–313.

Davies, J. (1989). *Computing fundamentals: PageMaker.* Reading, MA: Addison-Wesley.

Davis, F. E., Barry, J., and Wiesenberg, M. (1986). *Desktop publishing.* Homewood, IL: Dow Jones-Irwin.

Dick, W., and Carey, L. (1990). *The systematic design of instruction* (3rd ed.). Glenview, IL: Scott, Foresman.

Doczi, G. (1981). *The power of limits.* Boulder, CO: Shambhala Publications.

Dreyfus, J. (1985). A turning point in type design. *Visible Language, 19*(1), 11–22.

Duchastel, P. C. (1978). Illustrating instructional texts. *Educational Technology, 18*(11), 36–39.

Duchastel, P., and Waller, R. (1979). Pictorial illustration in instructional texts. *Educational Technology, 19*(11), 20–25.

Dunn, R. (1988). Framed rectangle charts or statistical maps with shading: An experiment in graphical perception. *The American Statistician, 42,* 123–129.

Dwyer, F. M. (1978). *Strategies for improving visual learning.* State College, PA: Learning Services.

Ehrenberg, A. S. C. (1977). Rudiments of numeracy. *Journal of the Royal Statistical Society A, 140,* 277–297. Cited by Wright, P. (1982). A user-oriented approach to the design of tables and flowcharts. In D. H. Jonassen (Ed.), *The technology of text: Principles for structuring, designing, and displaying text* (pp. 317–340). Englewood Cliffs, NJ: Educational Technology Publications.

Felici, J., and Nace, T. (1987). *Desktop publishing skills: A primer for typesetting with computers and laser printers.* Reading, MA: Addison-Wesley.

Feliciano, G. D., Powers, R. D., and Kearl, B. E. (1963). The presentation of statistical information. *AV Communication Review, 11*(3), 32–39.

Fleming, M. (1984, January). *Visual attention to picture and word materials as influenced by characteristics of the learners and design of the materials.* Paper presented at the Annual Convention of the Association for Educational Communications and Technology, Dallas, TX. (ERIC Document Reproduction Service No. ED 243 420)

Fleming, M., and Levie, W. H. (1978). *Instructional message design.* Englewood Cliffs, NJ: Educational Technology Publications.

Foster, J. J. (1979). The use of visual cues in text. In P. A. Kolers, M. E. Wrolstad, and H. Bouma (Eds.), *Processing of visible language* (Vol. 1, pp. 189–203). New York: Plenum Press.

Foster, J., and Coles, P. (1977). An experimental study of typographic cueing in printed text. *Ergonomics, 20*(1), 57–66.

Frase, L. T., and Schwartz, B. J. (1979). Typographical cues that facilitate comprehension. *Journal of Educational Psychology, 71,* 197–206.

Gagné, R. M. (Ed.) (1987). *Instructional technology: Foundations.* Hillsdale, NJ: Lawrence Erlbaum Associates.

Gibaldi, J., and Achtert, W. S. (1988). *MLA handbook for writers of research papers* (3rd ed.). New York: Modern Language Association of America.

Glynn, S. M., Britton, B. K., and Tillman, M. H. (1985). Typographical cues in text: Management of the reader's attention. In D. H. Jonassen (Ed.), *The technology of text (volume two): Principles for structuring, designing, and displaying text* (pp. 192–209). Englewood Cliffs, NJ: Educational Technology Publications.

Gregory, M., and Poulton, E. C. (1970.) Even versus uneven right-hand margins and the rate of comprehension in reading. *Ergonomics, 13*(4), 427–434.

Gropper, G. L. (1991). *Text displays: Analysis and systematic design.* Englewood Cliffs, NJ: Educational Technology Publications.

Hannafin, M. J. (1984, January). The relative effectiveness of pictures versus words in conveying abstract and concrete prose. Paper presented at the Annual Meeting of the Association for Educational Communications and Technology, Dallas, TX. (ERIC Document Reproduction Service No. ED 243 422)

Hartley, J. (1978). *Designing instructional text.* London: Kogan Page.

Hartley, J. (1982). Designing instructional text. In D. H. Jonassen (Ed.), *The technology of text: Principles for structuring, designing, and displaying text* (pp. 193–214). Englewood Cliffs, NJ: Educational Technology Publications.

Hartley, J. (1987). Designing electronic text: The role of print-based research. *Educational Technology and Communication Journal, 35,* 3–17.

Hartley, J., and Burnhill, P. (1977a). Fifty guidelines for improving instructional text. *Programmed Learning and Educational Technology, 14,* 65–73.

Hartley, J., and Burnhill, P. (1977b). Understanding instructional text: Typography, layout and design. In M. J. A. Howe (Ed.), *Adult learning* (pp. 223–247). London: John Wiley and Sons.

Hartley, J., and Jonassen, D. H. (1985). The role of headings in printed and electronic text. In D. H. Jonassen (Ed.), *The technology of text (volume two): Principles for structuring, designing, and displaying text* (pp. 237–263). Englewood Cliffs, NJ: Educational Technology Publications.

Hartley, J., and Trueman, M. (1983). The effects of headings in text on recall, search and retrieval. *British Journal of Educational Psychology, 53,* 205–214.

Hartley, J., and Trueman, M. (1985). A research strategy for text designers: The role of headings. *Instructional Science, 14,* 95–155.

Hartley, J., Young, M., and Burnhill, P. (1975). On the typing of tables. *Applied Ergonomics, 6*(1), 39–42.

Hawk, P., McLeod, N. P., and Jonassen, D. H. (1985). Graphic organizers in tests, courseware, and supplemental materials. In D. H. Jonassen (Ed.), *The technology of text (volume two): Principles for structuring, designing, and displaying text* (pp. 158–186). Englewood Cliffs, NJ: Educational Technology Publications.

Hewson, D. (1988). *Introduction to desktop publishing.* San Francisco, CA: Chronicle Books.

Hooper, S., and Hannafin, M. J. (1986). Variables affecting the legibility of computer generated text. *Journal of Instructional Development, 9*(4), 22–28.

Hurt, J. A. (1987). Assessing functional effectiveness of pictorial representations used in text. *Educational Communications and Technology Journal, 35,* 85–94.

Johnsey, A. L., Wheat, N. H., and Morrison, G. R. (1990, January–February). *Layout design making: The placement of illustrations.* Paper presented at the Annual Convention of the Association for Educational Communications and Technology, Anaheim, CA.

Kleper, M. L. (1987). *The illustrated handbook of desktop publishing and typesetting.* Blue Ridge Summit, PA: Tab Books.

Lang, K. (1987). *The writer's guide to desktop publishing.* London: Academic Press.

Latif-Pembry, R. (1989). *Desktop publishing with WordPerfect.* Terra Cotta, ON: Norbry Publishing.

Levie, W. H. (1987). Research on pictures: A guide to the literature. In D. M. Willows and H. A. Houghton (Eds.), *The psychology of illustration, volume 1* (pp. 1–50). New York: Springer-Verlag.

Levie, W. H., and Lentz, R. (1982). Effects of text illustrations: A review of research. *Educational Communications and Technology Journal, 30,* 195–232.

Levin, J. R. (1981). On functions of pictures in prose. In F. J. Pirozzolo and M. C. Wittrock (Eds.), *Neuropsychological and cognitive processes in reading* (pp. 203–228). New York: Academic Press.

Levin, J. R., and Berry, J. K. (1980). Children's learning of all the news that's fit to picture. *Educational Communications and Technology Journal, 28,* 177–185.

Levin, J. R., and Lesgold, A. M. (1978). On pictures in prose. *Educational Communications and Technology Journal, 26,* 233–243.

Levin, J. R., Anglin, G. J., and Carney, R. N. (1987). On empirically validating functions of pictures in prose. In D. M. Willows and H. A. Houghton (Eds.), *The psychology of illustration, volume 1* (pp. 51–86). New York: Springer-Verlag.

Lichty, T. (1989). *Design principles for desktop publishers.* Glenview, IL: Scott, Foresman and Co.

Macdonald-Ross, M. (1977a). Graphics in text. In L. S. Shulman (Ed.), *Review of research in education, vol. 5.* Itasca, IL: F. E. Peacock.

Macdonald-Ross, M. (1977b). How numbers are shown: A review of research on the presentation of quantitative data in texts. *AV Communication Review, 25,* 359–409.

Marland, P. W., and Store, R. E. (1982). Some instructional strategies for improved learning from distance education materials. *Distance Education, 3*(1), 72–106.

Merrill, P. F., and Bunderson, C. V. (1981). Preliminary guidelines for employing graphics in instruction. *Journal of Instructional Development, 4*(4), 2–9.

Miles, J. (1987). *Design for desktop publishing.* San Francisco: Chronicle Books.

Misanchuk, E. R. (1989). *Learner preferences for typeface (font) and leading in print materials.* Saskatoon, SK: Division of Extension and Community Relations, The University of Saskatchewan. (ERIC Document Reproduction Service No. ED 307 854)

Moore, D. W., and Readence, J. E. (1984). A quantitative and qualitative review of graphic organizer research. *Journal of Educational Research, 78,* 11–17.

Moriarty, S. E., and Scheiner, E. C. (1984). A study of close-set text type. *Journal of Applied Psychology, 69,* 700–702.

Morrison, G. R. (1986). Communicability of the emotional connotation of type. *Educational Communications and Technology Journal, 34,* 235–244.

Muncer, S. J., Gorman, B. S., Gorman, S., and Bibel, D. (1986). Right is wrong: An examination of the effect of right justification on reading. *British Journal of Educational Technology, 17,* 5–10.

Ogunyemi, O. A. (1983). *An analytic study of the efficacy of black-and-white pictorial instruction on achievement.* (ERIC Document Reproduction Service No. ED 286 252)

Parker, R. C. (1988). *The Aldus guide to basic design* (2nd ed.) Seattle, WA: Aldus Corporation.

Parrish, P. (1990). *Illustrations for instruction: A guide for instructors.* Westminster, CO: Front Range Community College.

Paterson, D. G., and Tinker, M. A. (1932). Studies of typographical factors influencing speed of reading: X. Styles of type face. *Journal of Applied Psychology, 16,* 605–613.

Paterson, D. G., and Tinker, M. A. (1940). *How to make type readable.* New York: Harper and Row. Cited by Tinker, M. A. (1965). *Bases for effective reading.* Minneapolis: University of Minnesota Press.

Peeck, J. (1987) The role of illustrations in processing and remembering illustrated text. In D. M. Willows and H. A. Houghton (Eds.), *The psychology of illustration, volume 1* (pp. 115–151). New York: Springer-Verlag.

Peng, C. Y., and Levin, J. R. (1979). Pictures and children's story recall: Some questions of durability. *Educational Communications and Technology Journal, 27,* 39–44.

Printing layout and design. (1968). Albany, NY: Delmar Publishers.

Publish! (1989a). *101 best desktop publishing tips, vol. 1.* San Francisco, CA: PCW Communications.

Publish! (1989b). *101 best desktop publishing tips, vol. 2.* San Francisco, CA: PCW Communications.

Rickards, J. P., and August, G. J. (1974). Generative underlining strategies in prose recall. *Journal of Educational Psychology, 67*(6), 860–865.

Rieber, L. (1991, January–February). Chairman's concluding remarks at the session *The effects of pictures and illustrations in learning* at the Annual Convention of the Association for Educational Communications and Technology, Orlando, FL.

Romiszowski, A. J. (1981). *Designing instructional systems: Decision making in course planning.* London: Kogan Page.

Salomon, G. (1984). Television is "easy" and print is "tough": The differential investment of mental effort in learning as a function of perception and attributions. *Journal of Educational Psychology, 76,* 647–658.

Sans, J. C. (1988). *Handbook of desktop publishing.* Dallas, TX: Wordware Publishers.

Schallert, D. L. (1980). The role of illustrations in reading comprehension. In R. J. Spiro, B. C. Bruce, and W. F. Brewer (Eds.), *Theoretical issues in reading comprehension: Perspectives from cognitive psychology, linguistics, artificial intelligence, and education* (pp. 503–524). Hillsdale, NJ: Lawrence Erlbaum Associates.

Schriver, K. A. (1990). *Document design from 1980 to 1990: Challenges that remain* (Tech. Rep. No. 39). Berkeley, CA/Pittsburgh, PA: Center for the Study of Writing, University of California/Carnegie-Mellon University. (ERIC Document Reproduction Service No. ED 320143)

Sewell, E. H., and Moore, R. L. (1980). Cartoon embellishments in informative presentations. *Educational Communications and Technology Journal, 28,* 39–46.

Shushan, R., and Wright, D. (1989). *Desktop publishing by design.* Redmond, WA: Microsoft Press.

Simonsen, R. (1985). The elements of design. *Popular Computing,* November, 59.

Spiegelman, M. (1987). Interior design for documents. *PC World*, March, 178–185.

Swann, A. (1987). *How to understand and use design and layout.* Cincinnati, OH: North Light Books.

Tajika, H., Taniguchi, A., Yamamoto, K., and Mayer, R. E. (1988). Effects of pictorial advance organizers on passage retention. *Contemporary Educational Psychology, 13*, 133–139.

Tankard, J. W. (1986, August). *Quantitative graphics in newspapers.* Paper presented at the Annual Meeting of the Association for Education in Journalism and Mass Communication, Norman, OK. (ERIC Document Reproduction Service No. ED 272 871)

The Chicago manual of style (13th ed.). (1982). Chicago: University of Chicago Press.

Tinker, M. A. (1955). Prolonged reading tasks in visual research. *Journal of Applied Psychology, 39*, 444–446.

Tinker, M. A. (1957). Effect of curved text upon readability of print. *Journal of Applied Psychology, 41*, 218–221.

Tinker, M. A. (1963). *Legibility of print.* Ames, IA: Iowa State University Press.

Tinker, M. A. (1965). *Bases for effective reading.* Minneapolis: University of Minnesota Press.

Tinker, M. A., and Paterson, D. G. (1928). Influence of type form on speed of reading. *Journal of Applied Psychology, 12*, 359–368.

Tordella, S. J. (1988). How to create good graphics. *American Demographics, 10*(10), 40–41.

Trollip, S. R., and Sales, G. (1986, January). *Readability of computer-generated fill-justified text.* Paper presented at the Annual Convention of the Association for Educational Communications and Technology, Las Vegas, NV.

Tufte, E. R. (1983). *The visual display of quantitative information.* Cheshire, CT: Graphics Press.

Turabian, K. L. (1976). *Student's guide for writing college papers* (3rd ed.). Chicago: University of Chicago Press.

van Dam, G., Brinkerink-Carlier, M., and Kok, I. (1986). Influence of visual and verbal embellishment on free recall of the paragraphs of a text. *American Journal of Psychology, 99*, 103–110.

Vinberg, A. (1980). *Designing a good graph.* (ERIC Document Reproduction Service No. ED 222 192)

Waddill, P. J., McDaniel, M. A., and Einstein, G. O. (1988). Illustrations as adjuncts to prose: A text-appropriate processing approach. *Journal of Educational Psychology, 80*, 457–464.

Wainer, H. (1984). How to display data badly. *The American Statistician, 38*, 137–147.

Walker, P. (1990). A lesson in leading. *Aldus Magazine*, March/April, 45–47.

Waller, R. (1977). *Three functions of text presentation.* (Notes on transforming, 2). Milton Keynes, England: Institute of Educational Technology, The Open University, mimeograph. Cited by Marland, P. W., and Store, R. E. (1982). Some instructional strategies for improved learning from distance teaching materials. *Distance Education, 3*(1), 72–106.

Waller, R. H. W. (1979). Typographic access structures for educational texts. In P. A. Kolers, M. E. Wrolstad, and H. Bouma (Eds.), *Processing of visible language* (Vol. 1, pp. 175–187). New York: Plenum Press.

Waller, R. (1982). Text as diagram: Using typography to improve access and understanding. In D. H. Jonassen (Ed.), *The technology of text: Principles for structuring, designing, and displaying text* (pp. 137–166). Englewood Cliffs, NJ: Educational Technology Publications.

West, S. (1987). Design for desktop publishing. In The Waite Group (J. Stockford, Ed.), *Desktop publishing bible* (pp. 53–72). Indianapolis, IN: Howard W. Sams.

White, J. V. (1983). *Mastering graphics.* New York: Bowker.

Winn, W., and Holliday, W. (1982). Design principles for diagrams and charts. In D. H. Jonassen (Ed.), *The technology of text: Principles for structuring, designing, and displaying text* (pp. 277–299). Englewood Cliffs, NJ: Educational Technology Publications.

Wright, P. (1968). Using tabulated information. *Ergonomics*, *11*(4), 331–343.

Wright, P. (1982). A user-oriented approach to the design of tables and flowcharts. In D. H. Jonassen (Ed.), *The technology of text: Principles for structuring, designing, and displaying text* (pp. 317–340). Englewood Cliffs, NJ: Educational Technology Publications.

Wright, P., and Fox, K. (1970). Presenting information in tables. *Applied Ergonomics,* *1*(4), 234–242.

Wright, P., and Fox, K. (1972). Explicit and implicit tabulation formats. *Ergonomics*, *15*(2), 175–187.

Zimmerman, B. B. (1989). *Working with WordPerfect* (3rd. ed.). Chicago, IL: Scott, Foresman.

Author Index

Feliciano, G. D., Powers, R. D., and Kearl, B. E. 189, 190, 200, 202, 225, 227

Fleming, M. 250

Fleming, M., and Levie, W. H. 264

Foster, J. J. 113

Foster, J., and Coles, P. 114

Frase, L. T., and Schwartz, B. J. 111, 178

Gagné, R. M. 26

Gibaldi, J., and Achtert, W. S. 59

Glynn, S. M., Britton, B. K., and Tillman, M. H. 114, 146

Gregory, M., and Poulton, E. C. 7

Gropper, G. L. 176, 180

Hannafin, M. J. 245

Hartley, J. 6, 73, 130, 175, 177, 178, 198, 199, 201, 218

Hartley, J., and Burnhill, P. 7, 55, 79, 110, 114, 175, 178, 180, 191, 200, 202, 218

Hartley, J., and Jonassen, D. H. 101, 102, 106, 178

Hartley, J., and Trueman, M. 101, 106

Hartley, J., Young, M., and Burnhill, P. 201

Hawk, P., McLeod, N. P., and Jonassen, D. H. 272

Hewson, D. 2, 8, 29, 60, 61, 138, 163, 255

Hooper, S., and Hannafin, M. J. 140

Hurt, J. A. 239, 243, 244, 245

Johnsey, A. L., Wheat, N. H., and Morrison, G. R. 106, 270

Kleper, M. L. 2, 6, 17, 94, 110, 126, 137, 138, 156, 164

Lang, K. 2, 58, 73, 86, 87, 90, 92, 93, 103, 105, 106, 117, 120, 130, 142, 143, 156, 181, 261

Latif-Pembry, R. 2

Levie, W. H. 242

Levie, W. H., and Lentz, R. 239, 242, 243, 249

Levin, J. R. 247, 249

Levin, J. R., and Berry, J. K. 244

Levin, J. R., and Lesgold, A. M. 244

Levin, J. R., Anglin, G. J., and Carney, R. N. 248

Lichty, T. 2, 5, 8, 60, 73, 86, 90, 93, 94, 110, 125, 130, 137, 139, 143, 156, 157, 174, 183, 184, 219, 221, 224, 226, 229, 230, 248, 268

Macdonald-Ross, M. 189, 190, 207, 208, 209, 210, 211, 221, 223, 225, 229, 230, 232, 234

Marland, P. W., and Store, R. E. 97

Subject Index